International Business Contracts Training Course

国际商务合同
实训教程

杨静　主编

東北財經大学出版社　｜　大连
Dongbei University of Finance & Economics Press

图书在版编目（CIP）数据

国际商务合同实训教程 / 杨静主编 . —大连 : 东北财经大学出版社，2019.12

（21世纪高等院校国际经济与贸易专业精品教材）

ISBN 978-7-5654-3749-6

Ⅰ . 国… Ⅱ . 杨… Ⅲ . 国际贸易-贸易合同-英语-高等学校-教材 Ⅳ . ①F740.4 ②D996.1

中国版本图书馆CIP数据核字（2020）第020814号

东北财经大学出版社出版

（大连市黑石礁尖山街217号　邮政编码　116025）

网　　址 : http://www.dufep.cn

读者信箱 : dufep@dufe.edu.cn

大连永盛印业有限公司印刷　东北财经大学出版社发行

幅面尺寸：185mm×260mm　　字数：288千字　　印张：11.25

2019年12月第1版　　　　　2019年12月第1次印刷

责任编辑：蔡　丽　　　　　　　　　责任校对：蓝　海

封面设计：冀贵收　　　　　　　　　版式设计：钟福建

定价：32.00元

前　言

《国际商务合同实训教程》与东北财经大学出版社出版的《国际商务合同双语教程》既互为补充，又自成体系，突出技能与知识的应用，实用性强，在一定程度上填补了国内类似教材的出版空白。

一、本教材的主要内容

本教材共分3篇：

第一篇为阅读篇，主要是国际商务合同的语言特征实训，主要包括国际商务合同的词语、句式、时态和语态的实训。

第二篇为写作篇，主要是撰写国际商务合同条款及案例分析的实训。

第三篇为实战篇，对各类合同及协议进行练习，主要是对国际商务合同条款起草进行实训。

二、本教材的特色

（1）本教材在内容的安排上，以"范本+技能"为编写思路，以"必需、够用"为基准，突出实用性、时代性、技能性，遵循全面、系统、简明、规范的原则，收录了大量具有代表性的国际商务合同示范文本，并将其合理地分类，以方便读者查阅使用。

（2）本教材以案例为主线，导入相关的实训项目。本教材中的30个实训项目训练学生的国际商务合同实际应用能力，使学生能够系统地、准确地掌握国际商务合同的具体法律制度及相应的规范，并能够在实践中灵活地运用、分析和处理各种合同实务问题。

本教材的编者是长期从事商务英语专业教学的高校教师，具有商务和语言的双重专业背景，教学与实践经验丰富。杨鑫坡、戴君益、罗攀、刘艳萍、陆秋娥参与了本教材的资料搜集工作，在此一并表示感谢。

本教材可作为高等院校商务英语、国际经济与贸易、国际商务、工商管理等专业相关课程的教材，也可作为企业各类管理人员的培训教材或辅导资料，以及广大商务英语学习者的自学教程或读物。

　　本教材借鉴、吸收了同行的观点和其他教材的精华，由于篇幅所限，无法一一注明出处，敬请谅解，在此一并致谢。本教材的错漏之处在所难免，希望各位读者指正。

编　者

2019年9月于南宁

目　录

阅读篇　国际商务英文合同的语言特征实训

实训项目1

国际商务英文合同结构练习①

实训目标

掌握国际商务英文合同的基本结构。

一、阅读下列英文内容，并指出它们分别属于合同结构中的哪个部分（A.标题；B.导言；C.正文；D.结尾与附录）

1. After friendly consultations conducted in accordance with the principles of equality and mutual benefit, the Parties have agreed to describe subject matter of the Contract in accordance with Applicable Laws and the provisions of this Contract.　　　　　　　　　　（　　）

2. No lawsuit arbitration or other legal or governmental proceeding is pending or, to its knowledge, threatened against it that would affect its ability to perform its obligations under this Contract.　　　　　　　　　　（　　）

3. Joint Venture Contract.　　　　　　　　　　（　　）

4. IN WITNESS WHEREOF, each of the Parties hereto has caused this Contract to be executed by its duly authorized representative on the date first set forth above.　　　　（　　）

---

① 乔焕然. 英文合同阅读指南：英文合同的结构、条款、句型与词汇分析 [M]. 最新增订版. 北京：中国法制出版社，2015.

二、对下面的英文合同进行结构划分

Stock Purchase Agreement

THIS AGREEMENT, made on the _____ th/rd/nd day of _____ [month], _____ [Year], by and between ×××, a corporation authorized to do business in YYY (the Corporation) and the individual listed in Exhibit A attached hereto (each individually a Shareholder and collectively the Shareholders).

RECITALS

A. The issued and outstanding capital stock of the Corporation currently consists of one thousand two hundred thirty one (1,231) shares of common stock (the Shares). The Shareholders currently own all the issued and outstanding Shares.

B. The Shareholders and the Corporation desire to make provisions for future disposition of the Shares in order to prevent interference with the orderly conduct of the business of the Corporation.

C. The Shareholders and the Corporation desire that each Shareholder shall be prohibited from engaging in any business or activity that competes with the business of the Corporation, as long as he holds Shares of the Corporation.

NOW THEREFORE, in consideration of the mutual premises and covenants made herein, and for other good and valuable consideration, the receipt and sufficiency of which are hereby acknowledged, the parties do hereby agree as follows:

RESTRICTIONS ON TRANSFER

1. Restrictions on Transfer. No Shareholder will sell, transfer, donate, exchange, pledge or assign or in any way alienate, encumber or dispose of his ownership of any of his Shares of capital stock of the Corporation, whether now owned or hereafter acquired, either voluntarily or by operation of law, without the prior written consent of the Corporation and all the Shareholders, unless such transfer is in accordance with the provision of this Agreement.

1.1 Void Transfers. The Corporation shall not transfer on its books any Shares sold or transferred other than pursuant to the provision of this Agreement. No transferee of Shares in violation of the provision of this Agreement shall be a record owner of such Shares nor will such transferee have the right to receive dividends or other distributions payable to the record owner of such Shares. Any transfer of Shares in violation of the terms and conditions of this agreement shall be void and without effect in transferring any interest in such Shares to the transferee.

1.2 Lifetime Transfers. Any Shareholder desiring to transfer Shares of the Corporation during his lifetime (the Transferring Shareholder) must give notice (the Notice) of intent to transfer in writing to the Corporation and to the remaining Shareholders at least ninety (90) days before the date of the proposed transfer. The Notice shall specifically name the proposed transferee, the number of Shares to be transferred and the proposed price and terms of the transfer. The following procedure shall be followed:

(A) Purchase by Corporation. Within thirty (30) days after receipt of the Notice, the

Corporation may elect to purchase the Shares of the Transferring Shareholder at the price and terms indicated in the Notice, or, at the option of the Corporation, the price and terms indicated in paragraph 1.4 herein. The Transferring Shareholder shall abstain from participating in any decision of the Corporation to exercise or refrain from exercising the purchase options provided herein, except that at the direction of the holders of the majority in interest of the outstanding Shares not held by the transferring Shareholder, the Transferring Shareholder will vote its Shares and take such other action as may be required by such majority.

(B) Purchase by Shareholders. In the event that the Corporation either affirmatively elects not to exercise the above-described option or allows the period for exercise of the option to lapse, the remaining Shareholders shall have an additional sixty-day period beginning with the end of the thirty-day period specified in subsection (A) above in which to elect to purchase all the Shares of the Transferring Shareholder at the price and terms indicated in the Notice, or at their option, the price and terms indicated in paragraph 1.4 herein. Any Shareholder so electing shall deliver to the president of the Corporation a written notice indicating the Shareholders intent to purchase such Shares and the number of Shares which such purchasing Shareholders exceed the number of Shares to be transferred by the Transferring Shareholder, the Shares of the Transferring Shareholder shall be allotted among the purchasing Shareholder in any manner on which the purchasing Shareholder may agree; however, if they are unable to agree the shares shall be allotted among them so that each Purchasing Shareholder shall purchase the fractional portion of the Shares to be transferred which is equal to the fractional portion of the total number of outstanding Shares held by the respective purchasing Shareholder (the Pro Rata Amount). Should the Pro Rata Amount of a respective Shareholder exceed the Purchase Commitment of the respective Shareholder, the excess of each Pro Rata Amount exceeding the Purchase Commitment shall be allocated among the remaining Purchasing Shareholder in any manner on which the remaining Purchasing Shareholder may agree; however, if they are unable to agree, the Shares shall be allotted among them as equally as possible per capital without creating fractional Shares, preference shall be given to the Purchasing Shareholder in order of their respective holdings of Shares of the Corporation, with the holder of the greatest number of shares receiving the first preference.

(C) Interim Death of Transferring Shareholder. In the event a Shareholder dies or dissolves after having sent the Notice but prior to the transfer of ownership of the Shares pursuant to the terms of this Agreement, this paragraph 1.2 shall cease to be effective and the provisions of paragraph 1.3 shall be in effect.

(D) Lapse or Refusal. If the options to purchase all the Shares of the Transferring Shareholder are not exercised by neither the Corporation nor the remaining Shareholders, the Transferring Shareholder may then transfer its shares pursuant to the provision described in the Notice, but such transfer must be to the original transferee at the purchase price and under the provision specified in the Notice within one hundred (100) days following the original date of receipt of the Notice by the Corporation. Additionally, such transfer will not be effective unless the transferee executes and becomes bound by this Agreement prior to the transfer of the Shares to such transferee.

1.3 Death or Dissolution of a Shareholder. In the event of the death or dissolution of a Shareholder, the executor or personal representative or corporate representative of the deceased or dissolved Shareholder shall sell and the Corporation shall purchase all of the Shares then owned by the deceased or dissolved Shareholder at the price and terms provided in paragraph 1.4 of this Agreement. The Corporation may, however, at its option, assign the right to purchase such Shares to the surviving Shareholders on a basis proportional to their respective ownership of Shares in the Corporation.

1.4 Purchase Price and Closing. In the event of the purchase of Shares under paragraph 1.3, or at the option of the Corporation or the purchasing Shareholder under paragraph 1.2, the purchase price to be paid for each of the Shares shall be the net book value as of the end of the month preceding the month Shareholder notifies the Corporation of its desire to sell then begins the process of dissolution. Net book value shall be determined from the Corporations regular financial statement as prepared in accordance with Section 1.5 by subtracting the total amounts of its liabilities from the total net book value of its assets and dividing the difference thereby obtained by the number of shares of capital stock of the Corporation issued and outstanding as of the date of valuation. Appropriate adjustments shall be made, however, for dividends and other distributions to Shareholders which occur after the valuation date.

The closing of the transfer of Shares pursuant to this Agreement (the Closing) shall take place within ten (10) days following the date on which the determination of the purchase price for the Shares to be transferred has been completed. The closing shall take place at the principal office of the Corporation at 12:00 noon or at such time and place as may mutually agree upon by the parties. The selling Shareholder or its personal or corporate representative shall deliver to the Party A at closing the certificates representing the Shares being purchased along with such additional documentation and endorsements as the Party A may reasonably request. The purchase price for any shares purchased pursuant to this Agreement shall be paid in cash or by check payable to the selling Shareholder.

1.5 Financial Statements. The Corporation shall cause its financial condition and the results of its operations to be compiled at the end of each fiscal year by its accountant. The Corporation shall prepare or cause to be prepared financial statements as of the end of each month including the month that corresponds to the end of its fiscal year. These statements need not be audited and shall consist of a balance sheet and the profit and loss statement which shall contain all appropriate adjustments necessary to present fairly the financial condition and results of operations of the Corporation as of the end of each month and for the interim period then ended. Such year-end and monthly financial statements shall be prepared in accordance with generally accepted accounting principles consistently applied.

1.6 Company shall provide the Shareholder with _____ shares of the company's outstanding stock for the payment of $_____ . The Shareholder shall relinquish his/her voting right and elect

_____ to represent Shareholders voting rights, (excluding rights to dividends and other rights of holders of Shares). If _____ leaves the employment of the Corporation (for any reason) before one year from _____ nd/rd/th of _____[month]_____[year], the payment of $_____could be returned to the Shareholder by the company with 12% interest due 30 days after employees' departure. Should a forfeiture result in the creation of fractional share(s), the number of share(s) to be forfeited shall be rounded out to prevent the creation of fractional share(s). All stocks distributed under this agreement shall be adjusted to preserve the value of the bonus in the event of a stock dividend, stock split or reverse stock split, recapitalization, merger, consolidation, reorganization, cash or properly dividend exchange of share, repurchase of shares or any other changes in corporate structure of or by company that in any such event materially effects the outstanding shares of stock.

Party A

Name of Company:

By: (Signature)

(Name, Title of person signing)

Party B

Name of Company:

By: (Signature)

(Name, Title of person signing)

三、翻译

(一) 将下列合同标题翻译成英文

封面：中国浙江宁波化工厂与韩国 Hives 化学公司关于建设浙江天堂聚酯项目的合同，签字时间为 2019 年 6 月。

(二) 将下列技术合同中的英文目录翻译成中文

TABLE OF CONTENTS

(三) 将下列英文当事人条款翻译成中文

This Contract is made and entered into at Chengdu of Sichuan on the fifth day of May 2019 by and between Company A (hereinafter referred to as "Party A") and Company B (hereinafter referred to as "Party B").

(四) 将下列英文证明及签字条款翻译成中文

IN WITNESS WHEREOF, the Principal and the Consultant hereto have caused this Consulting Agreement to be executed in accordance with their respective laws the day and the year first above written.

Qi Yinchuan (Signature)   Habibi (Signature)

Managing Director   General Manager

Orient Lion Trading Company   Dal Handles Consultants Partnership

四、辨别并略过累赘词的阅读练习 (快速阅读后翻译下面的句子)

Termination of this Agreement pursuant to Section ×× does not terminate, limit or restrict the rights and remedies of Party A. In addition to Party A's right under common law to redress for any breach or violation, Party B shall indemnity and defend Party A against all losses, damages (including, without limitation, consequential damages), costs and expenses including, without limitation, interest (including prejudgment interest in any litigated mailer), penalties, court cost of and attorney's fees and expenses asserted against imposed upon, or incurred by Party A, directly or indirectly, arising out of or resulting from the breach or violation and the enforcement of this Section.

实训项目 2
国际商务英文合同规范用词与用语练习①

实训目标

1. 掌握国际商务英文合同的规范用词与用语的基本词汇。
2. 掌握国际商务英文合同的重点用语。
3. 掌握国际商务英文合同的语言特点及翻译策略。

一、选词填空

1. At the request of Party B, Party A agrees to send technicians to _____ (assist, help) Party B to install the equipment.

2. The Employer may _____ (require, ask) the Contractor to replace _____ (forthwith, at once) any of its authorized representatives who is incompetent.

3. The Sellers shall not be held responsible for late delivery or nondelivery of the goods owing to the generally recognized "Force Majeure" causes. However, in such cases, the Sellers shall telegraph the Buyers a certificate of the occurrence issued by the government authorities or the Chamber of Commerce at the place where the accident occurs as evidence.

4. This contract is made by and _____ (thereof, hereof) between the Buyers and the Sellers _____ (whereby, hereby) the Buyers agree to buy and the Sellers agree to sell the undermentioned commodity according to the below. The terms shall include a provision / terms and conditions stipulated _____ (whereby, hereby), in the event of any claim in respect of which the Contractor would be entitled to receive indemnity under the policy being brought or made against Employer, the insurer will indemnify the Employer against such claims and any costs, charges and expenses in respect _____ (thereof, hereof).

5. From the date on and from which the contract comes into effect to the termination _____ (thereof, hereof), the two Parties _____ (hereto, thereto) shall hold a meeting every year to discuss

① [1] 乔焕然. 英文合同阅读指南：英文合同的结构、条款、句型与词汇分析 [M]. 最新增订版. 北京：中国法制出版社，2015. [2] 王相国. 鏖战英文合同：英文合同的翻译与起草 [M]. 最新增订版. 北京：中国法制出版社，2014. [3] 刘庆秋. 国际商务合同的文体与翻译 [M]. 北京：对外经济贸易大学出版社，2011.

problems in the execution _____ (thereof, hereof).

6. The balance shall be settled _____ (upon, on) the arrival of the goods at the port of destination.

二、翻译下列句中下划线词语

1. Party B shall train Party A's technical personnel so as to enable them to master Party B's design, moulds design, performance test and technology in machining, erection and inspection of the contracted product so that Party A can use the technical documents and know-how supplied by Party B to produce the same product and moulds in Party A's factory.

2. To promote the cooperation between both parties hereto, for the convenience of the capital flow of Party B, Party A agrees to offer certain line of credit about the credit sales. Party B shall provide its written application for the credit sales in accordance with the procedures as required by Party A and provides material as required by Party A. Party A shall determine the line of credit as RMB yuan (subject to the credit and the purchase capability) in accordance with the credit certification provided by Party B and with the previous account settlement. With the development of the business, this credit line can be changed in accordance with the negotiation between both parties.

3. The date of receipt issued by transportation department concerned shall be regarded as the delivery of goods.

4. This contract is made by and between the buyers and the sellers; whereby the buyers agree to buy and the sellers agree to sell the under mentioned commodity in accordance with the terms and conditions stipulated below.

5. The Contractor shall be responsible for the true and proper setting-out of the Works in relation to original points, lines and levels of reference given by the Engineer in writing and for the correctness, subject as above mentioned, of the position, levels, dimensions and alignment of all parts of the Works and for the provision of all necessary instruments, appliances and labor in connection therewith.

6. After accepting or confirming the order of Party B, Party A shall deliver goods to Party B according to the agreed delivery method. Party B shall examine and accept the goods before signing the delivery documents of Party A. If, due to force majeure or other uncontrollable reasons, Party A cannot deliver the goods in accordance with the agreed delivery method, Party A shall not assume the financial losses.

7. Should an export licence be required in order to ship goods of the contractual description, it shall be the duty of the seller at his own expense to apply for the licence and to use due diligence to obtain the grant of such a licence.

8. Subject to the above stipulations, the profits, losses and risks of the Joint Venture Company shall be borne by the Parties in proportion to their respective contributions to the registered capital of the Joint Venture Company.

三、翻译下列合同术语词组

1. sign the contract/agreement
2. equality mutual benefit and friendly consultation
3. breach the contract
4. breaching party
5. observant party/non-breaching party
6. liability for breach of the contract
7. terms and conditions
8. registered capital
9. fixed assets
10. compensate for the loss
11. disclose the confidential information
12. terminate the contract
13. arbitration
14. settlement of disputes
15. come into effect/come into force
16. binding force
17. compensation
18. infringement
19. violation
20. warrant
21. waiver

四、翻译下列句子

1. The following documents shall be deemed to form and be read and construed as an integral part of this contract.

2. Party B shall deliver the finished products to Party A at the former's own expense and risk not later than ten (10) days after the end of each calendar quarter and shall advise Party A by telex, within three (3) days after loading, of the quantity, vessel's name, port of shipment, date, estimated date of arrival to the destination and other information regarding the shipment.

五、翻译下列同义词/近义词词组

1. null and void, terms and conditions, provisions and stipulations
2. on or off the site
3. plus or minus 5%
4. null and void
5. furnish and provide
6. claims and debt

7. customs and usage

8. fixed and settled

9. alteration, modification or substitution

10. any part or parts of it

11. defaced or altered

12. compensation or damages

13. use, misuse or abuse

14. express or imply

15. claim or allegation

16. insufficiency or inadequacy

17. arrest or restraint

六、翻译下列句子

1. Normally, Party B, if it refuses to deliver the said goods, shall be subject to a penalty per day equaling twenty percent (20%) of the total value of the goods; if the goods fail to have the expected quality, the price shall be redefined; if the delivery is delayed, a penalty for the delay shall be charged at a rate equal to five percent (5%) per day.

2. If requested by the Supplier, the Distributor shall give all reasonable assistance in locating and recovering any defective products and preventing their sale to the third parties and, in particular, shall comply with any product recall procedures adopted by the Supplier and shall make its best efforts to ensure that its customers cooperate in a similar manner.

3. Buyer shall give Seller notice of any claim within 30 days after arrival of the goods at the port of destination. Unless such notice, accompanied by proof certified by an authorized surveyor, arrives at the Seller's office during such 30 days, Buyer shall be deemed to have no claim.

七、翻译下列特殊用词（注意词的单数和复数在词意上的差异）

1. import, imports

2. export, exports

3. stock, stocks

4. flow, flows

5. reserve, reserves

6. holding, holdings

7. shipment, shipments

8. sale, sales

9. supply, supplies

10. damage, damages

11. earning, earnings

12. effect, effects, no effects

13. liability, liabilities

14. engagement, engagements

八、翻译下列下划线的情态动词

1. The parties hereto <u>shall</u>, first of all, settle any dispute arising from or in connection with the contract through friendly negotiations. <u>Should</u> such negotiations fail, such disputes <u>may</u> be referred to the People's Court having jurisdiction on such disputes for settlement in the absence of any arbitration clause in the disputed contract or in default of agreement reached after such disputes occur.

2. This agreement <u>shall</u> come into effect upon the signature by the parties hereto, and the effective period of the agreement <u>shall</u> cover 5 years. In case both parties find it desirable to carry on the cooperation between them upon the expiration of the agreement, an application to the effect <u>shall</u> be submitted to the competent authorities under the Chinese Government for an extension thereof the agreement <u>may</u> then be extended for another 5 years, or a new similar agreement <u>shall</u> be signed between the parties.

3. The indemnitee <u>shall</u> notify the indemnitor in writing, and with reasonable promptness, of any claim that does not involve a Third Party Claim (a "Claim").

4. Neither the exercise nor the failure to exercise the right of set-off constitutes an election of remedies, nor does it limit in any way any other right Party A <u>may</u> have to enforce a claim for indemnification whether under this Article, applicable law or otherwise.

5. Either party has the right to appeal the arbitration panel's award to an appellate arbitrator by filing with the AAA, no later than 20 days after transmittal of the award, a written brief, not to exceed 20 pages, stating the reasons why the panel's decision <u>should</u> be reversed or modified.

九、阅读以下合同条款，说出其中下划线单词的含义

1. Termination of the license under the <u>provisions</u> of paragraph 12 shall be without prejudice to any rights which Licensor may otherwise have against Licensee. Upon the termination of this license, notwithstanding anything to the contrary herein, all royalties on sales theretofore made shall become immediately due and payable and no minimum royalties shall be repayable or avoidable.

2. Licensee shall be <u>released</u> from its obligations hereunder and this license shall terminate in the event that governmental regulations or other causes arising out of a state of national emergency or war or causes beyond the control of the parties render performance impossible and one party so informs the other in writing of such causes and its desire to be so released. In such events, all royalties on sales theretofore made shall become immediately due and payable and no minimum royalties shall be repayable.

3. This Note means the Note mentioned in the Loan Agreement and is entitled to all the benefits provided <u>therein</u>. This refers to the rights and obligations therein of advance payments, default and acceleration of the maturity in the event of default.

4. The developer may enter into a contract for construction project with a prime contractor, or

enter into contracts for survey, design, and construction with the surveyor, designer, and constructor respectively. The developer may not divide a construction project which should be completed by one contractor into several parts and contract them out to several contractors.

Subject to consent by the developer, the prime contractor or the contractor for survey, design, or construction may delegate part of the contracted work to a third person. The third person and the prime contractor or the contractor for survey design, or construction shall be jointly and severally liable to the developer in respect of the work product completed by such third person. The contractor may not assign in whole to any third person the contracted construction project, or divide the whole contracted construction project into several parts and separately assign each part to a third person under the guise of sub-contracting.

The contractor is prohibited from sub-contracting any part of the project to an entity not appropriately qualified. A sub-contractor is prohibited from further sub-contracting its contracted work. The main structure of the construction project must be constructed by the contractor itself.

5. Unless another provision of this Agreement specifically provides to the contrary, the rights of termination as herein provide shall be in addition to all other rights and remedies which either party may have to enforce this Agreement or to secure damages for the breach hereof, and the exercise of any right of termination as herein obligations under this Agreement accruing prior to the effective date of termination, including, but not limited to, the obligation to pay fees and any applicable royalties or to render reports with respect thereto.

实训项目 3
国际商务英文合同句子的翻译①

实训目标

1.掌握国际商务英文合同的句子特点。
2.掌握国际商务英文合同的句子的翻译原则和翻译策略。

一、翻译下列英文商务合同常用语句

1. The undersigned buyer and seller have confirmed in accordance with the following terms and conditions.

2. In witness whereof, the parties have executed this contract in duplicate upon the signature by the authorized representatives on the date first above written.

3. Through friendly negotiations, Party XX and Party YY, on the principle of mutual benefits, have hereby reached the contract as follows:

4. Whereas..., an agreement has been reached as follows:

5. This agreement is signed by..., with the intention to...

6. This agreement shall come into force on and from the day of signature.

7. The undersigned buyer and seller have confirmed... in accordance with the following terms and conditions.

8. any failure or delay in the performance of the contract

9. obligations under this Agreement

二、翻译下列句子

1.董事会表决中如遇投票数均等平分,主席(董事长)可投决定票。

2.如果任何一方有任何违反本协议之处,一方有权向另一方索取因违反协议而造成的损失赔偿费。

3.合同价格意指第×款中所提及的总计价格,可根据下文所列条款酌情予以增减。

---

① [1]吕昊,刘显正,罗萍. 商务合同写作及翻译 [M]. 武汉:武汉大学出版社,2005. [2]王相国. 鏖战英文合同:英文合同的翻译与起草 [M]. 最新增订版. 北京:中国法制出版社,2014. [3]刘川,王菲. 英文合同阅读与翻译 [M]. 北京:国防工业出版社,2010. [4]索普,贝利. 国际商务合同 [M]. 段佳陆,等,译. 中英文双语版 [M]. 北京:华夏出版社,2004. [5]乔焕然. 英文合同阅读指南:英文合同的结构、条款、句型与词汇分析 [M]. 最新增订版. 北京:中国法制出版社,2015.

4. 对于最低产量或有关专利费的支付的要求必须按比例分配。

5. 此种买卖应服从下列条款。

6. 考虑到包含于此的相互协议，缔约双方特此同意如下。

7. 该项不动产包括土地连同地面上的一切建筑物和辅助设施。

8. 工程师应该按公司规定的标准价格得到报酬。

9. 高级职员或董事不得在卖方业务中使用的或从属于该业务的商标或商号中占有任何利益。

10. 由于没有满足该项要求，这笔债务应被视为到期应付款。

三、从句翻译练习（指出下列英文合同复合句中包含的从句类型，并翻译成中文）

1. While every employee is encouraged to exercise his/her political rights and responsibilities as an individual, either party or any employee may use resources of respective party to make any political contributions to any political party or to any person seeking political office.

2. In the event that the Company's operations are reduced substantially from the scale of operation originally anticipated by the parties, or the Company experiences substantial and continuing losses resulting in negative retained earnings not anticipated by the Parties in the agreed Business Plan, or in any other circumstance permitted under Applicable Laws or agreed by the Parties, the Parties may agree to reduce the registered capital of the Company on a pro rata basis.

3. Either Party may terminate the contract in case of failure on the part of the other Party to fulfill or perform any of its obligations hereunder and in the event that such failure remains un-remedied sixty (60) days after the service of a written notice as described in Article × below by the non-defaulting Party to the other Party specifying the failure in question and requiring it to be remedied.

4. Party B guarantees that Party B is the legitimate owner of the know-how and technical documentation supplied by Party B to Party A in accordance with the stipulations of the Contract, and that Party B is lawfully in a position to transfer the above-mentioned know-how and technical documentation to Party A. If any/a third party brings a charge of infringement, Party B shall be responsible for dealing with the third Party and bear the full legal and financial responsibility which may arise therefrom.

5. Upon the expiration or earlier termination of the Strategic Alliance Agreement, all Confidential Information, together with all transcripts, reproductions or physical reproductions thereof in any form then in the Transferee's custody, control or possession shall be promptly returned or destroyed in accordance with the request of the Transferor, except an original writing may be retained for archival purposes in the files of the Transferee's Legal Department.

四、翻译下列句子（注意规范句型的翻译）

1. The surety who pays the principal obligation is subrogated to the rights of the creditor.

2. Three partners own equal shares in a building from which a cornice falls and injures Tom. One partner pays the demand of $ 3,000 for Tom's injury; he is entitled to a contribution of $ 1,000 from each of his partners.

3. The Parties have any controversy, claim or dispute arising from or otherwise relating to this Agreement, such controversy, claim or disputes shall first be submitted to the Parties respective relationship coordinators.

4. If a technological achievement accomplished by an individual was an assignment from the legal person or other organization with which he formerly served and was chiefly accomplished by utilizing the material and technological resources of the legal person or other organization which he is currently serving, the rights and interests therein shall be determined in accordance with the agreement reached between the legal person or other organization with which the natural person formerly served and the one with which he is currently serving. If they fail to reach an agreement, the two parties shall share the technological achievement reasonably in proportion to their contributions to the accomplishment thereof.

5. The surveyor(s) shall surrender to the proper officer of the Corporation the certificates of the subscribers, and shall receive for them new certificates issued to them as trustee(s) under this agreement.

五、翻译下列句子中的下划线部分（注意被动语态的翻译）

1. The prices stated are based on current freight rates, and any increase or decrease in freight rates at time of shipment is to be the benefit of the buyer, with the seller assuming the payment of all transportation charges to the point or place of delivery.

2. If any terms and conditions to this Contract are breached and the breach is not corrected by any party within 15 days after a written notice thereof is given by the other party, then the non-breaching party shall have the option to terminate this Contract by giving written notice thereof to the breaching party.

3. In case the quality, quantity or weight of the goods is found not in conformity to those stipulated in this Contract after reinspection by the China Import and Export Commodity Inspection Bureau within 15 days after the arrival of the goods at the port of destination, the Buyer shall return the goods to, or lodge claim against the Seller for compensation of losses upon the strength of Inspection Certificate issued by the said Bureau, with the exception of those claims for which the insurers or the carriers are liable.

4. If a registered auditor is necessary to be employed to undertake annual financial checking and examination, Party A shall give its consent. All the expenses thereof shall be borne by Party B.

5. All disputes arising from the execution of, or in connection with the Contract shall be settled through friendly consultation between both parties hereto. In case no settlement can be reached, the disputes shall be submitted for arbitration.

六、翻译下列句子（注意"的"字结构的翻译）

1. 有下列情形之一的，不得就损失索赔。

2. 货物运输需要办理审批、检验等手续的，托运人应当将办理完有关手续的文件提交承运人。

3. 没有采取措施致使损失扩大的，应该承担对损失的赔偿责任。

七、翻译下列句子（注意下划线部分介词短语的翻译）

1. Shipment during the period beginning on April 1 and ending on Oct. 20, both dates inclusive, subject to Buyer's Letter of Credit reaching Seller on and before Mar. 20.

2. Party A shall be unauthorized to accept any orders or to collect any account on and after September 20.

3. The terms are cash within three months, i. e. on or before May 1.

4. Payment: By irrevocable L/C at sight to reach the sellers 30 days before the time of shipment. The L/C shall be valid for negotiation in China until the 15th day after the date of shipment.

八、将下列长句子翻译为中文

1. Assignment and Delegation.

(1) No Assignments. No party may assign any of its rights under this Agreement except with the prior written consent of the other party. The party shall not unreasonably withhold its consent. All assignments of rights are prohibited under this subsection, whether they are voluntary or in voluntary, by merger, consolidation, dissolution, operation of law, or any other manner. For purposes of this Section:

(a) A change of control is deemed an assignment of rights;

(b) "Merger" refers to any merger in which a party participates, regardless of whether it is the surviving or disappearing corporation.

(2) No Delegations. No party may delegate any performance under this Agreement.

(3) Ramifications of Purported Assignment or Delegation. Any purported assignment of rights or delegation of performance in violation of this Section is void.

2. Should any purported obligation or liability of the Customer (which, if valid or enforceable, would be the subject of this Deed) be or become wholly or in part invalid or unenforceable against the Customer on any ground whatsoever including any defect in or insufficiency or want of powers of the Customer, or irregular or improper purported exercise thereof or breach or want of authority by any person purporting to act on behalf of the Customer, or any legal limitation, disability, menial or other incapacity, or any other fact or circumstance, whether or not known to you, or if, for any other reason whatsoever, the Customer is not or ceases to be legally liable to discharge any obligation or liability undertaken or purported to be undertaken on the Customers behalf, the Covenanter shall nevertheless be liable to you in respect of that obligation or liability or purported

obligation or liability as if the same were wholly valid and enforceable and the Covenanter was the principal debtor in respect thereof.

3. Any failure or delay in the performance by either party hereto of its obligations under this Agreement shall not constitute a breach hereof or give rise to any claims for damages if and to the extent that it is caused by occurrence beyond the control of the party affected, including, but without limiting the generality of the forgoing, acts of governmental authority, acts of god strikes or concerted acts of workmen, fires, floods, explosions, wars, riots, storms, earthquakes, accidents, acts of a public enemy rebellion, insurrection, sabotage, epidemic quarantine restrictions, shortages of labour, materials or supplies, failures by contractors or subcontractors transportation embargoes, failures or delays in transportation, rules regulations, orders, or directives of any government or any state, subdivision, agency or instrumentality thereof or the order of any court of competent jurisdiction.

4. In the event that any party hereto is prevented from executing the contract or executing it in accordance with the agreed terms and conditions by force majeure, such as earthquakes, typhoon, flood, fire, wars or any other unforeseen accidents, whose occurrence and consequences are unpreventable and unavoidable, the prevented party shall inform the other party thereof by telegram without delay, and within 15 days thereafter provide detailed information of the events and a valid document as evidence issued by the competent notary authorities explaining the reason for its failure to execute or delay in executing the whole contract or part of it.

5. Section 2.1 Agreements to Supply

Subject to the terms and conditions of this Agreement, Supplier shall harvest, prepare, process and sell to Buyer Biomass in such quantities and at such times as are specified in Purchase Orders placed by Buyer pursuant to this Agreement and on the other terms and conditions set forth in this Agreement. The Biomass shall be supplied dried and ground in bulk form and packaged in bulk containers in accordance with the Harvesting Guidelines.

Section 2.2 Purchase Price

The purchase price to be paid by Buyer to Supplier for Biomass shall be $ 8,200 per ton (the "Initial Purchase Price"). Sales of Biomass shall be CIF from supplier site, wherever it would be, cleared for export to the site designated by Buyer in Chongqing, the People's Republic of China. After the twelve (12) month anniversary of the first delivery of Biomass to Buyer pursuant to this Agreement, Supplier may increase the Initial Purchase Price by the lower of (i) three percent (3%), or (ii) the percentage increase in the Consumer Price Index as reported by the United States Department of Labour for the corresponding period; provided, however, that a price increase may be made only one time during any twelve month period. Supplier shall give Buyer at least sixty (60) days prior a written notice of the increase and the increase will be effective for purchase orders issued after the effective date of the increase.

Section 2.3 Purchase Orders

Purchases and sales of Biomass hereunder shall be implemented by Buyer's issuance of individual purchase orders specifying the quantity, desired delivery date and delivery address of the Products. The terms of this Agreement shall not be amended or modified by any Purchase Order or invoice, unless agreed to by the parties. Buyer estimates in good faith that it will be able to utilize and purchase a minimum of 13.8 tons of Biomass per year; provided that the Biomass contains 0.03% of paclitaxel on an annual basis and is otherwise satisfactory to Buyer.

九、将下列中文翻译成英文

1. A. 甲方的权利和义务

（1）甲方负责向乙方提供具有国际领先水平的新型民用住宅建筑材料的专利技术资料及相关专用生产设备，并出具相关专利技术证书。

（2）甲方负责指导乙方掌握生产设备安装维修操作与新型建材的安装、修缮专业技术，并负责完成乙方员工的上述技能培训工作。

（3）在双方协作合同正式签订之后一个半月，甲方无偿向乙方提供一辆载重大卡车。

（4）甲方待产品正式投产后，将中国山西、河南、陕西三省的销售总代理权授予乙方。

（5）甲方负责向乙方提供厂房建筑设计图纸资料及新型板材环保证明材料，并为乙方提供生产厂房的安装技术培训。

（6）在正式投产后，甲方协助乙方降低成本，并包销该项目的全部产品，包销时间双方另行商定。

（7）甲方保证所提供的生产设备，按每日双班工作、每周5日工作制计算，年生产能力达到100万张新型建材板。

（8）甲方负责保证乙方按期、保质、保量供应原材料，并提供材料的真实价格资料。

B. 乙方的权利和义务

（1）乙方付款300万美元，购买甲方提供的生产设备。付款方式与时间如下：

①300万美元分两期付款，首期150万美元分两次支付：第1次付定金50万美元，通过中介银行汇入甲方账户；第2次款项为100万美元，通过开具信用证方式支付。

②第2期150万美元在5年内付清，从2014年到2019年，每年年底付30万美元。

（2）乙方负责提供生产流动资金500万元人民币。

（3）乙方负责提供生产场地、厂房。

（4）待双方合作项目正式签约后，乙方同意甲方以专利技术投资入股，占该项目纯利润的35%（按照国际惯例方法计算）。

（5）自本协议签订之日到正式合同签订期间，甲乙双方各自承担本方发生的费用。

（6）董事长、总经理由乙方选派，会计、审计由甲方选派。

（7）管理、生产由乙方负责。

上述条款经协商一致，签订正式文本后生效。

甲方代表：　　　　　　　　　　　乙方代表：

日　　期：　　　　　　　　　　　日　　期：

2. 甲乙双方应尽力以最有效、经济的办法实现合营公司的经营宗旨和目标，并在现行法律和允许的营业范围内选派有资格、有经验的管理人员和技术人员在公司工作。

3.本合同第2条中的设备费（青岛到岸价150万美元），货抵达青岛后，凭提单、商业发票、装箱清单，经甲乙双方银行审核与本合同规定的规格、型号、数量相符后，甲方按货价90%的金额兑现给乙方。

4.如果仲裁在中国进行，则应将案件提交北京或上海或深圳中国国际经济贸易仲裁委员会，适用该委员会的仲裁规则；如果仲裁在日本进行，则应将案件提交东京或大阪日本商事仲裁协会，适用该仲裁组织的仲裁规则。

5.合伙企业一经终止或解散，应立即对合伙企业进行清算，分配剩余资金前对所有债务应先予清偿，然后根据上文第5条规定的出资比例进行分配。

十、将下列短文翻译为中文

Invoices and Payment

1. Supplier shall invoice Buyer for the Biomass supplied to Buyer pursuant to this Agreement, referencing in each such invoice the shipment to which such invoice relates. Payments shall be made in U.S. Dollars at Supplier's address set forth in this Agreement for notices or, if requested by Supplier, by wire transfer of immediately available funds to an account designated by Supplier in written notice to Buyer. Any costs associated with the wire transfers shall be paid by Supplier.

2. Following the execution of this Agreement, Buyer will make, or cause one of its Affiliates to make, advance 30% to Supplier of the principal sum of $8,200 per ton, the remaining 70% will be made by L/C to the designated account upon receiving the lading document in the port of export. The minimum purchase is one container of dried biomass (approximately 13.8 tons). The advance payment shall be conditioned on Buyer or its Affiliate first having received from Supplier an invoice prior to the harvest of this product, which is usually 2-3 weeks (from the date of advance payment and date of shipment) depending on harvesting season.

Problems with Supply

As soon as it shall become apparent to Supplier that circumstances resulting in any failure or delay in delivery of Buyer's requirements of any Biomass will continue for more than thirty (30) days, Supplier shall promptly notify Buyer of the details thereof and as soon as possible thereafter have a meeting with Buyer to discuss the best method of resuming continuous supply. In the event that at any time Buyer is not reasonably satisfied that Supplier will be able to meet its supply obligations in strict compliance with this Agreement, then Buyer shall have, in addition to any other rights and remedies it may have, the right to terminate this Agreement upon thirty (30) days with written notice to Supplier.

十一、将下列短文翻译为英文

甲乙双方经协商，共同达成如下条款的约定：

1.甲乙双方本着互惠互利的原则，建立业务合作伙伴关系，签订本销售合作协议书。

2.本协议代表了双方平等的贸易关系，双方共同承诺的权利与义务有：

甲方的义务：

1.不定期向乙方提供甲方新的商品信息。

2. 提供所售商品的销售许可证、技术标准、质检证明、产品说明书。

3. 按乙方需求提供合格的商品，及时交货，并提供必要的商品售后服务。

甲方的权利：

1. 审核乙方资信情况，确定赊销信用额度及赊销期。

2. 根据双方的约定向乙方收取销售款。

乙方的义务：

1. 向甲方如实提供乙公司营业执照复印件、银行开户许可证复印件、委托签约的法人授权委托书及甲方合理要求的其他材料。

2. 以清楚规范的形式，向甲方提出订货单。

3. 按规定的期限和结算方式向甲方支付已购商品的货款。

乙方的权利：

1. 要求甲方按照订单准确及时地提供商品，但乙方的订单需得到甲方的确认，甲方可根据其库存或乙方的要求来决定是否接受乙方订单。

2. 对有质量问题或不符合订单要求的商品，可在交付货物后30天内带原包装按甲方"退换货制度"给予退换。

3. 甲方应乙方要求向乙方提供产品报价、订货期及相关资料。

写作篇　撰写合同条款及案例分析练习

实训项目4

合同结构条款练习①

实训目标

1. 掌握英文合同结构条款的内容。
2. 掌握英文合同结构条款撰写的注意事项。

一、选择同义词或近义词填空并翻译句子

1. During the term of this Agreement, Party A shall undertake, _____ (extend, renew) and maintain for its benefits and interest, and _____ (at its own cost and expense, on one's account) of the following primary insurance _____ (policies, certificates).

2. Words importing the singular include the plural and _____ (vice versa, in reverse order from that stated).

3. Party forever _____ (releases, discharge) any discharges the other _____ (from, out of) all claims, debts, allegations, actions, causes of action and demands, whether known or unknown, arising from or in connection with the Claim and existing as at the date of this Settlement Agreement, including without limitation any liability for legal costs connected with or _____ (arising out of, rising from) the subject matter of the Claim.

---

① [1] 乔焕然. 英文合同阅读指南：英文合同的结构、条款、句型与词汇分析 [M]. 最新增订版. 北京：中国法制出版社，2015. [2] 王相国. 鏖战英文合同：英文合同的翻译与起草 [M]. 最新增订版. 北京：中国法制出版社，2014. [3] 吴敏，吴明忠. 国际经贸英语合同写作 [M]. 广州：暨南大学出版社，2002. [4] 刘川，王菲. 英文合同阅读与翻译 [M]. 北京：国防工业出版社，2010. [5] 王立非，国际商务合同实践教程 [M]. 上海：上海外语教育出版社，2012.

4. The express warranties in this Agreement shall be _____ (in lieu of, instead of) all other warranties, express or implied, including the implied warranties of merchantability non-infringement, interoperability and fitness for a particular purpose.

5. The local court is the _____ (competent, jurisdictional) court to deal with the case.

6. All the relevant taxes shall be levied _____ (on, against) Party B.

The judge levied a $ 5 million fine _____ (on, against) the factory for polluting the river.

7. The examination and approval authority shall, _____ (in, within) three months of the receipt of all the documents set out in Article 5 of these Regulations decide whether to approve or not to approve such documents.

8. This contract needs _____ (confirmed, confirmation) by the manager.

Before entering into a formal contract, I will send you a _____ (confirmation, agreement).

9. The Party A lodged a _____ (compensation, claim) against the Party B for his breach of contract.

Party A claimed $ 1,000 _____ (for, against) Party B.

10. In consideration of the exclusive right herein granted, Party A shall _____ (in no way, not in any way) directly or indirectly sell or export products to territory through any other channel than Party B.

二、选用正确的词及形式填空

1. withdraw, revoke, rescind

(1) application for _____ of an action

(2) An offer may be _____. The revocation notice of an offer shall reach the offeree prior to the dispatch of an acceptance notice by the offeree.

(3) The other party may demand that the legal agent ratify the contract within one month. Where the legal agent fails to manifest its intention, it shall be deemed as refusal to ratify the contract. Prior to ratification of the contract, the other party in good faith is entitled to _____ the contract. Rescission shall be affected by notification.

2. terminate, cancel, rescind

(1) An invalid, _____ or terminated contract does not influence the enforceability of any relevant disputes resolution Article which exists independently.

(2) _____ a contract

(3) To _____ a collective contract through written agreement

3. competent, eligible

(1) _____ authority

(2) the right to be _____ for public office

(3) The purpose of a flexible spending account is to permit _____ employees to elect to defer part of their pay on a pre-tax basis to defray the cost of their unreimbursed medical and dental care, the cost of the unreimbursed medical and dental care for their refuse and dependents and dependent care expenses.

(4) If for any reason any court of _____ jurisdiction shall find any provisions of this Section 15 unreasonable in duration or geographic scope or otherwise, the Executive and the Company agree that the restrictions and prohibitions contained herein shall be effective to the fullest extent allowed under applicable law in such jurisdiction.

4. bear, assume

(1) The Company shall _____ and pay directly all costs and expenses (including additional interest and penalties) incurred in connection with such contest and shall indemnify the Executive.

(2) The Party A may withhold consent on any of the following grounds: the Party B is in default of an obligation of this Agreement when consent is requested, the proposed assignee cannot financially perform the Party B's obligations remaining under this Agreement, the proposed assignee refuses to _____ all of the Party B's remaining obligations under this Agreement, or the proposed assignee fails to meet the Party A's standards for new Party B's in effect at the time consent is requested.

5. construe/construction, interpret/interpretation

(1) Nothing expressed or implied in this Agreement is intended or shall be _____ to give to any person or entity, other than the parties and the Party A's permitted assignees, any rights or remedies under or by reason of this Agreement.

(2) In the literature on legal drafting, a singular _____ typically works better than a plural one.

(3) The statutes are sometimes written in terms of presumed intention, and they are sometimes properly _____ as imposing the same legal consequences as if one of the parties to a contract had made a promise in the prescribed terms. If so, rules stated here may be applicable.

(4) If there is no explicit promise, and no government liability, the question whether a particular claimant is an intended beneficiary is one of _____ , depending on all the circumstances of the contract.

三、翻译下列结构条款中的下划线部分

1. (1) We have instructed our hank to open an irrevocable documentary letter of credit <u>in your favor</u> (in favor of you). The amount is $ 1,300.00.

(2) "The balance of power between contracting parties usually tips <u>in favor of</u> the party who drafts the written contract. "

2. In case her age exceeds 15 years, the extra average insurance premium thus <u>incurred</u> shall be home by the Party B.

3. (1) The judge asked <u>counsel</u> for the defense to explain his point.

(2) The United Nations Security <u>Council</u>.

(3) The <u>councilor</u> in charge of the contract objected to the plan.

(4) He is an excellent <u>counsellor</u>. I'd listen to him if I were you.

四、翻译下列常用合同结构条款（注意下划线部分句型/词在不同语境中的用法）

1. (1) Should the Party A be unable to arrange insurance in time owing to the Party B's failure to give the above-mentioned advice of shipment by cable or telex, the Party B shall be held responsible for any and all damages and/or losses attribute to such failure.

(2) Crime of being defaulted due to professional misconduct in signing and executing contract.

(3) In view of the personal nature of the service to be performed under this Agreement by you, you cannot assign or transfer any of your obligations under this Agreement.

(4) The purpose of the contract cannot be realized by virtue of force majeure.

2. (1) Notwithstanding Provision 16.1, Party B shall not be entitled to claim for itself in respect of any Force Majeure in Provision 16.1.

(2) Party C or New Company shall retain all rights with respect to the specifications, plans, drawings and other documents and Party B undertakes not to disclose the same or any information contained therein to any third party without the prior written consent of Party C or New Company.

(3) Broker is in the business of brokering real estate loans and engages sales representative to perform services pertaining to such business.

(4) All activities of the Cooperative venture company shall be governed by the laws, decrees and pertinent rules and regulations of the Peopled Republic of China.

3. (1) Whereas/while other countries were inspired by the Enlightenment to codify laws and written constitutions, Britain clung to a common law tradition.

(2) Many countries differ from/are different from England in that they have written constitutions.

(3) The English judge takes no part in deciding guilt or innocence. The French judge, in/by contrast, readies a verdict together with the jury.

(4) The American legal system, as distinct from the British one, allows lawyers to charge contingency fees.

4. (1) Party A's right to reject is prior to acceptance of goods.

(2) Upon acceptance, does this offer form the basis of a binding contract?

(3) If under the terms of the agreement the order of performance depends on an event subsequent to the time of making the contract, that event is to be taken into account.

五、用英文撰写下列导言条款

（一）开场白条款（合同的当事人背景介绍）

1. 本合同依照_____州法律组织设立，于_____［国籍］的____年____月____日签订。

双方当事人为：_____公司（以下简称"甲方"），主营业地为____

____；_____（以下简称"乙方"），居住于_____。

2.本合同由_____［地址］的_____

_____［自然人或实体类型以及国籍或成立地点］

（甲方）和_____［地址］的_____

_____［自然人或实体类型以及国籍或成立地点］（乙方）订立于

_____［日期］。

（二）序言条款

1.（1）双方同意由甲方生产并销售_____［描述货物或附件中列明的当前产品目录］，并且在将来可能开发并生产具有类似功能的其他_____
［货物种类］。

（2）甲方希望指定乙方作为在_____州或国（"区域"）内的独家的并且排他的经销商。

（3）乙方希望成为该区域内的销售甲方货物的独家排他性经销商。有鉴于此，双方同意如下：

2.甲方任命乙方作为其在该销售区域内的独家排他性经销商，以从事货物转卖、租赁。乙方接受此任命。

（三）用英文撰写下列过渡条款

因此，双方基于各自提供之对价订立本合同，并作如下约定：

六、用英文撰写下列通用条款

（一）用英文撰写下列定义条款

1.本合同于201____年____月____日由以下两方在_____［地点］签订。_____［甲方名称］，一家根据中华人民共和国法律组建及存续的_____［甲方组织形式］，［注册］［主要营业场所］地址为_____；_____［乙方名称］，一家根据_____［乙方所在国］法律组建及存续的_____［乙方组织形式］，［注册］［主要营业场所］地址为_____。双方以下单独称为"一方"，合称为"双方"。

2.本合同中所提到之任何一方当事人之"关联企业"，系指直接或间接控制该当事人，或受该当事人控制，或与该当事人受控于同一企业。前述"控制"指通过合同或其他方式，掌握受控制企业51%以上之股东投票权，从而拥有主导该企业之经营与政策的能力与权力。

（二）用英文撰写下列陈述与保证条款

1.甲方陈述和保证，构成土地全部或任何部分的房地产，其内部、上面、下面或其相关的部位现在不存在，也不可能存在危害人身健康或环境的情况(无论是否符合法律规定），且土地上从未生产、使用、处理、储存、运输或处置过任何危险的或有毒的物质、污染物或致污物，土地内部、上面或上空亦未曾释放过任何危险的或有毒的物质、污染物或致污物。

甲方进一步陈述和保证，土地不存在任何权利主张、抵押、地役权、权利负担、租约、契约、担保权益、留置权、购买权、质押、他人权利或限制，无论是以协议、谅解、普通法、衡平法还是其他方法设定的。

2. 担保。甲方应为每个货物给予乙方如甲方提供给自己的客户的有限担保。乙方必须将甲方的担保提供给每一个购买其商品的人。乙方不得对甲方的担保条款作出任何变更。甲方应立即修理或退还任何出现故障或其他任何担保之下的缺陷的货物，无论乙方或乙方的顾客在此时是否拥有该货物。

（三）用英文撰写下列补偿条款

1. 各方谨此表示，因一方被指控违反、实际违反或未遵守本协议条款和条件，包括但不限于由于该方与项目相关的过错、不作为或活动导致对另一方的知识产权或其他权利的侵犯，而引起的任何和所有索赔、诉讼、损害、支出（包括律师费和管理费），均由该违约方向另一方作出赔偿，且违约方承诺使另一方免受损害，并为其进行抗辩。

2. 补偿

双方约定如下互惠补偿条款：

（1）乙方将对甲方补偿可以归因于乙方行为、操作或履行义务过程中导致的人身伤亡、财产损失。

（2）甲方将对乙方补偿可以归因于甲方的产品缺陷、失误、故障，而并非乙方造成的索赔，但因乙方所致或可归因于乙方行为、操作或履行除外。在本协议的期间内，甲方负责对销售给甲方产品的质量责任投保，至少每次的总额为_____［货币与数量］，并且保单应当以乙方作为额外被保险人。

（四）用英文撰写下列保密条款

1. 甲方已经提供并且在本协议有效期间内继续向乙方提供与被许可软件以及甲方服务相关的技术、商业信息以帮助乙方履行其项下的义务。上述信息包括包含在与被许可软件、甲方服务设计、生产相关说明书及图纸中的信息。甲方对这些信息享有所有权。乙方具有如下权利和义务：

（1）仅为该等目的使用该等信息；

（2）由于这些信息不为公众所知，乙方不得复制、散布、披露任何上述信息（包括但不限于具有上述性质的信息，甲方可以随时特别指定信息具有保密性质）；

（3）本协议终止后，应向甲方公司返还所有包含由甲方公司所指定为机密的资料及其副本；

（4）确保与本许可软件相关之人员知悉并遵守本条款。

2. 保密义务

在本协议约定的保密期间，信息接收方应采取所有必要的（商业）（合理）手段，以保持保密信息的保密性［包括但不限于其用来保护自己的（性质类似的）保密信息的所有手段]。除此之外，信息接收方还应促使其代表遵守本协议之规定并且阻止任何的代表对保密信息进行任何披露。

3. 无权使用

信息接收方应立即将任何对保密信息的无权使用（披露）通知公司，且应协助公司对该种无权使用或披露进行救济。进行协助并不代表接受方不违反本条规定，接受协助也不代表对该违反的豁免。

（五）用英文撰写下列期间与终止条款

1. 期间与续展

（1）本合同期间为合同生效之日起____［年数］年，但当事人提前终止合同则不受此限。

（2）本合同期间届满后，除非当事人于期间届满之日前60日通知对方当事人表示不再续约，否则本合同期限自动延长一年。

2. 甲方终止

在下述情况下，甲方有权以叫乙方发出书面通知的形式终止本协议，该终止效力见本协议之第一条：

（a）乙方实质违背或违反本协议中的任何合意、陈述或保证，且甲方在成交之时或成交之前未书面放弃就该种违背或违反所享有的权利；

（b）乙方未能满足甲方履行义务的任一条件，且甲方未在成交之时或成交之前对此进行豁免。

（六）用英文撰写下列合同转让与变更条款

1. 被禁止转移合同权利的当事人（比如许可合同中的乙方）除非经过受保护的当事人（比如许可合同中的甲方）事先书面同意，不得将本合同及本合同项下的权利转移给任何第三人（包括企业与个人），但（受保护的当事人）非有正当理由不得拒绝同意。

2. 协议的变更

本协议只有经过双方书面签字的形式才能进行变更。

（七）用英文撰写下列合同完整性条款

1. 本合同的所有附件是合同不可分割的一部分。本合同及其附件构成双方就本合同规定的标的达成的完整协议，并取代双方先前与该标的相关的一切口头和书面的洽谈、谈判、通知、备忘录、文件、协议和合同。

2. 完整协议

本协议、本协议中提及的文件以及本协议的附件构成甲方和开发人就本协议之标的的完整、全部和完全的合意，并取代所有的先前合意。除本协议规定可由甲方单方面进行之外，未经双方同意并且其授权管理人或代理书面签署，任何对本协议的修订、改变或变动都对双方当事人没有约束力。

（八）用英文撰写下列合同可分性条款

1. 若本协议之任何条款被认定为无效、非法或不可强制执行，本协议的其他条款仍将保持全部效力，但前提是本协议的基本条款和条件仍然有效、合法和可强制执行。双方当事人承认并同意第____、____和____条构成本协议标的，即双方同意的交换之基本要素（该种承认和同意不构成对上一句的限制）。相应地，若这些条款的任何实质方面被认定为无效、非法或不可强制执行，本协议的其他部分对任一方都不具有强制执行力。上述具体列举的条款并不意味着也不暗示本协议的其他条款都不构成本协议的标的，即双方同意的交换之基本要素。

2. 可分性

若本协议之任何条款成为或被有管辖权的法院宣布为非法、不可强制执行或无效，本协议之其余部分应继续保持完全效力。但该种条款分离实质上改变了任一方本协议下的经济利益的除外。

（九）用英文撰写下列合同不弃权条款

1. 一方当事人对他方当事人违背或不执行本合同约定之情形表示放弃追究法律责任的权利的，该弃权不得被解释为连续性弃权。对他方将来可能发生的违约行为，守约方仍有权追究其责任。

2. 弃权与履行迟延。如果一方当事人对另一方当事人的某些违约行为弃权，或者未能、拒绝或疏于行使本协议赋予的权利或权力，或者未坚持要求严格履行本协议，任何一方不得仅仅因此而认为该方放弃其根据本协议条款寻求违约救济的权利或要求严格履行本协议的权利。

3. 弃权。本协议中的任何条款都不得被放弃，除非由该种放弃所试图针对的一方当事人签署书面文件进行。

（十）用英文撰写下列合同不可抗力条款

1. 除付款义务外，任何一方当事人均不因超出其可合理控制的因素造成的未能履行或迟延履行负责。这些因素包括但不限于供应商或分包商违约、各种类型的产业纠纷、雇佣关系僵局、罢工。

2. （同意对方免责的当事人）同意（得以免责的当事人）不必为非（得以免责的当事人）所能控制的因素而引起的损失、现在或将来发生的伤害、扣留、全部或部分的给付迟延或给付不能而负责。此等因素包括但不限于：天灾、（同意对方免责的当事人的）作为或不作为、火灾、罢工、叛乱、暴动、禁运、运输迟延、无法取得原料、（国名）政府或其他军事或一般机关之法令规定。当事人依本条款免除给付迟延或债务不履行之责任者，他方当事人支付买卖价款之义务并不因此而减免。

（十一）用英文撰写下列合同竞业禁止条款

1. 乙方承诺，在本合同及本合同终止后两年的期间内，不得以在生产、销售或经销过程中作为委托人、合伙人、代理人、承包人或雇员，从事乙方根据本合同已经经销的任何产品。

2.竞业禁止约定

任何竞争企业或任何竞争企业的关联公司、相关实体、继受者或受让人合作（包括但不限于作为独资人、所有人、雇主、合伙人、本人、投资者、合资人、股东、合作人、雇员、成员、顾问、承包商或其他身份进行合作），以及与上述合作相关，从事咨询服务，但就任何竞争企业的公开交易的或成为公开交易的股票而言，合伙人作为被动投资者拥有一个竞争企业已发行的公开交易的股票不足1%时，不得被视为违反本协议。

（十二）用英文撰写下列合同知识产权条款

1.知识产权保护

甲方知晓乙方对其所售商品的设计、专利、商标、商号及公司名称（知识产权）拥有排他性权利。甲方无权拥有乙方的任何知识产权。甲方不得如使用乙方的财产那样使用乙方的知识产权，亦不得如属于自己的财产那样对乙方知识产权在任何国家进行注册。甲方承认其如使用或注册乙方知识产权，或者与乙方知识产权混淆的知识产权将构成侵害乙方的专有权。

2.知识产权

双方同意：

（1）甲方拥有与产品相关的所有商标、名称、设计、专利和商业秘密的知识产权。该等权利没有被授予乙方。乙方不得声称已拥有甲方的知识产权，亦不得使用甲方的名义作为自己的名义。知识产权均保留于甲方。

（2）乙方在进行经销、转销、租赁货物时，有权使用该等知识产权，但不得再将该等知识产权用于其他任何目的。

（3）所有的广告、促销材料、报价单、发票、标志以及其他所有与产品相关的其他材料必须包括表明甲方拥有该等知识产权的通知，并且这些材料必须声明乙方是被授权的销售者。

（4）乙方不得在使用与产品相关的知识产权过程中对其进行任何改变。所有的细节、色彩和设计必须与甲方规定的完全一致。

（5）只有在货物使用与甲方的知识产权相关的情况下，乙方才可以转售、租赁货物。乙方不得销售非由甲方提供而使用甲方的知识产权的任何产品。

（6）乙方不得仿冒或试图仿冒任何货物，不得向其他意图仿冒的人提供产品，或生产或制造任何与产品相混淆或会引起欺骗后果的产品。

（7）乙方不得从事可能会损害甲方知识产权的注册或产权的行为。乙方不得试图改变或取消知识产权的任何登记。乙方不得协助他人从事此等行为。

（8）违反本条款将立即导致本协议的终止。同时，双方同意违反本协议将导致对甲方声誉、商誉、知识财产价值的损害，从而会引发实质损害赔偿。此等损害将是无法估量的，因为难以计算无形财产价值。因此，双方同意如果乙方违反本条款，则甲方有权对乙方主张约定违约金，违约金数量等于甲方当前产品目录上所列明的被侵犯产品价格的百分之_____〔数字〕。

（十三）用英文撰写下列合同违约条款

1. 如果甲方实质性违反本合同，乙方或其权利的继受人有权终止本合同。如果乙方实质性违反本合同，甲方如发出书面通知，有权要求乙方在收到书面通知后15天内改正违约行为。如果乙方在15天期限内未予改正，甲方则有权解除合同，并要求得到违约赔偿。

2. 如果一方实质上未履行其在本合同项下的任何义务，或一方在本合同项下的陈述或保证实质上是不真实的或不准确的，该方应被视为违反了本合同。违约方应在收到另一方指明其违约行为的通知后30日内，纠正其违约行为（若该违约行为是可以纠正的）。无论如何，违约方有责任赔偿另一方因该等违约而造成的一切损害。如果守约方根据×条款终止本合同，违约方仍应给予损害赔偿。本合同规定的法律规定的一切救济应是累积的。

（十四）用英文撰写下列合同纠纷解决条款

1. 因本合同效力、解释或执行所发生之任何纠纷，双方同意以最大之善意与努力，在60日或双方同意之期限内，以友好的方式协商解决。

2. 任何由本合同引起或与本合同相关的协议，包括其是否存在、有效、终止等问题，均应提交给新加坡，根据新加坡国际仲裁中心当时有效的仲裁规则（SIAC规则）进行最终解决，该规则应被视为已经合并到本条款中。仲裁庭应由该中心主席指定的仲裁员组成。仲裁语言应当为（　　　）。

七、用英文撰写下列合同常用条款

（一）用英文撰写下列合同先决条件条款

1. 注册资本的缴付

如果批复、批准证书或营业执照（合称"批准文件"）中某一份含有对相关内容的实质性修改，则双方应共同协商并作出以下决定：

（1）接受这些实质性修改，并且放弃第2.1条所载相应的先决条件；

（2）向相关政府机关申请，对该份批准文件以双方均可接受的方式进行修订，并且重新颁发。

此外，如果所颁发的批复或批准证书含有实质性修改，且双方未能达成一致接受这些实质性修改并放弃相应的先决条件，则在就这些实质性修改以双方均可接受的方式得到解决前，双方不应向市场监督管理局申请颁发营业执照。

2. 先决条件

双方在此明确规定，本修订及本修订下双方义务之先决条件为：Cmiexis公司和出租方签署"交出空间"（定义见下文）及特定额外空间的新的书面租赁合同，且该合同在所有实质及形式方面均为出租方认可（是否认可完全由出租方自主决定）（下称"ABC租赁合同"）。若该先决条件未被满足，或出租方自主决定放弃该先决条件，则本修订无效，且不具有任何效力，但既存的租赁协议仍将保持完全效力，并不受本修订之影响。出租方应书面通知该先决条件已经被满足或被放弃。

（二）用英文撰写下列合同保险条款

1. 由买方委托卖方按发票金额的110%代为投保××险和××险，保险费由买方负担，按1981年1月1日中国人民保险公司海洋运输货物保险条款为准。

2. 保险由卖方按发票金额110%投保水渍险，保险期间为仓至仓，延伸至比利时布鲁塞尔，保险依据1981年1月1日中国人民保险公司海洋运输货物保险条款办理。

（三）用英文撰写下列独立合同关系条款

1. 独立的合同当事人关系

销售代理商认可并同意因本合同而成立的关系为独立承包商关系，而非员工雇佣关系。本合同不得解释为订立合伙和合营企业、信托关系或任何其他类似关系，任何一方对另一方的债务均不负任何责任，也无权约束另一方执行任何合同。销售代理商有权雇用员工或独立的承包商，并且甲方无权限制、解聘或雇用此等员工。保证在_____ ［国家］从事商业行为时符合当地法律的要求是销售代理商的职责。销售代理商另需对因货物在_____ ［国家］销售而产生的税收和费用等债务或责任负责。甲方无须对乙方因履行本合同而产生的损失、索赔或其他责任承担责任。销售代理商将根据甲方的合理要求帮助将货物运到消费者手中。

2. 双方的关系

双方均承认乙方是单独和独立于甲方的。本协议不得被解释为雇佣、合伙、合营企业、信托或其他任何相似的关系。一方对另一方的债务或责任不负责任，亦无权要求其承担任何合同义务。乙方可自行决定雇佣或与任何人员及独立的合同当事人订立协议，而且甲方无权限制、解聘或雇用这些人。确保在_____ ［国家］的经营符合当地法律的要求，是乙方的义务。对_____ ［国家］货物销售而引起的税务和费用的支付问题，亦应由乙方自行负责。甲方对乙方在转售、租赁货物过程中发生的损失、索赔或其他责任不负责任。

（四）用英文撰写下列合同税收条款

1. 合营企业进口下列物资，依照中国税法的相关规定减税、免税：

（1）按照合同规定作为外国合营者出资的机器设备、零部件和其他物料（其他物料系指合营企业建厂（场）以及安装、加固机器所需材料，下同）；

（2）合营企业以投资总额以外的资金进口的机器设备、零部件和其他物料；

（3）经审批机关批准，合营企业以增加资本所进口的国内不能保证生产供应的机器设备、零部件和其他物料；

（4）合营企业为生产出口产品，从国外进口的原材料、辅料、元器件、零部件和包装物料。

上述减税、免税进口物资，经批准在中国国内转卖或者转用于在中国国内销售的产品，应当照章纳税或者补税。

2. 依照本协议应给付顾问的一切服务费、开支和其他费用，均不包括任何销售税、使用税、消费税、增值税或其他适用的税收、关税或税项，该等税款应由客户独家负责缴纳

（顾问净收入使用的税收或因顾问与其人员的雇佣关系或独立承包人关系而发生的税收除外）。如果该等税收、关税或税项向顾问征收，则客户须偿还顾问缴纳的该等税款，或在顾问缴纳该等税款前，向顾问提供该等税款予以豁免的有效证明。若法律规定客户须从根据本协议付给或应付给顾问的任何款项中扣除、代扣或缴纳税款，付给或应付给顾问的金额应返计还原，以确保顾问收到和保留的总额，相等于如同在不扣除或代扣税款情况下收到和保留的净收入，而无须缴纳该等税收。

（五）翻译下列税收条款

1. TAXES

Any and all payments under this Contract shall be made free and clear of any restriction, counterclaim, set off, deductions or withholdings (except to the extent required by law) on account of any tax or expenses charged, imposed, levied, collected, withheld or assessed by any person. If (a) any payment to be made under this Contract is subject to any deduction or withholding or, (b) the Company (or any person on its behalf) is required by law to make any deduction or withholding from, or (except on account of tax on the overall net income of the Company) any payment on or calculated by reference to the amount of, any sum received or receivable by the Company under this Contract, the Contractors hereby jointly and severally undertake to pay to the Company forthwith on demand such additional amounts as may be necessary to ensure that the net amounts received by the Company are equal to the amounts which the Company would otherwise have received.

2. TAXES

Each party shall be responsible for its own applicable taxes imposed upon it resulting from its performance of its part of this Agreement. Neither party shall be responsible for any unpaid taxes of the other party.

Should a governmental body mandate that Customer withhold or should have withheld tax from payments to Company, the invoiced amount payable, without regard to taxes, shall be adjusted in favor of Company, such that the amount received by Company after deduction of such withholding tax shall be equal to the amount it originally invoiced Customer with regard to taxes. Where the Customer withholds tax from payment to Company, the Customer will provide to Company a withholding tax certificate in a timely manner as evidence that the tax has been remitted to the relevant Governmental authority.

In the event that there is a change in the legislation of the country (ies) of operations or origin of payment, or in the interpretation of such legislation, including but not limited taxes or customs and excise duties of whatever nature, after the effective date of this Agreement, which results in an increase in the costs to Company of performing this Agreement, the Customer shall reimburse Company the amount of the increase in such costs.

The party responsible for notifying the tax authorities in the relevant jurisdiction where the services are being performed shall be governed by the tax legislation in that jurisdiction. The other party shall provide reasonable assistance for such matters, including the supply of relevant information in a timely manner.

（六）实务思考

案例1

代办保险不当致损案

中国某公司（卖方）曾按 CFR 条件和信用证付款方式向西非某国商人（买方）出售一批商品。由于目的港盗窃比较严重，故买方开来的信用证中要求卖方代其投保 WPA，并提供保险单，保险费可在信用证金额中支取。卖方为避免改证，遂同意代办保险。卖方即按我国过去出口此类商品的习惯做法，投保了 ALL RISKS 及 WAR RISK，发票金额和保险费总数未超过信用证金额。中国银行议付时已发现险别不符，但卖方认为 ALL RISKS 的承保责任范围大于 WPA 对买方有利，可不必改正。开证行收到单据后，表示拒付。后来，卖方只好用批单方式将险别改为 WPA 及 WAR RISK，保险费当然也相应减收。待更正的单据寄出后，卖方虽收到了货款，但蒙受晚期收汇的损失。

问题：导致卖方延迟收汇和蒙受利息损失的主要原因是什么？

案例2

误解加保战争险而引起的争议案

中国某公司（卖方）曾按 CIF 条件向澳大利亚某商人（买方）出售一批货物，买卖合同中没有约定投保的具体险别，卖方按合同规定发运了货物，并按国际惯例代买方投保了基本险中的平安险。后买方指责卖方漏保战争险，其理由是，既然货价中包括保险费，卖方就应加保战争险，双方因此产生争议。后经卖方有理有据地说明，买方终于消除误解。

问题：为什么说本案合同项下的买方指责卖方漏保战争险，完全是一种误解？

八、用英文撰写下列合同的操作性条款

1. 乙方的义务

（1）乙方应当积极向该经销区域内的消费者推广、销告、租赁其从甲方处购买的货物，并提供服务。

（2）乙方应当自行决定在经销区域内使用的各种销售策略，包括价目表、邮购订单、电话以及网络销售等。

（3）乙方应在经销区域内的选定地点至少开设一家销售店，以销售或租赁货物。该销售店必须在协议生效日期后_____［数字］日内开设。乙方有权自行决定在经销区域内开设其他零售店。

（4）乙方不得销售、租赁任何非由甲方生产的具有与甲方货物相同或易混淆相似功能的货物，以冒充甲方的货物。

（5）乙方不得向其他已经从事相同或混淆、欺骗性的货物销售、租赁的任何其他公司销售、租赁甲方的货物。

（6）乙方自行负责经营过程中产生的各种成本，包括税费、劳动成本以及相关的罚款。

（7）乙方负责获取所有的进口、运输、仓储以及货物在乙方国家销售的相关进口许可

证、运输许可证、营业执照以及其他类似许可。乙方亦有责任向甲方提供所有货物进口到乙方国内的进口及运输文件。如果乙方因甲方交付时限而未能提供文件，则因乙方造成的交付迟延不得被视为违约。

2.甲方的义务

（1）除非因乙方的过错造成延误或按照本协议的规定无法履行，甲方应当于_____〔数字〕日内向乙方交付其订购的货物。

（2）甲方将以船舶运输的方式将订购的货物运至销售区域内由乙方指定的地点，但是乙方应遵守进口方面的义务。甲方对在运输时间内取得出口许可证和检验以及完成出口要求负责。

（3）如果甲方因任何原因停止任何货物的生产，则其应立即通知乙方，同时在合理时间内继续提供替代货物，并提供已经销售货物的服务。

（4）除乙方之外，甲方不得将货物出售给其他任何在经销区域内销售、转销、租赁与甲方的货物相同或混淆的或欺骗性货物的人或企业。

（5）甲方不得在经销区域内将货物出售给除乙方之外的任何人或企业，或者为直接使用而进行交付。

（6）甲方应将其获知的关于在经销区域内潜在客户的所有潮流、趋势以及相似信息及时通知/提交乙方。

（7）甲方应提供建议零售价和租赁价，但该价格对乙方无约束力。

（8）甲方应向乙方及其员工提供关于货物使用、操作、维护、维修等方面的培训和技术指导。

（9）甲方应在行业、公众范围保持旨在提高货物质量形象和商誉的广告宣传。

（10）甲方应向乙方提供其要求的销售原材料和技术说明书。

九、用英文撰写下列合同订货条款

订　货

双方对订货条款约定如下：

1.初始订单在本协议生效日期后_____〔数字〕日内，乙方初始订货的总购买价格应当不少于_____〔货币与数量〕。甲方将按照本协议中的规定交付货物，乙方亦应按照本协议规定支付价款。初始订单中的价格为_____〔货币与单价，或本协议所附当前产品名录中的规定〕。

2.后续最小额订单为保持在经销区域内独家销售的权利，乙方必须在初期订单之后继续订购货物的数量和次数至少应为：

（1）在本协议生效日期后第一个_____〔数字〕月内，订购一份或多份总额至少为_____〔货币与数量〕的货物。

（2）在本协议生效日期后第二个_____〔数字〕月内，每个_____〔数字〕月内订购至少一份总额至少为_____〔货币与数量〕的货物直至本协议终止。

（3）在本协议生效日期后第三个_____〔数字〕月内，每个_____〔数字〕月内订购至少一份总额至少为_____〔货币与数量〕的货物直至本协议终止。

（4）在本协议生效日期后第四个_____〔数字〕月内，每个_____〔数字〕月内订购至少一份总额至少为_____［货币与数量］的货物直至本协议终止。

（5）在本协议生效日期后第五个_____［数字］月内，每个_____［数字］月内订购至少一份总额至少为_____［货币与数量］的货物直至本协议终止。

3. 不可抗力。如果因任何超过乙方控制的原因，经销区域内的市场需求下降，致使乙方按照本协议中规定订货不再具备商业可行性，则只要该等情形继续存在，乙方的最小订单要求就不再适用。

十、用英文撰写下列合同价格与付款条款

甲方应向乙方主张当前产品目录上的价格，直至甲方决定变更价格时止。甲方保留为其货物变更价格的权利，但对价格进行调整时，甲方应当立即将新价格单提供给乙方。货物价格不包括运输成本、保险成本、进口关税，所有该等费用应单独向乙方收取。甲方应对出口许可证费用负责。如果乙方在甲方通知调整价格之前发来订单，则甲方应遵从调价前的原价格。乙方对所有交付的货物均应以现金于_____［数字］日交付。乙方自发票日后的_____［数字］日内支付货款的，有权享受百分之_____［数字］的折扣。

十一、用英文撰写下列合同中外汇管制下的付款方式条款

如果任何一方的所在国限制向对方国家汇款，则甲方可以指示乙方将相关款项存到以甲方的名义在乙方所在国开立的账户中。此账户必须在由甲方选定的银行开立。乙方向甲方提供存款的证明文件后，甲方将提供给乙方相应的收据。

十二、用英文撰写下列合同结尾条款

本合同由被正当授权之人，于本协议在上述记载之日期代表双方当事人订立，特此证明。

十三、翻译下列条款名称并找出其中的通用条款、常用条款和操作性条款

1. identification of parties
2. payment-method of payment
3. payment-medium of exchange
4. payment-exchange rate
5. costs and charges-duties and taxes
6. costs and charges-handling and transport
7. delivery-transfer of title
8. transportation-notice provisions
9. transportation-insurance or risk of loss protection
10. import/export documentation
11. invoice preparation and delivery
12. reexportation prohibition
13. inspection rights
14. indemnities

15. intellectual property rights

16. warranties

17. enforcement and remedies

18. arbitration provisions

19. time is of the essence

20. modification of contract

21. liquidated damages

22. attorneys' fees

23. inurement and assignment

24. conditions precedent

25. governing law

26. choice of forum

27. severability of provisions

28. integration of provisions

29. authority to bind

30. independent counsel

实训项目 5
合同法规与国际惯例条款练习①

实训目标

1. 掌握国际商务合同中的法规与国际惯例条款内容。

2. 掌握草拟国际商务合同中的法规与国际惯例条款的注意事项。

一、翻译以下法规与国际惯例中的词组

1. sino-foreign contractual enterprise

2. escrow agreement

3. deposit agreement

4. venture capital management agreement

5. share transfer agreement/agreement on assignment of equity interests

6. enterprise contracting management contract

7. contract of mortgage loan

8. contract for prospecting and design of construction project

二、撰写以下法规与国际惯例中的合同条款

1. 当事人可以约定一方违约时应当根据违约情况向对方支付一定数额的违约金，也可以约定因违约产生的损失赔偿额的计算方法。约定的违约金低于造成的损失，当事人可以请求人民法院或者仲裁机构予以增加；约定的违约金高于造成的损失，当事人可以请求人民法院或者仲裁机构予以适当减少。当事人迟延履行约定违约金的，违约方支付违约金后，还应当履行义务。

2. 涉外合同的当事人可以选择处理合同争议所适用的法律，但法律另有规定的除外。涉外合同的当事人没有选择的，适用与合同有最密切联系的国家的法律。

在中华人民共和国境内履行的中外合资经营企业合同、中外合作经营企业合同、中外合作勘探开发自然资源合同，适用中华人民共和国法律。

① [1] 哈格德 T R. 法律写作 [M]. 影印版. 北京：法律出版社，2003. [2] KIAN C T S, CHIM T S. Contract law, a layman's guide [M]. London：Time Books International，2000. [3] BLACK H C. Black's law dictionary [M]. 5th ed. St. Paul：West Publishing Co.，1979. [4] SITARZ D. The complete book of small business legal forms [M]. 3rd ed. Carbondale，IL：Nova Publishing Co. , 2001.

3.未经银行事先同意，货物不得以银行的地址直接发送给该银行，或者以该行作为收货人，或者以该行为抬头人。

然而，如果未经银行事先同意而将货物以银行的地址直接发送给了该银行，或以该行为收货人或抬头人，并请该行付款或承兑或凭其他条款将货物交付给付款人，该行将没有提取货物的义务，其风险和责任仍由发货方承担。

4.被保险人提出保险要求，经保险人同意承保，并就海上保险合同的条款达成协议后，海事保险合同成立。

保险人应当及时向被保险人签发保险单或者其他保险单证，并在保险单或者其他保险单证中载明当事人双方约定的合同内容。

合同订立前，被保险人应当将其知道的或者在通常业务中应当知道的有关影响保险人据以确定保险费率或者确定是否同意承保的重要情况，如实告知保险人知道或者在通常业务中应当知道的情况；保险人没询问的，被保险人无须告知。

5.（1）若卖方按合同或本公约的规定将货物交付给承运人，如果没有在货物上加标记或在装运单据或以其他方式清楚地注明有关合同，卖方必须向买方发出说明货物的发货通知。

（2）若卖方有义务安排货物的运输，其必须订立必要的合同，按通常运输条件，用适合的运输工具，将货物运到指定地点。

（3）若卖方无义务对货物的运输办理保险，其必须在买方提出要求时，向买方提供一切现有的必要资料，使买方能够办理这种保险。

实训项目 6
合同常用条款练习①

实训目标

1.掌握国际商务合同常用条款的内容。

2.掌握撰写国际商务合同常用条款的注意事项。

一、翻译下列效力条款

1.本协议是第×××号机器合同和第×××号羽绒合同不可分割的组成部分。双方应该执行所达成的全部条款。在全部条款执行完毕前，任何一方不得终止本协议。

2.本合同用中英文两种文字写成，每种有正本两份，由各方各持一份。如中文版本与英文版本有异议，以英文版本为准。

3.本合同自受聘方到校之日起生效，到聘期届满时失效。如果一方要求延长聘期，必须在合同期满前1个月以书面形式向对方提出，经双方协商同意后另签延聘合同。

4.本合同经双方签署后立即生效，有效期为3年，自2020年1月1日至2022年12月31日止。本合同经双方协商同意时可以顺延两年。

5.本合同经双方签署后立即生效，有效期为2年，自2020年2月1日至2022年1月31日止。期满前1个月，如果双方均没有提出书面异议，本协议将自动延长1年。如一方未按本条款执行，则另一方有权终止本协议。

二、翻译下列转让条款

1.转让

未经另一方事先书面许可，任何一方均不得转让本合同。任何一方均不得无理拒绝同意。甲方可以拒绝的理由有：乙方在要求同意转让时怠于履行义务，拟受让人在财力上不能按照本协议要求履行乙方的权利和义务，拟受让人拒绝承担乙方在本协议下所有未履行义务，或者拟受让人在请求同意时事实上未能满足甲方对于新的乙方的要求。

---

① [1] 陶博. 法律英语：中英双语法律文书制作 [M]. 上海：复旦大学出版社，2004. [2] KARLA C, SHIPPEY J D. International contracts [M]. 上海：上海外语教育出版社，2000. [3] 乔焕然. 英文合同阅读指南：英文合同的结构、条款、句型与词汇分析 [M]. 最新增订版. 北京：中国法制出版社，2015. [4] 吴敏，吴明忠. 国际经贸英语合同写作 [M]. 广州：暨南大学出版社，2002. [5] 王相国. 鏖战英文合同：英文合同的翻译与起草 [M]. 最新增订版. 北京：中国法制出版社，2014. [6] 吕昊，刘显正，罗萍. 商务合同写作及翻译 [M]. 武汉：武汉大学出版社，2005.

2. 如甲方或乙方要转让其全部或部分出资额给予第三者,应事先向合营他方转让,合营他方在收到转让方发出书面转让通知之日起 3 个月内有权决定是否优先购买。过了 3 个月以后,有意转让其全部或部分出资额的一方可将其出资额转让给予第三者,但出让方得遵守下列各项规定:

(1) 合营他方没有行使其优先购买权;

(2) 转让出资额给予第三者的条件不能比向合营他方转让的条件优惠;

(3) 转让已获审批机关批准。

如果对上述规定的条款有所违反,合同转让无效。

三、翻译下列保证条款

1. 卖方应该保证货物品质规格必须符合本合同及质量保证书之规定,品质保证期为货物到达目的港 3 个月内。在保证期限内,因制造商在设计、制造过程中的缺陷造成的货物损害,应由卖方负责赔偿。

2. 乙方保证所提供的技术资料是乙方实际使用的最新技术资料,并保证在合同有效期内向甲方及时提供任何关于合同中所列产品的改进和发展的技术资料。

乙方保证所提供的技术资料完整、正确、清晰,并保证按合同规定的时间及时交付。如果乙方提供的技术资料不符合本合同附件的规定,乙方必须在收到甲方书面通知后最短时间(不迟于 30 天)内免费将所缺的技术资料或正确、清晰的技术资料寄给甲方。

3. 公司应从每年的生产总值中抽出 8% 以偿还外方投资,用以更新和大修设备。支付各种开支后的余额作为利润,按照第 2 条第 3 款规定的比例分给双方。

四、翻译下列保密条款

1. 乙方同意其在签订本合同后的任何时间内,都不得泄露任何与公司生产、设计或乙方经销产品的方法相关的信息。

2. 信息接收方承诺,提供的保密信息只会披露给那些为履行与该协议所规定的目的有关的义务而合法且绝对必要知晓该保密信息的员工。

3. 除非事先获得信息披露方许可,否则,信息接收方不得将该保密信息披露给除其他员工以外的任何人。

4. 在没有预先取得另一方书面同意的情况下,本协议中提供的一切资料必须严格保密,不得向任何第三方泄露。唯一例外是在政府或者有关的权力机构制定的法律、命令、规章强制之下泄露,这种泄露不得视为对本协议条款的违反。

5. 在本合同有效期内,甚至在其终止或者撤销后,乙方仍需注意保密,不得将该项技术资料泄露给任何第三方。

五、国际货物运输条款的练习

(一) 翻译下列运输条款

1. The sellers shall immediately, upon the completion of the loading of the goods, advise the buyers of the Contract No. , names of commodity, loaded quantity, invoice values, gross weight,

names of vessel and shipment date by TLX/FAX.

2. 100 M/T ± 5% of the goods should be shipped in March, 200 M/T ±5% in April and 300 M/T ±5% in May.

3. On ship's arrival at the port of discharge, lay time shall commence at 13:30, if Notice of Readiness to Discharge is tendered by the Master to the Buyers within ordinary business hours from 8:30 AM to 11:30 AM, or at 8:30 AM next working day if Notice of Readiness to Discharge is tendered within ordinary business hours from 13:30 to 17:30 to the effect that the vessel is in every respect and fit to discharge cargo, whether in berth or not, the Buyers have the option to use one or two berths for discharging and time for shifting from the first berth to the second berth is not to count as lay time. Where more than two berths are used, time for shifting to further berths is to count Cargo to be discharged at the average rate of metric tons per weather working days of 24 consecutive hours, Saturdays, Sundays and Holidays excepted, unless used, in which case, half of actual time used to be counted. If the Buyers fail to discharge cargo at the aforementioned average rate, demurrage is to be paid by the Buyers to the Sellers at the rate which exceeds the aforesaid quantity per day if the discharging. The Sellers are to pay the Buyers dispatch money at half of the demurrage rate, fraction of a day to be counted pro rata.

（二）实务思考

案例1

某公司向德国出口某冷冻商品1 100箱，合同规定1—5月按同等量装运，每月300箱，凭不可撤销即期信用证付款。客户按时开来信用证。该公司1—3月交货正常，顺利结汇，但在4月时，由于船期延误，推迟到5月6日才装运出口，而海运提单则倒签为4月30日，并送银行议付，议付行也未发现问题。后在5月10日，该公司又同船装运300箱运往目的地，开具的提单为5月10日。进口商取单时发现问题，拒绝收货。

问题：

（1）该公司的失误在哪里？

（2）进口商为何拒收货物并拒付？

案例2

中国A公司与加拿大J公司经磋商成交进口小麦30 000公吨，贸易术语为每公吨250美元FOB多伦多，目的港为北海港，11月、12月装运，卖方船舱交货并平舱、理舱。A公司负责租船订舱，并与某运输公司签订了定程租船运输合同，其中合同部分内容作如下规定："船东不负责装卸、理舱、平舱，按连续24小时晴天工作日计算，装货率为每天2 200公吨，星期六、星期日和节假日除外（不用不算，用了也不算）。递接备装通知书后从次日上午8时开始，如通知书于下午4时以后送达则于次日下午2时开始起算装货时间，滞期费为每天800美元，速遣费为600美元，不足1天按比例计算，滞期按连续计算，速遣按节省工作时间计算。"

A公司希望把这些奖罚转移给卖方，以对卖方有所约束。

问题：A公司与J公司的交易合同中的装运条款应有哪些内容？

（三）用英文撰写以下装运条款

1. 我国上海 Q 公司向美国 R 公司出口一批自行车，数量为 20 000 辆，用木箱装，9—12 月装运，允许分批装运，每月平均装运，贸易术语为每辆 50 美元 CFR 纽约。

2. 我国北京东方进出口有限公司与日本某公司经洽谈成交出口东北大豆 1 100 公吨，数量和金额总值允许有 5% 增减，大路货，用塑料编织袋包装，每袋装 100 千克，2019 年 12 月前装运，允许分批装运和转船，贸易术语为每公吨 200 美元 CIF 横滨。

六、支付条款的练习

（一）实务思考

案例1

国内用户擅自改变其代理人对外约定的价格和付款条件致损案

2018 年 9 月 14 日，吉林省某外贸公司（买方）代该省某用户向韩国某厂商（卖方）订购一批管道疏通剂，买卖合同规定：单价为 USD 1.10 CIF 大连，总价款为 3.3 万美元，付款条件为买方用户售完后付款。2018 年 9 月 19 日，该用户又擅自与卖方商谈，改变原买卖合同中的单价和付款条件，并重新签订购入管道疏通剂的合同书，其中约定，用 60 万元人民币购入价值 3.3 万美元的管道疏通剂，并于签约当天用 60 万元人民币现金直接交付给卖方。后来，因卖方交付的货物存在严重质量问题，根本起不到疏通管道的作用，用户无法销售出去，买方即向卖方提出损害赔偿要求，卖方不理，买方遂向中国国际经济贸易仲裁委员会提请仲裁，要求卖方退回用户交付的 60 万元人民币和赔偿因品质不符合同要求而给买方造成的损失。在仲裁审理过程中，作为被申请人的卖方却下落不明，既不作书面答辩，也不派人出席庭审，致使买方用户的实际损失难以挽回。

问题：从该案例中我们应该吸取什么教训？

案例2

拖欠货款争议案

2018 年 3 月 16 日和 2018 年 7 月 8 日，交易双方分别签订两份买卖合同。合同订立后，卖方先后于 2018 年 6 月 5 日和 2019 年 3 月 4 日分别将这两份合同项下的货物，按约定时间先后运抵天津新港，并向买方办理了交接手续，买方实际上也分别收到了这两份合同项下的货物。买方收到货物后，对第一份合同项下的货款没有全部付清，尚拖欠货款 600 021.13 美元；对第二份合同项下的货款 1 102 267.71 美元则全部未付。卖方虽多次催交货款，买方仍拖欠未付，于是卖方依约向中国国际经济贸易仲裁委员会提请仲裁，作为被申请人的买方对申请人提出的上述事项未否认或提出答辩，且未正式派人参加庭审。后经仲裁庭开庭审理，裁决买方如数偿还其拖欠的货款，支付逾期付款的利息，并承担全部仲裁费，以了结此案。

问题：从该案例中我们应该吸取什么教训？

（二）试用英文撰写下列付款条款

1. 我国 A 公司与日本 B 商社经洽谈成交大同煤炭 50 公吨，6 月装运，每公吨 100 美元

FOBC1秦皇岛。以汇付方式支付（电汇）货款，规定买方先预支货款。

2. 我国上海A公司向美国B公司出口一批自行车，数量为2 200辆，用木箱装，12月装运，贸易术语为每辆50美元CFR纽约，支付方式为托收中的承兑交单，远期汇票的付款期限为见票后60天付款。

（三）翻译下列付款条款

1. 买方对卖方开具的见票后××天付款的跟单汇票，于第一次提示时即予承兑，并应于汇票到期日即予付款，付款后交单。

2. 买方应通过卖方可以接受的银行于装运月份前××天开立并送达卖方不可撤销的见票后30天付款的信用证，有效期至装运月份后15天在北京议付。

七、数量条款的练习

（一）根据下列情境用英文撰写成交合同中的数量条款

1. （1）每袋黄豆净重100千克，共1 100袋，合计100公吨。

（2）我国H公司进口俄罗斯产尿素20 000公吨，塑料编织袋包装，每袋重50千克。

2. 在我国广州长城进出口有限公司与日商就出口东北大豆事宜进行磋商的过程中，双方的一些洽谈细节如下：

中方代表：每公吨220美元是我们的底价。

日方代表：你方报价太高，我方认为每公吨180美元才算合理。

中方代表：此价格已很优惠，鉴于我们的长期合作关系，如果你方能增大购买量，比如说1 100公吨以上，我方可作一定让步，每公吨200美元，但是数量和金额允许5%增减，并且由我方决定。

经过多次磋商，双方终于达成以下协议：

价格：每公吨200美元。

品质：大路货。

数量：1 100公吨。

包装：塑料编织袋包装，每袋装50千克。

数量和金额允许5%增减，由卖方决定。

（二）翻译下列数量条款

1. 中国大米10万公吨，卖方可溢交或短交5%。

2. 中国茶叶150公吨，卖方有权在合同规定交付货物数量的基础上多装或少装5%，视货船舱容而定，溢短装的差额部分按所签订的FOB合同价计算。

（三）实务思考

案例1

未按约定的品种和数量均衡搭配交货致损案

买卖双方按CIF条件和信用证付款方式达成一项服装交易。2018年11月，卖方收到从科威特开来的信用证，证中规定目的港达曼，见票后120天付款，货物品种数量为：

（1）约9 900打阿拉伯男服 ART NO. 1295

（2）约1 100打阿拉伯男服 ART NO. 1297

（3）约2 200打阿拉伯童服 ART NO. NF124

上述货物，须分大约等量2批出运：第1批约50%，在11月30日前装运；第2批约50%，在12月31日前装运。每批都要提供单独完整的装运单据。

上述货运数量共12 200打。卖方第1批装运6 600打，其中包括：第1项为4 400打，第2项为1 100打，第3项为1 100打。卖方第2批装运6 600打，其中包括：第1项为5 500打，第3项为1 100打。

卖方每批装运货物总数量虽相等，但每批装货的品种数量没有平均搭配，与信用证规定不符，故首批交单议付时，出口地议付行即拒绝议付。后卖方征得买方同意后，向银行出具保函，银行才同意改在信用证项下办理托收。第2批发货时，各方也按同样方式处理。这2批货款虽如数收回，但遭受晚收回货款的利息损失。

问题：从该案例中我们应该吸取什么教训？

案例2
<h3 style="text-align:center">错误引用国际贸易惯例而减少交货致损案</h3>

某外贸公司出售2 200打纺织品给加拿大某商人，买方依约开来信用证，证中规定不准分批装运。卖方发运时，发现有部分货物品质较差，故未予交足，只装运1 100打。卖方原以为少装100打是可以的，其根据是，按《跟单信用证统一惯例》规定："……在所支付款项未超过信用证金额的条件下，货物数量亦允许有5%的增减幅度……"银行在审单过程也忽略了这点，直到单据寄到开证行时，遭到拒付。后经卖方与开证人交涉，并说明情况，开证人员最后虽接受了单据，但卖方遭受晚收货物款1个月的利息损失。

问题：从该案例中我们应该吸取什么教训？

八、包装条款的练习

（一）翻译下列包装条款

1 每一纸板箱衬以塑料纸，全箱用铁箍加固，以防内装货物受潮及因粗暴搬运可能引起的损坏。

2. 国际标准茶叶纸箱，24个纸箱装1个托盘，10个托盘装1个集装箱（整箱）。

（二）根据下列情境用英文撰写包装条款

1. 我国广州长城进出口有限公司与越南海防远大公司就出口"飞宇"牌50英寸彩色电视机3 300台达成交易，每台价格为160美元，每台先装入1个大塑料袋，再装入1个纸外箱，外箱内衬塑料泡沫，在每个外箱正面的右边都要印有"小心轻放""防潮"指示性标志。唛头由卖方决定，但一定要把"飞宇"牌商标改为买方的"星空"牌商标。

2. 某公司生产知名品牌"永固"牌门锁。某日一外商前来参观，打算订购门锁一批，但是在内外包装上均不得出现"Made in China"字样，同时必须使用客商指定的"守护神"牌商标。要求：（1）客商此举用意何在？（2）该公司如与其达成交易，在包装条款中要注意什么问题？（3）如果要为客商设计一标准唛头要包含哪些内容？（4）请你制定完整的包装条款。

（三）实务思考

案例1

对不定量包装货物提供包装单的争议案

买卖双方按信用证付款方式签订一份买卖鱼粉的合同，买方依约开出信用证，证中规定鱼粉重量和包装重量共约250吨，用新麻袋，每麻袋不定量包装，除要求提交发票、运输单据外，还要求提供包装单和重量检验证书。卖方出运后，即向议付行办理议付，开证行收到信用证项下的全套单据后经审查，认为单证相符，即将票款偿付给议付行。当银行向买方提示单据时，买方认为，货物总重量为249.773吨，包装单中的计算有误，便向开证行提出不同意付款。同时，买方向卖方提出了同样的意见，也表示拒付货款。针对买方的意见开证行作出了答复，其大意是："单据经我行审核，我行认为单证相符。按惯例，我银行对于类似包装单这样单据上的数字不负运算之责。我银行只管单据是否表面上一致和单据之间是否表面上一致。你公司须按时付款，即使有虚假情况，可在付款后直接与卖方交涉甚至索赔。"买方对开证行的答复不满意，认为开证行偏袒一方，指责开证行未能合理谨慎地审核单据，甚至要求开证行向议付行提出拒绝接受单据，冲回账款。开证行就此又作了一些解释。

与此同时，买方也收到卖方的答复："关于单据重量问题，完全系你方的误解。该批货物总重量确实为249.973吨，它是经公证行对货物进行实际衡量出来的结果，它并非以每袋的重量计算出来的总重量。由于该批货物系不定量包装，每袋重量最低有的82千克，最高有的85千克，多数在82至83千克。因包装单内容要求列明总数量、总重量和包件的重量，所以我们根据实际衡量的总重量除以总件数得出每袋净重（249.973÷3.313=82.298（千克））。在包装单上表示每袋净重82.298千克属于平均重量。我们实际货物总重量就是249.973吨，并无虚假情况，也未多计收你方货款。

买方在先后接到开证行和卖方的答复与详细具体的解释之后，消除了误解，认为单证确实相符，最后同意付款赎单，了结此案。

问题：从该案例中我们应该吸取什么教训？

案例2

卖方未按合同包装条款改证和发货致损案

买卖双方按CFR条件和信用证付款方式签订一份买卖50吨蜂蜜的出口合同，合同包装条款规定木条箱（wooden crate）装，实货本来也是木条箱包装。2018年4月5日，买方开出信用证时，误将木条箱写成木箱（wooden case）。卖方直到装船前两天才发现信用证规定的包装与合同规定的包装及实货包装不一致。卖方认为，修改信用证已来不及了。如先装船，等修改后议付，风险太大；如退载，需承担空舱费损失，经济上又不合算。于是卖方决定按原计划装船，因为仓库还有木箱的货物，既不影响按时装运，又符合信用证要求，能安全收汇。

在卖方办完装运的翌日，即4月25日接到买方来电，承认因其疏忽，误将木条箱写为木箱，要求依照合同修改信用证，同时接到银行关于木箱装改为木条箱装的信用证修改书，但卖方拒不同意，硬将修改书退回，仍坚持按木箱装的单据办理寄单议付。4月29日，买方来电，表示对卖方如此违反合同规定，无法接受。后虽经卖方与开证行和买方反复交涉，均无效果。最后，卖方只得被迫派人去进口国与买方面谈，结果，处于被动的卖方只好答应自费在目的港加工更换包装，了结此案。

问题：从该案例中我们应该吸取什么教训？

九、价格与付款条款的练习

（一）翻译下列价格及付款条款

1. 单价：每公吨145美元秦皇岛港离岸价（含理舱费），条件是粉尘含量在6%～100%。如果粉尘低于6%，每低于1个百分点，价格提高10便士；如果粉尘高于10%，每高于1个百分点，价格降低10便士；少于1%的部分，根据上面提到的比例给予考虑。

2. 按货物金额的90%开立以卖方为受益人的不可撤销信用证，凭卖方即期汇票向银行议付，其余10%的货款在货物到达目的地检验合格后付清。

3. 贸易术语暂定为CIF伦敦，每公吨200.00美元，在装运期10~15天前由买卖双方经协商确定最终价格，买方按本合同规定的暂定价开立信用证。

（二）根据下列条件用英文撰写付款条款

1. 我国K公司与美国L公司经磋商，决定以FOB条件进口小麦3 300公吨，每公吨60美元，装运港为纽约，目的港为上海。散装舱运，货到目的港后卸货时再用麻袋包装，每袋装50千克，包装袋上印刷L公司标志，并由L公司提供随船装运。

2. F公司与新加坡G公司经磋商成交中国东北大豆10 000公吨，单层新麻袋包装，每袋重约50千克，以毛作净，9—10月装运，贸易术语为每公吨483美元CIF新加坡，装运港为中国大连。

3. 以贸易术语DAF为例，在汽车运输到中越边境友谊关就一台不可拆散但易损的3.3吨重机电产品以每台88 800港元价格成交，10月20日交货。请说明并掌握：（1）DAF交货价格描述。（2）交货合同中具体地点的描述。（3）贸易双方责任费用、风险的划分，如交货日期的确定、卸装费用负担、出口和进口手续办理等。

（三）实务思考

案例1

2018年，中国某出口公司（卖方）销售一批供鸟食用的食品。当年7月2日，瑞典某商人（买方）来电要求按CIF斯德哥尔摩条件购买25长吨，并主动报价每长吨为59英镑。卖方则误认为，对方将每长吨35英镑错报为59英镑，并于7月8日给对方复函称："据我们所知，此价与国际市场价格悬殊，恐系电文有误……如贵方还有兴趣，请来函或者电告。"7月24日，卖方接到对方7月21日来函，重申订购25长吨，并再次重复递价每长吨为59英镑，函中还称："我于7月2日收到你方6月25日来函后，立即用密码给你方回电，按CIF斯德哥尔摩59英镑递价。"这再次证明，对方报价59英镑为实际购货价格。但卖方仍向对方复函，再次要求对方查对电码是否有误。7月29日对方再复函，再次重申7月2日递价59英镑是对的，并称："我们有点惊奇，因为我们的递价肯定符合国际市场价格……我们还接到乌干达产品56英镑的报价。"卖方不仅对买方一再重申的上述报价和说明始终抱怀疑态度，而且竟然在7月29至30日两天内，以每长吨39英镑报出150长吨，8月1日又以每长吨41英镑报出13吨，均为受盘人立即接受。随后，虽有人建议提高报价，但该公司领导仍不敢按59英镑报价；直至12月下旬，才将价格逐步提至60英镑报价，也照样被外商接受。如按每长吨59英镑计算，这段时期少收外汇5 557英镑。

问题：从该案例中我们应该吸取什么教训？

案例2

某年，中国某出口公司（卖方）与科威特某中间商按CFRC5%的价格条件出售一批货物，合同总金额为52 200元。国外开来的信用证金额为49 975元，并注明"议付时扣5%系给某商号（中间商）的佣金"。由于卖方审证时忽视了核对信用证金额，故在缮制发票和汇票时，都以合同金额52 200元为准。议付时，中国银行扣除5%的佣金，即按49 975元借记开证行北京账户。开证行接单后，以发票金额超过来证金额为由拒付。后经与开证行及中间商多次交涉无效，只好在信用证有效期内，另行按来证金额49 975元再扣去5%佣金赶制发票和汇票，结果重复支付了一笔佣金。

问题：从该案例中我们应该吸取什么教训？

十、分析下列品名条款案例

案例1

错订成交商品名称的争议案

冷暖机是一种具有不同款式和技术规格的产品。中国某外贸进出口公司曾按国内用户要求向外商洽购一批"豪华式"冷暖机。买卖双方谈妥后，买方洽谈人员草拟合同时，粗心大意，竟将"豪华式"冷暖机误写为"手提式"冷暖机。在正式签约时，交易双方当事人对合同内容和各项条款都未表示异议，并同时分别签署了合同。后来，卖方按合同规定发了货。货到后，国内用户拒收货物，要求退货，卖方则认为其交付的货物符合买卖合同的规定，并坚持以合同条款为准，各持己见，导致贸易纠纷。

问题：从该案例中我们应该吸取什么教训？

案例2

卖方错交约定货物被拒收案

中国某公司曾向科威特出售一批冻北京鸭200箱，合同要求屠宰鸭要按伊斯兰教的用刀方法，其中具体规定："需由伊斯兰协会出具证明，证实鸭是按照伊斯兰教方法用刀屠宰。"合同订立后，卖方所交的北京冻鸭，在其颈部无任何刀口痕迹，这显然违反了伊斯兰教的用刀方法。由于中方误将普通冻鸭装运出去，违反了科威特买方的特定要求和说明，致使对方拒收货物，并要求退回货款。中方为避免进一步扩大不良影响，及时同意了对方要求，以了结此事。

问题：从该案例中我们应该吸取什么教训？

十一、品质条款的练习

（一）用英文撰写下列品质条款

1. 广州长城进出口有限公司是广东省广州市的一家中等规模的进出口公司。公司从事进出口业务已达20余年，经营的产品包括日用品、农副产品、机电产品等，产品畅销世界，受到客户好评。公司地址：北京路330号××大厦10楼（×× Building 10，330 Beijing Road，Guangzhou，Guangdong Province，P. R. China）。

3月5日，该公司业务代表与英商通过互联网就出口20英寸儿童长绒玩具熊进行磋商，并向英商提供样品照片。寄送样品后，英商确定以样品规定了原料、款式、颜色与尺寸，并达成交易，成交5 500件，并要求中方速寄合同。

2. 某外商预测其国内市场，认为某种印刷某种符号标记的旅行箱具有一定的销售潜力，于是向我国南方进出口有限公司提供该项商品的样品，要求我方按样品中的面料、辅料、颜色与尺码制作，交易数量为3万只。

3. 我国某进出口公司向瑞士某公司询盘："感谢贵公司多年来对我公司的支持！现欲购名牌手表，公差为48小时可误差1秒。请报实盘。"后来经双方就各项交易条件进行磋商，达成了交易。

4. 广州大阳进出口有限公司接到芬兰A.C.E公司的信后，经研究同意降低价格，以便打开芬兰市场。于是5月9日公司去信芬兰A.C.E公司如下：

敬启者：

你方5月5日信收悉，谢谢！

我方在欧洲销售××牌服装价格均不低于你方提出的价格，考虑到贵公司首次与我方合作，并对我方产品有信心，我方愿适当降低售价，接受你方报价。

同时，我方要求以不可撤销即期信用证支付，现寄去合同，我方保证在6月交货。正像你方所看到的那样，我方产品质优，在欧洲地区享有盛名，无疑将有助于你方开拓市场。

请贵方尽快答复。

张山
2019年5月9日

（二）实务思考

案例1

进口交货品质争议案

2018年，我某进出口公司（以下简称S公司）与德国某跨国钢铁公司新加坡公司（以下简称M公司）签订进口1万吨拉丝盘条合同，金额为USD 341 100，付款方式为L/C 180 DAYS SIGHT。检验条款规定以SGS验货报告为付款依据，以出入境检验检疫局（CIQ）商检结果作为索赔依据，同时约定如有争议在中国香港仲裁，以中国香港的相关规定为准。M公司收到S公司开证后，及时发运货物并提供了全套单据，S公司接受了单据，并指示银行承兑。

货物到港后，S公司发现到货数量、质量均与合同不符，便立即通知对方。一周后M

公司德国总部通过其北京办事处转来传真答复，认为CIQ的检验方法有问题，并声称其提供的货物与合同相符。后经S公司多次交涉，对方仍无解决问题的诚意。在此情况下，S公司及时制订索赔计划并采取措施，多方调查取证，向中国香港国际仲裁中心提交仲裁申请，并向当地法院通报此案，以寻求支持。后由于合同中没有订明仲裁机构的具体名称，而M公司又不同意再签仲裁协议，故中国香港国际仲裁中心不受理本案。

根据上述情况，S公司立即向当地法院提出诉讼申请，同时向法院申请诉讼保全，并就法院签发的止付令，命令开证行暂时停止支付本案项下全部货款。当对方银行提示付款时，开证行回复："由于接到法院止付令，该笔货款已被冻结，请速洽出口商，尽快解决其法律纠纷。"至此，案情急剧变化，S公司由被动反而变为主动。

这时，M公司一反常态，每天电话、传真不断，并主动派人来S公司面谈，一再表示道歉，强烈要求S公司撤诉。最后，M公司新加坡总裁亲自来北京谈判，双方终于达成和解协议。本案以M公司同意退货50%，其余货物每吨降价69美元了结。

问题：从该案例中我们应该吸取什么教训？

案例2

我国出口白砂糖一批，合同规定质量以96°旋亮度为标准。若货物的旋亮度不足96°，每低1°按FOB出口价降价1.1%，不够1°时按比例计算。若货物的旋亮度低于96°，则买方有权拒收。

问题：订立这样的品质条款合理吗？

案例3

我国A公司向美国B公司出口一批自行车共计3 300辆，合同中规定黑色、墨绿色和湖蓝色各1 100辆，不得分批装运。A公司在发货的时候，发现墨绿色的自行车库存只有950辆，考虑到短缺数量不多，于是便以50辆黑色自行车补够数量。

问题：这样做妥当吗？

十二、单据条款的练习

（一）翻译下列单据条款

Ⅰ.商业发票条款

1. Beneficiary's original signed commercial invoices in quintuplicate indicating the merchandise country of origin and other relevant information.

2. Commercial Invoice in 8 copies price CIF Bangkok showing FOB value, freight charges and insurance premium separately.

3. The commercial invoices should bear the following clause: we certify that this invoice is authentic that it is the only invoice issued by us for the goods described herein. That it shows their exact value without deduction of any discount and the goods are of Chinese origin.

4. Commercial Invoices in 5 fold evidencing developing country clause: I declare that these goods are traditional, handmade products of a cottage industry. The final process of manufacture of the goods has been performed in China for which special rates are claimed that not less than one

half of the factory or works cost of the goods which is represent by the value of labour or materials of China or of China and Australia.

Ⅱ.运输单据条款

1. Full set of 3/3 originals plus 3 non-negotiable copies clean on board ocean B/L, consigned to order and blank endorsed. Marked "Freight Prepaid" showing shipping agency at destination. Notify Applicant and evidence the goods have been by full container load.

2. Shipment from Chinese Port to London/ Rotterdam/Hamburg in buyer's option.

3. Shipment must be effected in three equal lots by separate steamers with an interval of at least 30 days between shipments. Documents must be separately negotiated.

4. Shipment on or before May 31st from Shanghai to Wellington, allowing partial shipment and transshipment.

5. Beneficiary's certified copy of telex addressed to applicant; telex must be within two working days after shipment date indicating B/L No.

Ⅲ.保险单据条款

1. Insurance Policy is covered for ×% of total invoice against ×× as per Institute Cargo Clauses ×× dated ××.

2. Policy of Insurance in duplicate issued to the order of ×× Ltd., in the currency of the credit for the CIF value of the shipment plus 10 percent covering all risks with extended cover war clause of the People's Insurance Company.

3. Insurance Policy/Certificate in 2 fold issued for 110% of the invoice value, covering Institute Cargo Clause A and War clause, stating claims payable in Holland by claims paying agent.

4. Insurance Policy or Certificate in negotiable form evidencing premium plus 10% CIF value.

5. Insurance Policy or Certificate issued in assignable form for 150% of CIF value covering All Risks and War Risk as per China Insurance Corporation, from the seller's warehouse to the buyer's warehouse, with claims payable at the destination.

Ⅳ.金融单据条款

1. Documentary Credit available with yourselves by payment against presentation of the documents detailed herein.

2. Credit available with any bank by negotiation of Beneficiary's Drafts at 60 days after sight drawn on ××.

3. Drafts to be drawn at sight for 95 percent of Invoice value of goods on us.

4. You are authorized to draw on HongKong Food Company, Vancouver for a sum not exceeding CAD 120,000.

5. Drafts must bear the clause "Payable at the Bank's current selling rate of exchange on New York with charges and interests at the current rate from the date of negotiation until the payment."

Ⅴ.其他单据条款

1. G.S.P. Certificate of Origin, Form A in duplicate and shows importing country.

2. Special U.S. Customs Invoice 5515 showing CIFC5% San Francisco for each item in 3 copies.

3. Beneficiary's Certificate indicates cable copy of shipping advice dispatched to the accountee

immediately after shipment.

4. Beneficiary's Certificate certifies that full set of non-negotiable copies of documents sent to Applicant immediately after shipment.

5. King/Weight List issued by Applicant in three photocopies, showing Carton Marks, Style No. , Color, Size, Quantity, G-WT, N-WT. Dimension Per Carton (s) , Packing Method and Breakdown of total quantity shipped in pieces, per style, per color, per size and must not show Invoice No. and description of goods.

（二）实务思考

案例1

发票地址不符遭银行拒付案

某外贸公司按信用证付款方式向外商出售一批纺织品，2018年卖方收到巴基斯坦一家银行依约开来的信用证，随后不久又接到开证人来电称，因纺织品市价下降，要求卖方降价，卖方未予同意，仍依约发运货物。当单据寄到开证行后，该行竭力配合开证人从单据中找漏洞，以发票上受益人的地址为"623 Road"，与来证规定的"Loti Nee San Road"不符为由，拒付货款，这实际上是因市价下降，故意找借口，拖延付款。后经银行复电说明：信用证上的英文路名就是广州方言623的译音。最后，开证行只好承付，但使我方晚收货款达一个半月之久。

问题：从该案例中我们应该吸取什么教训？

案例2

邮寄单据失误致损案

中国某外贸公司曾向美国某商出售5批货物，美国洛杉矶银行于2018年6—7月先后开来5张信用证，卖方凭证出运5批货物，并及时交单议付。出人意料的是，2个月之后，国外银行尚未收到单据，买方也多次来电催问，经议付行多方查询未果。直到10月份，邮局陆续将原件退回，信封上均盖有"地址不全，无法投递"的印章。由于原来信封上面只有开证行名称和洛杉矶地名，而未写路名、门牌号或信箱号以及邮区号码等详细地址，议付行只得另换封套再次投邮。由于寄单失误，货到后，无法提取，为急于应市，买方只好从其他方面购进一批同样的货物应市销售，并决定不要这批货物。后经双方反复协商，买方虽同意接受货物，但数千美元的库存费用均由我方负担，货款到12月底才支付。由于此次寄单失误责任在银行，经银贸双方协商和有关方面调解，上述损失，卖方和银行各负担一半，了结此案。

问题：从该案例中我们应该吸取什么教训？

十三、违约金与定金条款的练习

（一）翻译下列违约条款

1. 除合同第21条不可抗力原因外，如卖方不能按合同规定的时间交货，买方应同意在卖方支付罚款的条件下延期交货。罚款可由议付银行在议付货款时扣除，罚款率按每天收＿＿＿％，不足1天时以＿＿＿天计算。但罚款不得超过迟交货物总价的＿＿＿。如卖方延期交货超过合同规定____天，买方有权撤销合同，此时尽管合同撤销，卖方仍应不延迟地按上述规定向买方支付罚款。

买方有权对因此遭受的其他损失向卖方提出索赔。

2. 如果在发票载明的付款期后15日内仍未付款，则未付款部分将被视为付款延迟，卖方保留按照延迟的期间对已经延迟的部分按照最高利息率加收延迟付款利息的权利。

（二）实务思考

案例1

卖方支付违约金与买方退货谁先谁后的争议案

2018年12月8日，买方与卖方签订一份购买VSAT网络设备的合同。在履约过程中，双方发生争议。买方以卖方未在合同规定期限内完成有关设备安装、调试及开通义务等为由，要求卖方支付违约金，买方同时宣布取消合同并拟退回货物，卖方也表示同意买方的主张。但是，双方对先支付违约金还是先退货的问题存在分歧。双方经协商未达成共识，买方遂向中国国际经济贸易仲裁委员会深圳分会提请仲裁。经两次开庭审理结果，仲裁庭认为，在合同规定期限内，卖方没有完成合同义务，已构成违约。由于卖方违约，其应向申请人支付违约金，不应以买方先退货为支付违约金的条件，因此，卖方关于应先退回或同时退回设备再支付违约金的主张不能成立。仲裁庭判决结果是，卖方应按合同规定向买方支付违约金及违约金的利息损失，买方应做好在其公司所在地向卖方返还设备的准备。由于卖方违约，仲裁庭支持买方的请求，本案仲裁费全由卖方承担。

问题：从该案例中我们应该吸取什么教训？

案例2

关于返还定金与支付违约金争议案

买卖双方签订一份价款为10万美元的购销合同，合同规定，签约后1周内，买方向卖方支付1万美元定金，卖方在收到定金后，4个月内交付约定的货物。同时双方约定了违约金条款，规定任何一方违约，须向对方支付相当于合同价款8%的违约金。合同签订后，买方依约交付了定金，卖方收到定金后，因市场变化和经营状况不佳，不能依约交货，买方遂向卖方要求双倍返还定金并赔偿约定的违约金，卖方只同意支付违约金和退回原收入的1万美元定金，双方因此产生争议。买方便向某法律专家咨询，准备提请仲裁。后经这位专家提示，买方改变主意，仅要求对方双倍返还定金，撤销了赔偿违约金的要求，卖方对此表示同意，于是双方友好地解决了本案争议。

问题：从该案例中我们应该吸取什么教训？

十四、分析下列不可抗力条款案例

案例1

政府调整出口退税率是否构成不可抗力争议案

2017年3月7日，买卖双方按信用证付款方式签订一份购销200吨镁锭的售货确认书。确认书签订后，买方依约通过银行开出了信用证，但卖方未交付货物。2018年12月25日，买方遂向中国国际经济贸易仲裁委员会提请仲裁，要求卖方赔偿其经济损失。在庭审过程中，作为被申请人的卖方辩称，本案确认书签订后，国家出口退税政策进行了重大调整，致使约定的货价发生重大变动，使卖方无能力继续履行合同。这是属不可抗力的影响，合同不能履行属免责范围，被申请人不负赔偿责任。作为申请人的买方则认为，政府退税率的变动与进口商无关，它不能构成不可抗力。后仲裁庭裁定，中国政府对出口退税率的调整，不构成不可抗力事件，不应成为被申请人不履行合同的免责理由，被申请人应负相应的赔偿责任。

问题：从该案例中我们应该吸取什么教训？

案例2
发生不可抗力事件后是免除交货义务还是推迟交货日期的争议案

2018年，中国某公司同国外某厂商签订一项化肥进口合同。订约后，卖方生产原料的两个工厂中，有一个工厂发生了爆炸事件。按合同规定，这一事件是属不可抗力事件范围。由于当时化肥市价上涨，卖方就利用这一事件，要求免除全部交货义务，中方不同意对方要求，只同意相应推迟交货的日期。双方经过反复协商和争辩，最后达成相应推迟交货日期的协议。

问题：从该案例中我们应该吸取什么教训？

十五、分析下列检验仲裁条款案例
案例1
仲裁庭对卖方指示船方无单放货给第三方的裁决案

2018年2月16日，买卖双方按CFR条件和信用证付款方式签订了买卖合同。合同订立后，买方依约开出了信用证，卖方依约装运货物并交付了包括提单在内的整套单据。随后，卖方向承运货物的船方出具保函，要求船方无单放货给汕头某公司。2018年3月24日，买方通过承兑赎单，得到了提单等整套单据，但货物已于3月18日在汕头港被无单提走。同年6月9日，卖方通过银行收取了本案合同项下的货款。后来，买方虽经多次交涉，却未收到本案合同项下的货物，买方遂于2019年3月14日向中国国际经济贸易仲裁委员会提请仲裁。后经2次开庭审理，仲裁庭多数意见认为，作为被申请人的卖方出具保函要求船方无单放货，致使作为申请人的买方在持有正本提单的情况下却提不到货，卖方的行为构成违约，应赔偿申请人由此产生的损失。申请人关于退还货款本金和赔偿利息损失的合理请求，仲裁庭予以支持。

问题：从该案例中我们应该吸取什么教训？

案例2
仲裁与调解相结合争议案

某外贸公司曾在广州秋交会上，按CIF条件和信用证付款方式同某外商签订一项出口童装兔毛衫的合同。签约后，买方依约开来了信用证，卖方也按约定期限交付了货物。在货物装船前，卖方还应买方要求航寄装船样品9件，买方收到装船样品后，未提出任何异议。11月15日，买方向卖方提出异议，认为卖方未能按约定的规格交货，提出退货要求，其所持理由是，该批童装兔毛衫的款式，由原设计的反面做成了正面，显然是由生产设计中的错误造成的。而卖方拒绝买方的退货要求，其理由是，童装的款式是应买方的要求特意制作的，实际交货与合同规定完全相符，根本不存在制作错误问题。此外，买方收到卖方装船样品后，也未就童装款式与规格提出任何异议。双方各持己见，争议悬而未决。12月20日，双方又就原先存在的争议再次进行协商。在协商过程中，卖方表示，愿在下一年春交会交易中给予适当优惠，以照顾买方困难。买方回国后，于第2年8月13日向中国仲裁机构提请仲裁，要求退回该批童装中的150打，并赔偿其全部进口关税费用。

仲裁委员会受理本案后，组成仲裁庭，一方面对案情进行调查研究，另一方面进行调解，推动争议双方继续进行友好协商。最后，双方终于达成了和解协议，作为申请人的买方主动撤回仲裁申请，了结此案。

问题：从该案例中我们应该吸取什么教训？

十六、分析下列订立履行合同的案例

案例1

交货不符与拖欠货款争议案

美国某公司（卖方）同中国浙江某公司（买方）于2017年4月22日订立了分销协议。根据协议规定，买方以独立签约人的身份与卖方先后签订了3份购销合同，然后将其采购的产品分销给中国各最终用户。在协议期间，双方约定："买方同意购买，卖方同意销售、认可，并提供合同确定的软件、硬件服务（指订购的产品及服务）。"买卖双方所签订的购销合同是分销协议的附件，在买卖过程中的权利与义务必须同时符合分销协议和购销合同的规定。当二者出现不同规定时，以分销协议的规定为准。本案3份合同签订后，卖方交付了货物，但到货质量存在缺陷，有的型号不统一，有的缺少配件，以致使某些最终用户无法安装、调试和保持正常运转，故最终用户扣留10%的货款不付，从而使被申请人受到损失。买方遂根据不同情况向卖方提出减价、退货和赔偿损失的要求，并以卖方未按合同规定交货和信用证因单证不符问题导致有效期已过为由而拖欠货款。卖方则以买方未按合同规定付款为由，单方面停止分销协议和售后服务，并直接通知了最终用户，从而导致买方无法转售其尚未转售出去的产品。在双方争议无法达成共识的情况下，卖方向中国国际经济贸易仲裁委员会提请仲裁。

仲裁庭受理本案后，经过开庭审理，根据不同情况作出了如下裁决：一是买方对已转售的货物按约定条件付款，并承担其晚付货款而给申请人造成的利息损失；二是买方未转售出去的货物，予以退货；三是卖方交付的有缺陷的货物适当减价，以补偿被申请人的实际损失。

问题：从该案例中我们应该吸取什么教训？

案例2

3月15日，A公司向新加坡客户G公司发盘："报童装兔毛衫200打，货号CM034，每打CIF新加坡100美元，8月份装运，即期信用证付款，25日复到有效。"3月22日收到G公司答复如下："你方15日发盘收到。你方报价过高，若降至每打90美元可接受。"A公司次日复电："我方报价已是最低价，降价之事歉难考虑。"3月26日G公司又要求航邮一份样品以供参考。29日，A公司寄出样品，并函告对方："4月8日前复到有效。"4月3日，G公司回函表示接受发盘的全部内容，4月10日送达A公司。经办人员视其为逾期接受，故未作任何表示。

7月6日，A公司收到G公司开来的信用证，并请求用尽可能早的航班出运。此时因原料价格上涨，公司已将价格调整至每打110美元，故7月8日回复称："我公司与你方此前未达成任何协议，你方虽曾对我方发盘表示接受，但我方4月10日才收到，此乃逾期接受，无效。请恕我方不能发货。信用证已请银行退回。如你方有意成交，我方重新报价每打CIF新加坡110美元，9月份交货，其他条件不变。"

7月12日G公司来电："我方曾于4月3日接受你发盘，虽然如你方所言，4月10日才送达你方，但因你我两地之邮程需3天时间，尽管我方接受在传递过程中出现了失误，你我两国均为《联合国国际货物销售合同公约》（以下简称为《公约》）的缔约方，按《公约》第21条第（2）款规定，你方在收到我方逾期接受后未作任何表示，这就意味着合同已经成立，请确认你方将履行合同；否则，一切后果将由你方承担。"

问题：G公司的上述观点是否正确？

十七、用英文撰写下列合同解除、终止、处罚违约条款

1.在本协议有效期间，当任何一方对本协议的条款有所违背时，缔约双方首先应尽可能迅速、友好地解决问题，使双方都能满意。另一方以书面通知后，如果30天内不能获得解决，则另一方有权取消本协议，由此而遭受的损害和损失应由违约的一方负责赔偿。

2.如果合同一方未能在合同规定的时限内履行合同义务，并在收到未违约方的通知后15天内未能消除违约或采取补救措施，而且在被允许推迟履行的期限内仍未履行合同，在此情形下，未违约的一方应书面通知违约方解除合同，同时有权要求违约方赔偿损失。

3.独家经销权的终止。如果乙方未能按照本协议的要求进行最小量订货，并且如果乙方的违约行为不得以本协议规定的超出乙方控制的不可抗力为借口，则甲方唯一的救济措施将是终止乙方在该销售区域内的独家经销权。甲方只有在提前_____［数字］日内关于未能履约及意图终止独家销售权利给予乙方通知的前提下，才可以行使终止的权利。如果乙方在规定的日期内对违约行为进行了补救，则乙方的独家销售权将不会被终止。独家销售权的终止并不自动导致本协议的终止。无论乙方是否拥有独家经销权，只要乙方未违反本协议的其他条款，则本协议将在下列问题上继续有效：乙方在销售区域内不拥有独家经销权，并且甲方无权限制乙方销售或在销售区域内与他人缔约进行销售，或者招揽新的潜在消费者客户的行为。

十八、用英文撰写下列合同通知条款（注意下划线部分的翻译）

通　知

本协议中规定的所有通知均应以书面形式在协议中规定的地址作出。一方必须在地址变更生效后_____［数字］日内，通知另一方其地址的变更。该通知在收到之日视为已经送达。

实训项目 7
合同特殊条款练习①

实验目标

1. 掌握国际商务合同特殊条款的内容。
2. 掌握撰写国际商务合同特殊条款的注意事项。

一、翻译下列货物所有权条款

1. The Seller reserves the Ownership of the Goods delivered until the Buyer has paid fully to the Seller. The Purchase Price and all related costs (shipping costs, custom duty, VAT, insurance costs, etc.) as stated in the Contract for such Goods. The risk of loss of the Goods shall be borne by the Buyer upon delivery.

2. The title with respect to each shipment shall pass from the seller to the buyer when the seller receives reimbursement of the proceeds from the opening bank through the negotiating bank against the relative shipping documents as set forth in clause 9 after completion of loading on board the vessel at loading port, with effect retrospective to the time of delivery of the goods.

二、翻译下列产品销售条款

1. The Products of Joint Venture will be sold both in and out of China. Those that are to be sold in China shall amount to no more than 45% while those to be sold outside of China shall account for no less than 55%.

2. The Products manufactured in the Joint Venture or the domestic workshop may be marketed by proxy or exclusively by Chinese commodity departments or commercial departments, or marketed directly by the Joint Venture.

3. The Products will be marketed to foreign countries through the following channels:

Those that will be marketed directly outside Chinese territory by Joint Venture account for 30%.

Those that will be marketed by proxy or exclusively by the Chinese foreign trade corporation with which the Joint Venture will make a sales agreement account for 35%.

---

① 刘川，王菲. 英文合同阅读与翻译［M］. 北京：国防工业出版社，2010.

Those that the Joint Venture will entrust any other party or agent to market account for 35%.

三、翻译下列信用证付款条款

1. The Buyer shall open through a bank acceptable to the Seller an Irrevocable Sight Letter of Credit to reach the Seller 15 days before the month of shipment, valid for the negotiation in China within 15 days after the month of shipment.

2. The Buyer shall arrange with ×× Bank for opening an Irrevocable (Transferable) banker's acceptance Letter of Credit in favor of the Sellers before ... (or within ... days after receipt of Sellers advice; or within ... days after signing of this contract). The said Letter of Credit shall be available by draft(s) at ×× day's sight (or ×× days after date of shipment) and remain valid for negotiation in China within 15 days after the aforesaid time of shipment.

3. The Buyer shall open through a bank acceptable to the Sellers an Irrevocable Revolving Letter of Credit at sight to reach the Seller 15 days before the month of first shipment. The Credit shall be automatically available during the period of 2019 for ×× (value) per month and remain valid for negotiation in Beijing until Jan. 15, 2019.

四、翻译下列货币与汇率条款

1. If, after the date ×× days tenders for the Works the Government prior to the latest date for submission of or authorized agency of the Government of the country in which the Works are being or are to be executed imposes currency restrictions and/or transfer of currency restrictions in relation to the currency or currencies in which the Contract Price is to be paid, the Employer shall reimburse any loss or damage to the Contractor arising therefrom, without prejudice to the right of the Contractor to exercise any other rights or remedies to which he is entitled in such event.

2. Where the Contract provided for payment in whole or in part to be made to the Contractor in foreign currency or currencies, such payment shall not be subject to variations in the rate or rates of exchange between such specified foreign currency or currencies and the currency of the country in which the Works are to be executed.

3. Where the Employer shall have required the tender to be expressed in a single currency but with payment to be made in more than one currency and the Contractor has stated the proportions or amounts of other currency or currencies in which he requires payment to be made, the rate or rates of exchange applicable for calculating the payment of such proportions or amounts shall be those prevailing, as determined by the Central Bank of the country in which the Works to be executed, on the date _____ days prior to the latest date for the submission of tenders for the works, as shall have been notified to the Contractor by the Employer prior to the submission of tenders or as provided for in the tender documents.

五、翻译下列税务、财务与审计条款

1. Joint Venture may, subject to the provisions of Act of _____ (Name of the Host Country)

foreign joint venture of the _____ (Name of the Host Country) , set aside out of the gains and profits of Joint Venture such sums used as reserves, development fund, employees' welfare or reward fund, the proportion of such sums shall be decided at the general meetings of the Board of Directors in accordance with the operations of Joint Venture.

2. Financial affairs of Joint Venture shall be examined and checked by accountants registered in China and the result of the audit shall be reported to Board of Directors and President of Joint Venture.

3. When _____ (Party B) thinks it proper to employ some foreign auditors other than the Chinese ones to make the annual financial examination and checking, no protest shall be made by _____ (Party A) and in this case_____ (Party B) alone shall bear all the charges in respect of the specially fixed audit.

六、翻译下列技术转让条款

1. _____ (Party A) and _____ (Party B) agree that Joint Venture may enter into Agreement of Assignment of Technology with _____ (Party B) (or with a third party) to get the sophisticated techniques in production indispensable for gaining the purposes provided in Chapter _____ of this Contract, including product designs, manufacturing skills, inspection methods, directions for producing materials, quality control, personnel training, etc.

2. As for technology and technical service provided by _____ (Party B) in a Usages according to the Agreement of Assignment of Technology, _____ (Party B) shall make detailed lists as appendices to the Agreement to guarantee the enforcement of the Agreement.

3. _____ (Party B) shall transfer all the technology to Joint Venture under the terms in this Contract and in the Agreement of Assignment of Technology, the technology transferred shall be the most advanced of the same category in _____(Party B) 's portfolio, the type and function of the equipment shall be good and shall meet the demand of technological process and practical usage.

七、翻译下列知识产权条款

1. Licensor guarantees that Licensor is the legitimate owner of all the Patented Technology and Documentation supplied by Licensor to Licensee in accordance with the Contract, and that Licensor is lawful in a position to transfer all such Technology and Technical Documentation to Licensee. In the course of implementation of the Contract, if any third party accuses Licensee of infringement, Licensor shall be responsible for approaching the third party about the accusation and bear all the economic and legal responsibilities which may arise.

2. Upon the terms and conditions hereinafter set forth, Licensee agrees to obtain from Licensor, and Licensor agrees to grant Licensee the right to utilize the Registered Trademark solely and only upon and in connection with the manufacture, sale and distribution of the Contract Products. The name, model, specification and technical notices of the Contract Products are detailed in Appendix 2 to the Contract. The license and right are exclusive and untransferable.

Licensor agrees that during the validity of this Contract, it will not authorize a third party to utilize the Registered Trademark upon and in connection with the manufacture, sale and distribution of the Contract Products in the same area specified in this Contract.

3. In the period of validity and one year after expiry, either party of this agreement shouldn't let out the business secret between both parties to the other person, if leading to the fact therefrom that the interests of another Party are lost, another party has right of demanding the economic responsibility of the party which lets out business secret.

八、翻译下列劳工条款

1. The Contractor shall make his own arrangements for the engagement of all labor, local or otherwise, and save insofar as the Contract otherwise provides, for the transport, housing feeding and payment thereof.

2. The Contractor shall not, otherwise than in accordance with the Statutes, Ordinances and Government Regulations or Orders for the time being in force, import, sell, give, barter or otherwise dispose of any alcoholic liquor, or drugs, or permit or suffer any such importation, sale, gift, barter or disposal by his subcontractors, agents or employees.

3. In the event of any outbreak of illness of an epidemic nature, the Contractor shall comply with and carry out such regulations, orders and requirements as maybe made by the Government, or the local medical or sanitary authorities for the purpose of dealing with and overcoming the same.

九、翻译下列竞业禁止条款

1. During the continuance of the employment, the Employee shall not be employed by, be engaged in or take an interest in any other business, unless a prior written consent of the partners is acquired.

2. _____ year after termination of this Contract, the Employee shall not be employed, be engaged in or take an interest in any other business, whether directly or through other persons or entities, which are in competition with or related to the Company's business, provided that the Company provides the Employee with an appropriate compensation. The compensation in the amount of monthly salaries (excluding social insurance contributions) shall be deemed as appropriate.

3. Employee Non-compete Agreement

In consideration of my being employed by_____ (Company), I, the undersigned, hereby agree that upon the termination of my employment and not-withstanding the cause of termination, I shall not compete with the business of the Company or its successors or assigns, to _____and shall not directly or indirectly, as an owner, officer, director, employee, consultant, or stockholder, engage in the business of _____ or a business substantially similar or competitive to the business of the Company.

The non-compete agreement shall extend for a radius of _____ miles from the present location of the Company, and shall be in full force and effect for _____ years, commencing with the date of employment termination.

Signed and sealed this _____th day of _____[month], 2019.

十、翻译下列不形成劳动关系的声明条款

1. During this Agreement, the Contractor shall be an independent Contractor and nothing contained herein shall be construed as creating an employer–employee relationship between the Company and the Contractor.

2. The Agreement shall not create a partnership, joint venture, agency, employer/employee or similar relationship between Company and Sales Representative. Sales Representative shall be an independent contractor. Company shall not be required to withhold any amounts for state or federal income tax or for FICA taxes from sums becoming due to Sales Representative under this agreement. Sales Representative shall not be considered as employee of Company and shall not be entitled to participate in any plan, arrangement or distribution by Company pertaining to or in connection with any pension, stock, bonus, profit sharing or other benefit extended to Company's Employees. Sales Representative shall be free to utilize his time, energy, and skill in such manner as he deems advisable to the extent that he is not otherwise obligated under this Agreement.

3. The Agreement is entered by two separate companies and each of them is liable for the obligation herein described. Manufacturer is the only responsible for the employees it may use for the manufacturing and supply of the Products, and for all legal, labor, occupational health and safety, environmental, and consumer protection obligations and claims. There is no labor relationship between the Purchaser and the Manufacturer's employees. The Manufacturer shall indemnify and hold harmless the Purchaser against any labor, environmental, occupational health and safety, and the consumer's protection liability. Taxes incident upon the Products shall be paid according to the applicable legislation.

十一、翻译下列设备、材料和工艺条款

1. All samples shall be supplied by the Contractor at his own cost if the supply thereof is clearly intended by or provided for in the Contract, but if not, then at the cost of the Employer.

2. All workmanship, materials, equipment and articles shall be new and unused and shall be subject to the inspection, examination and test by the Owner (or its nominee) at any time and at any place during the manufacture, installation or construction thereof. The Owner shall have the right to reject or require the correction of the materials and workmanship, at the Contractor's expense, which are not in strict accordance with the Contract Documents. If the Contractor fails to proceed at once with the replacement of rejected material, equipment or articles, or the correction of defective workmanship, the Owner may replace such material or correct such workmanship and charge the cost thereof to the Contractor.

3. The Contractor shall, upon demand of the Owner, and at the Contractor's expense, repair and/or replace to the Owner's satisfaction any Work and/or material furnished by the Contractor

which does not conform to the requirements of the Contract Documents, and/or where such repair or replacement is required in order for the plant, equipment or other material furnished hereunder to function in accordance with and as contemplated by the Contract Documents, the Contractor shall have such obligation to repair or replace with respect to any such deficiencies in the Work which appear within the time period specified in the Construction Agreement from the last to occur of the completion of the Work final acceptance of the Work by the Owner, or the initial commercial operation of the plant, equipment or other materials furnished hereunder.

十二、翻译下列临建工程、设备和材料条款

1. All Constructional Plant, Temporary Works and materials provided by the Contractor shall, when brought on to the Site, be deemed to be exclusively intended for the execution of the Works and the Contractor shall not remove the same or any part thereof, except for the purpose of moving it from one part of the Site to another, without the consent, in writing, of the Engineer, which shall not be unreasonably withheld.

2. Upon completion of the Works the Contractor shall remove from the Site all the said Constructional Plant and Temporary Works remaining thereon and any unused materials provided by the Contractor.

3. In respect of any Constructional Plant which the Contractor shall have imported for the purposes of the works, the Employer will assist the Contractor, where required, in procuring any necessary Government consent to the re-export of such Constructional Plant by the Contractor upon the removal thereof as aforesaid.

十三、翻译下列维修及缺陷条款

1. To the intent that the Works shall at or as soon as practicable after the expiration of the Period of Maintenance be delivered to the Employer in the condition required by the Contract, fair wear and rear excepted, to the satisfaction of the Engineer, the Contractor shall finish the work, if any, outstanding at the date of completion, as certified under Clause 2 hereof, as soon as practicable after such date and shall execute all such work of repair, amendment, reconstruction, rectification and making good defects, imperfections, shrinkage or other faults as maybe required of the Contractor in writing by the Engineer during the Period of Maintenance, or within _____ days after its expiration, as a result of an inspection made by or on behalf of the Engineer prior to its expiration.

2. All such work shall be carried out by the Contractor at his own expense if the necessity thereof shall, in the opinion of the Engineer, be due to the use of materials or workmanship not in accordance with the Contract, or to neglect or failure on the part of the Contractor to comply with any obligation, expressed or implied, on the Contractor's part under the contract. If, in the opinion of the Engineer, such necessity shall be due to any other cause, the value of such work shall be ascertained and paid for as if it were additional work.

3. If the Contractor shall fail to do any such work as aforesaid required by the Engineer, the

Employer shall be entitled to employ and pay other persons to carry out the same and if such work is work which, in the opinion of the Engineer, the Contractor is liable to do at his own expense under the Contract, then all expenses consequent thereon or incidental thereto shall be recoverable from the Contractor by the Employer, or may be deducted by the Employer from any monies due or which may become due to the Contractor.

十四、翻译下列工程计量条款

1. The quantities set out in the Bill of Quantities are the estimated quantities of the work, but they are not to be taken as the actual and correct quantities of the Works to be executed by the Contractor in fulfillment of his obligations under the Contract.

2. The Engineer shall, except as otherwise stated, ascertain and determine by measurement the value in terms of the Contract of work done in accordance with the Contract. He shall, when he requires any part or parts of the Works to be measured, give notice to the Contractor's authorized agent or representative, who shall forthwith attend or send a qualified agent to assist the Engineer or the Engineer's Representative in making such measurement, and shall furnish all particulars required by either of them. Should the Contractor not attend, or neglect or omit to send such agent, then the measurement made by the Engineer or approved by him shall be taken to be the correct measurement of the work. For the purpose of measuring such permanent work as is to be measured by records and drawings, the Engineer's Representative shall prepare records and drawings month by month of such work and the Contractor, as and when called upon to do so in writing, shall, within days, attend to examine and agree such records and drawings with the Engineer's Representative and shall sign the same when so agreed. If the Contractor does not so attend to examine and agree such records and drawings, they shall be taken to be correct. If, after examination of such records and drawings, the Contractor does not agree the same or does not sign the same as agreed, they shall nevertheless be taken to be correct, unless the Contractor shall, within ×× days of such examination, lodge with the Engineer's Representative, for decision by the Engineer, notice in writing of the respects in which such records and drawings are claimed by him to be incorrect.

十五、翻译下列特殊合同条款

Where the Contractor provides for payment in more than one currency, the proportions or amounts to be paid in foreign currencies in respect of Provisional Sum items shall be determined in accordance with the principles set forth in subclause (1) and (2) of this Clause as and when these sums are utilized in whole and in part in accordance with the provisions of Clause 58 and 59 hereof.

实战篇　各类合同及协议练习

实训项目 8

销售代理协议练习①

实训目标

1. 掌握销售代理合同的基本词汇和重点句子。
2. 熟悉销售代理合同的结构和重点条款的起草和翻译。

一、翻译下列代理协议

Sole Agency Agreement

8th December, 20＿＿＿

    This Agreement is hereby entered into through friendly negotiation by and between China National Native Produce and Animal By-products Import and Export Corporation, ×× Street, Beijing, China (hereinafter referred to as Party A) and WXY Co., Anzio Avenue, Auckland, New Zealand (hereinafter referred to as Party B) for further cooperation in extending the volume of China tea business, whereby Party A agrees to appoint Party B as sole Agent in New Zealand under the terms and conditions set forth below:

    1. Commodity: All kinds of China tea handled by Party A and its Branches.

    2. Territory: Mainland of New Zealand.

    3. Price: When Party A and/or its Branches make an offer or a quotation to Party B, the price

――――――――――
①　[1] 徐良霞，李海燕. 实用英语教你写合同 [M]. 北京：北京航空航天工业大学出版社，2004. [2] 张林玲. 商务英语合同翻译与写作 [M]. 北京：机械工业出版社，2009.

shall be CIFC5% main port, New Zealand for Party B to promote the sale at that price. If Party B alters the price, the alteration is subject to Party confirmation.

4. Commission: Party A shall remit Party B a commission of 5% on the invoice value of each individual transaction after negotiation of shipping documents.

5. Payment: Payment is to be made against documents upon arrival of the goods and documents will only be delivered against payment. Party B shall be responsible for urging the buyers to make payment immediately after the carrying vessel reaches the port of destination.

6. Delivery: Goods are to be shipped from the Port(s) of China to the Main Port(s) of New Zealand. Partial shipments and transshipment are permitted.

7. Inspection: Both parties agree to take as final the Inspection Certificate of Quality and Inspection Certificate of Weight issued by the China Commodity Inspection Bureau and/or its Branches at the Port(s) of China.

8. Mutual Obligation:

(1)During the period of validity of this Agreement, Party B agrees not to act as agent for and/or undertake to sell any kind of tea originated from other countries.

(2)During the period of validity of this Agreement, Party A and its Branches shall pass on to Party B enquiries, if any, received from commercial shops or clients within the territory represented by Party B for the purchase of the said commodities.

(3)Party B shall furnish Party A and its Branches concerned for reference purposes at the end of each quarter with information regarding the activities of the agency, market trends, competitor's prices, saleable items, import rules and regulations as well as suggestions for development of mutual business. Party B shall also forward to Party A and its Branches promptly any information that is important.

(4)Party A shall supply Party B with catalogues, illustrated pamphlets relating to the commodities concerned. Party B shall do its utmost in advertising and promoting the sale of China tea by way of display in show cases or windows. If Party A is required to pay the cost of advertising and promoting, Party B shall submit the scheme to Party A for approval beforehand.

9. Effective period of the Agreement: This Agreement is effective from ... to ...

10. Any terms and conditions of this Agreement may be revised or supplemented with mutual approval through consultation.

11. This Agreement is drawn up in both the Chinese and English languages, each in two originals and one original of each is to be held by Party A and Party B. Both versions are equally effective.

二、翻译下列句子

1.关于你们希望做我公司代理的问题，我们认为商讨此事的时机尚未成熟。

2.请继续努力推销，以便我们考虑建立代理关系。

3.尽管我们的价格已很低，但我们例外地给你方2%的折扣作为特殊照顾。

4.如数量超过1 000打，我们可以给5%折扣。

5.我们对所有客户都按同样的佣金率付给佣金。

6.按照我们的记录，应付你们的佣金总额为588英镑。

7.我们愿指出此项限制不仅仅是针对你们的。

8.在这种情况下，我方歉难照顾，但相信你方应能理解我们的处境。

9.我们获悉，你方在我国尚未委任代理，我们愿意提供服务以推销你们的产品。由于我公司有30多年经营此类产品的丰富经验，因此相信在为你方获得订单、经营销售以及办理单证等事宜方面能提供最优良的专业知识。销售可按你方喜欢的方式进行，或者寄售，或者由我方向你方订购。如果你方对我方建议有兴趣，我们将乐于向你方提供银行及贸易资信证明书。

三、用适当的介词填空

A. Sole Agency: Under sole agency a sole agent is appointed. He is entitled an exclusive right to sell the designated goods for the principal in a specified area within a stated period of time.

Once a sole agent is appointed, according to general practice, the principal is no longer a position to sell directly or indirectly the same kind of goods _____ any other buyers in that specified area within the validity of the sole agency agreement. In this sense, it is understood that if there is any sale of the goods made through others in that area, the sole agent is entitled a commission though the business is not canvassed through him. And, equally, before the termination of the sole agency agreement the sole agent is obliged not to sell any similar or competitive goods from other sources in that particular area. He should devote himself _____ promoting the sale of the designated goods in the specified principal.

B. Exclusive Sale: Exclusive sale is established a seller and an exclusive distributor by means an exclusive sales agreement, under which the exclusive distributor is authorized by the seller an exclusive right to buy, and then, sell the designated goods in the specified area within a specified period of time. With such an arrangement the seller should no means make use _____ the area, and the exclusive distributor, reciprocally, should guarantee to buy a specified amount of the designated goods the seller within a certain period.

四、选择适当的选项

1. If the buyer _____ concluding business directly with Party A, Party A may do so.

A. insist in　　　　　B. insist to　　　　　C. insist on　　　　　D. insist of

2.　During the period of this Agreement, both Parties should strictly _____ the terms and conditions of this Agreement.

A. abide by　　　　　B. abide with　　　　　C. abide of　　　　　D. abide in

3.　In the event of any breach of the terms by one party, the other party _____ to claim the termination of this Agreement.

A. are entitled　　　　　B. be entitled　　　　　C. is entitled　　　　　D. entitles

4. If the business had been carried out to our satisfaction, we _____ to sign the Agency Agreement.

A. had agreed　　　B. already agreed　　　C. shall agree　　　D. should have agreed

5. This Agreement may be _____ 6 months before its expiry.

A. renewed　　　B. delayed　　　C. expanded　　　D. postponed

6. ABC Company will tender _____ the construction of a new railway.

A. in　　　B. for　　　C. by　　　D. on

7. We have completed the above shipment in accordance with the stipulations set _____ in L/C No.

A. on　　　B. forth　　　C. back　　　D. off

8. We would like to barter farm's products _____ your TV sets.

A. at　　　B. on　　　C. to　　　D. for

9. You must be responsible for all the loss _____ from your delay in shipment.

A. arising　　　B. rising　　　C. arousing　　　D. have arisen

10. This Agreement is made out in _____ Chinese _____ English languages, each in two originals and one original of each is to be held by Party A and Party B.

A. both;and　　　B. either;or　　　C. not only;but also　　　D. neither;nor

五、根据括号提示内容填空

1. Sales Representative Agreement

This AGREEMENT ("Agreement") is made and effective on _____ [MM/DD/YY], by and between DanceShoesOnline.com and _____ ("Representative") _____ [Address].

Company desires appoint Representative, and Representative desires to accept appointment, as a Sales Representative of Company to sell Company's products as set forth herein.

NOW, THEREFORE, in consideration of the mutual promises contained herein, the parties agree as follows:

...

2. Appointment

Company hereby appoints Representative as its (1)_____ (非独家销售代理) for the products in the Territory, and Representative hereby accepts such appointment. Representative's sole authority shall be to (2)_____ (寻求订单) for the Products in the Territory in accordance with the terms of this Agreement. Representative shall not have the authority to make any (3)_____(承诺) whatsoever on behalf of Company.

3. General Duties

Representative shall use its best efforts to promote the products and maximize the sale of the products in the Territory. Representative shall also provide (4)_____(合理协助) to company in promotional activities in the Territory such as trade shows, product presentations, sales calls and other activities of the company with respect to the products. Representative shall also provide reasonable (5)_____ (售后支持) to product purchasers and generally perform such sales related activities as are reasonable to promote the products and the goodwill of company in the territory. Representative shall (6)_____(每周向公司报告) concerning sales of the products and competitive promotional and pricing activities. Representative will devote adequate time and effort to perform its obligations. Representative shall neither advertise the products outside the Territory nor solicit sales from purchasers located outside the Territory (7)_____ (未经事先书面同意) of the company.

...

4. Independent Contractor

Representative is an independent contractor, and nothing contained in this Agreement shall be construed to (i) give either party the power to direct and control the day-to-day activities of the other, (ii) constitute the parties as (8)_____(合伙、合营、共有或其他关系), or (iii) allow Representative to create or assume any obligation on behalf of company for any purpose whatsoever. Representative is not an employee of company and is (9)_____(无权享有雇员利益). Representative shall (10)_____(负责支付) all income taxes and other taxes charged to Representative on amounts earned hereunder. All financial and other obligations associated with Representative's business are the sole responsibility of Representative.

六、将下列句子翻译成中文

1. The sales representative agrees to sell and market the goods aggressively within China on behalf of the manufacturer.

2. The sales representative shall forward all customer orders to the manufacturer in a timely manner.

3. The sales representative shall not promote, advertise, offer for sale, or sell any goods that are identical to, confusingly or deceptively similar to, or otherwise competitive with the goods.

4. The sales representative shall comply with the manufacturer's guidelines on prices, charges, terms, and conditions for the sale of the goods, which are subject to change from time to time.

5. The manufacturer shall give the sales representative the written notice of changes in the guidelines at least 60 days in advance of implementation.

七、将下列句子翻译成英文

1.针对销售代理可能销售的货物，制作商同意制造和保持足够数量的货物，并及时地交付。

2.制造商应根据"制造商手册"对客户的订单开具发票或以其他方式确认，并装运货物。

3.如果制造商修改或停止任何货物的生产，应立即告知销售代理并提供替代货物。

4.如果销售代理拒绝销售替代货物，本协议应终止，并且各方彼此间不再有索赔或责任。

5.对根据本协议所履行的服务，制造商应向销售代理支付占所销售货物批发价8％的佣金。

八、讨论

1. How do you define a sales representative contract?

2. What is the difference between sales representative contracts and relevant contracts?

3. What are the key obligations of the manufacturer and the sales representative?

4. What are the main clauses and the contents of a sales representative contract?

5. China Dragon Sales, Inc. was a party to a representative agreement with American Sam Corporation Inc. as an exclusive independent sales representative for the sale of LED products included in the representative agreement was the following split commission clause:" The parties recognize that sometimes the design, specification, justification and / or approval, purchase and installation of the products may be in different territories. In such cases, the Manufacturer reserves the right to split the commission ..." Is the said clause effective?

九、实务思考

案例1

未订代理合同，外贸公司受骗受损
——美国海维兰服装公司诉杭州东君外贸公司案

美国海维兰服装公司（以下简称海维兰公司）与杭州东君外贸公司（以下简称东君公司）有着长期的进出口服装业务往来。每年，海维兰公司给予东君公司的服装订单占到东君公司接到的所有订单的1/3以上，它是东君公司的一大主顾。2018年2月，海维兰公司向东君公司订购一批总价值达80万元人民币的真丝衬衣，并与东君公司签订了出口服装的协议，协议规定了双方的权利、义务，并约定最后交货期为2018年4月30日，最后一批货必须出运并货到纽约港。另外，双方对违约金作了明确规定：如出口方不能及时出运，应支付迟延交货的违约金，金额为迟延交付货物总价的4%；如出口方不能交货，应支付不能交货部分货款总价4%的违约金。当然，对于买方违约，该协议也明确地规定了相应的违约金额。合同签订后，东君公司将订单分配给几家熟悉的生产厂家生产。2018年2月中旬，杭州西子服装厂（以下简称西子厂）听说东君公司有许多订单，便通过关系从东君公司接来一批价值10万元的真丝衬衣订单。10万元的订单对于一个规模不是很大的生产厂家来说是个不小的数目。同年4月中旬，东君公司陆续配齐海维兰公司价值80万元服装的部分货物，并分阶段陆续出仓、装船出运。而此时，西子厂迟迟不见交货，东君公司几次电话催促，西子厂都称正在赶制。东君公司遂派员前去察看，发现大约有3/5的货物已经完成，经询问，西子厂称可以在4月30日前全部完工。至4月底，西子厂仍没有交货，东君公司遂又派人前去责问，见仓库内有4/5的货已备齐。东君公司此时考虑到如果再找其他生产厂家，时间上已经来不及，遂决定与海维兰公司协商，推迟交货。海维兰公司传真过来称"2018年5月4日以前必须全部装船出运"，东君公司遂继续用电话催促西子厂加紧赶制。5月3日，东君公司经理亲自到西子厂察看，却发现所有货物已经不见。据知情人士说，西子厂同时接到东君公司10万元的真丝衬衣订单和另一家外贸公司8万元的真丝衬衣订单，仓库内的真丝衬衣已由另一家外贸公司代理出口。东君公司气愤万分，但再找其他生产厂家已然不可能，只有跟海维兰公司协商。协商未成，东君公司终诉之法院。法院判决，终止履行未交货部分的合同，包括其他厂家已交货并已装船的15万元货物，由东君公司向海维兰公司支付违约金1万元。东君公司不但遭受了巨额损失，而且得罪了大客户，当然不甘心，遂向法院起诉西子厂。西子厂否认交货时间，否认东君公司曾经向他们几次催促的事实，又反称货早已配齐，东君公司迟迟未来提货、清点出仓（此时西子厂已经从其他厂家借来一部分货存放于仓库，制造有货的假象），故将部分货物转让他人，东君公司违约在先云云。因双方均无确凿证据，无代理合同，又考虑到西子厂是一个不大的厂家，在法院的主持下调解结案，西子厂象征性地向东君公司支付了违约金。

问题：从该案例中我们应该吸取什么教训？

案例2

双方代理，从中渔利

——中国济科联合化工厂有限公司诉美国加州温纳尔达公司案

原告中国济科联合化工厂有限公司（以下简称济科公司）为从美国进口5 300吨高压聚乙烯，委托被告美国加州温纳尔达公司（以下简称温纳尔达公司）在该地寻找货源，并代理进口。双方于2017年8月签署了一份委托代理协议，该协议对委托人要求的事项向代理人作了明确的授权，并对进口商品的名称、质量、浓度、密度、包装、熔融度、杂质含量等作了严格限制，并在协议中约定了双方各自详细的权利、义务，明确了代理期限为"2017年8月10日至2018年8月31日"，确定了"中英文两个版本具有同等的效力"。合同签订以后，双方各执中英文两个版本的合同4份。

2017年12月初，温纳尔达公司向济科公司称其货源已落实，该货主为美国VIS公司。济科公司为确保这项业务可靠，致电要求温纳尔达公司向它传真一份美国VIS公司的资信调查表。2017年12月29日，应济科公司之要求，温纳尔达公司传真了一份由美国资信调查中心出具的对VIS公司的资信调查表（英文）。根据该调查表，济科公司确信美国VIS公司具有丰厚的资产和极高的商业信誉，遂致电温纳尔达公司，可以与美国VIS公司签署合同，并重申了货到青岛港以及价格、质量要求等一定要符合代理协议中所称，同时要求合同签署后，立即传真一份副本给它。2018年1月20日，温纳尔达公司以济科公司代理人的身份，以济科公司的名义与美国VIS公司签署一份高压聚乙烯947号购销合同，并当即传真了一份合同（英文）给济科公司，济科公司派人对此合同进行审核，未发现有疏漏之处。2018年2月10日，济科公司收到货已装船的相关单据，遂向银行开出以温纳尔达公司为受益人的信用证，由温纳尔达公司扣除合同约定的佣金之后向美国VIS公司支付货款。2018年5月2日，5 300吨货物按约到达青岛港，济科公司派人前去检验，检验结果表明947号合同项下有6个批号的货物的熔融指数不符合合同的规定，其中有的批号混杂有不同品种的颗粒，且密度不一，系低密度聚乙烯。这样总计有10个批号的货物不符合同规定，涉及聚乙烯1 500吨左右，计价款约40万美元。济科公司当即与美国VIS公司、温纳尔达公司联系、交涉，称其合同项下货物不符合合同规定，要求两公司派员来再次检验、确认。两公司人员以种种理由推托，济科公司遂向美国VIS公司提出索赔，却发现该公司已于2018年4月申请破产，该笔货款已被其列入破产财产清偿了债务。同时，济科公司发现在该州并无美国资信调查中心这一部门，温纳尔达公司出具的对美国VIS公司的资信调查表纯系温纳尔达公司自己杜撰。另查证属实，温纳尔达公司作为美国 VIS 公司在加州的独家代理推销其化工产品的代理商，曾于 2017 年 10 月中旬与美国 VIS 公司签订一份独家代理协议，该协议的期限为 3 年。据此，济科公司以温纳尔达公司双方代理并进行商业欺诈为由诉之法院，法院判决济科公司胜诉，但判决书迟迟得不到执行。

　　问题：从该案例中我们应该吸取什么教训？

实训项目 9
保密协议练习①

实训目标

1.掌握保密协议的内容。

2.掌握撰写保密协议的注意事项。

一、将下列保密协议条款翻译成英文

1.本协议任何一方都可以在任何时候将其在本协议项下的全部或部分利益或权利进行转让。

2.本合同终止时，本保密义务应继续有效。

3.本合同条款中一部分或全部被法院判决无效，不影响其他有效部分条款的执行效力。

4.本协议一方因违反本协议约定未能行使本协议规定的权利的，不得视为放弃了该权利。

5.本协议可由当事人订立，副本不限。

二、将下列保密协议条款翻译成中文

1. The Party B agrees that it will not at any time after the signature of this Agreement disclose any information in relation to the Company's method of manufacture or design or the Party B's method of distribution in relation to the Products.

2. The Recipient undertakes to disclose the Confidential Information furnished to it only to its employees who have a legitimate and absolute need to know the Confidential Information in order to perform their duties relating to the purpose set out herein.

3. The nondisclosure provisions of this Agreement shall survive the termination of this Agreement and Receiving Party's duty to hold Confidential Information in confidence shall remain in effect until the Confidential Information no longer qualifies as a trade secret or until Disclosing Party sends Receiving Party a written notice releasing Receiving Party from this Agreement,

---

① [1] 兰天，屈晓鹏. 国际商务合同翻译教程［M］. 大连：东北财经大学出版社，2014.［2］王相国. 鏖战英文合同：英文合同的翻译与起草［M］. 最新增订版. 北京：中国法制出版社，2014.

whichever occurs first.

4. "Confidential Information" means any and all data, reports, records, notes, compilation, studies and other information disclosed directly or indirectly by one Party to the other Party relating to or in any way connected with the Work, whether such information is disclosed orally, in writing, or by any other means.

5. Nothing contained in this Agreement shall be deemed to constitute either Party a partner, joint venture or employee to the other party for any purpose.

三、实务思考
案例 1

Example of Breach of Non-Disclosure Agreement[①]

In 2003, Wall Street trader Lauren Brenner was inspired to start a physical fitness studio based on military boot camp-style programs. She visited Fort Knox on several occasions to learn and design materials she would use. After studying the program, she opened Pure Power Boot Camp in New York City. The studio used military colors and obstacles designed to fit an indoor space.

The studio employed a unique method of payment by clientele, in which no membership fee was charged, but the clients were referred to as "recruits" who signed up for returning "tours of duty." Brenner hired former marines as instructors to drill the recruits, two of which became her most trusted employees.

The studio was successful from the beginning, and Brenner planned to expand the operation. Her employees signed an employee agreement which contained non-disclosure, non-compete, and non-solicitation provisions. After opening a second location in Manhattan, Brenner invited one of the two top marines to become a partner. He refused, claiming he did not have the money to invest.

In reality, the two instructors were planning to open their own boot camp gym with investments from their girlfriends. They leased a space 15 blocks from Brenner's facility, and stole her Pure Power studio documents from her office, and destroyed their own employee agreements. The stolen documents included Pure Power Boot Camp business plan, its startup information, and its client list.

Before she learned about the stolen documents, Brenner got into an argument with one of the drill instructors and fired him. The other drill instructor promptly quit. The men used the stolen documents to open their own Warrior Fitness Boot Camp, going to far as to email Pure Power's clients in an attempt to get them to switch to their gym.

When Brenner learned the men had stolen her confidential information to form their own business, she filed a lawsuit seeking an injunction against the competing business. While the court denied her request for an injunction, finding that the non-compete agreement was not enforceable. The judge did order the men to return the stolen materials, and to alter their dress code for their

---

① ANON. Non disclosure agreement [EB/OL]. (2016-01-03) [2019-10-17]. https://legaldictionary.net/non-disclosure-agreement/.

clients.

The case was then taken to federal court where the parties eventually had a bench trial.

Questions:

(1)Did the two men breach the non-disclosure agreement portions of their employee contracts?

(2)Should the men pay punitive damages for their "egregious" betrayals of the plaintiff's trust?

案例 2

IDX V. Epic[①]

Background

In one case, a company learned that non-disclosure agreements were enforceable but found out the documents must be carefully worded. The case involved IDX Systems Corporation and Epic Systems Corporation, which both made software for use in managing the financial side of a medical practice including billing, insurance reimbursement and collections.

One of IDX's customers was the University of Wisconsin Medical Foundation, which was made up of more than 1,000 physicians. The Foundation used IDX software for many years after signing a non-disclosure agreement with the firm—and then switched to software developed by Epic.

IDX believed that two former Epic employees, who were hired to manage data processing at the Foundation, not only instigated the change but transferred valuable information to Epic.

According to IDX's complaint, the two employees and others working at the Foundation furnished Epic with details about how IDX software worked. This enabled Epic to enhance its own product enough to ultimately take the Foundation's business and match up better in the competition for other customers.

IDX filed suit, charging the Foundation and the employees with theft of trade secrets and breach of contractual covenants of confidentiality.

In the non-disclosure contract at issue, the Foundation agreed not to permit the software and related materials created by IDX to be "examined ... for the purpose of creating another system" and not to "use or disclose or divulge to others any data or information relating to" IDX's product or "the technology, ideas, concepts, know-how and techniques embodied therein."

Lower Court Ruling

The U.S. District Court held that IDX did not properly establish the existence of any trade secrets in the information disclosed to the Foundation. The court attempted to limit the scope of the non-disclosure agreement by drawing analogies to employee non-competition agreements. (Although the case was decided based on Wisconsin law, the concepts were general in scope.)

Confidentiality agreements protecting information that is not a trade secret are "suspect and must incorporate geographic or temporal limitations" the court stated, similar to non-compete agreements signed by employees.

---

① 　HALL A. Case study: IDX v. Epic〔EB/OL〕. (2016-12-02)〔2019-10-17〕. https://aaronhall.com/trade-secrets-ndas/.

Typically, when an employee challenges a non-compete covenant, courts look at whether the agreement is reasonably limited in terms of time and geographic scope. For example, a one-year agreement prohibiting a former employee from working for competitors within a 50-mile radius might be considered reasonable. A ten-year limit spanning several states may be deemed unreasonable because it inhibits the former employee's ability to earn a living.

In the case involving IDX, the lower court required these geographic and time limitations to apply to the non-disclosure agreement between a vendor and its customer.

Appeals Court Ruling

On appeal, the Seventh Circuit reversed on several key points. Here are two highlights of its decision:

The non-disclosure contract was enforceable despite being unlimited in time and geographic scope. "It is impossible to understand how a non-disclosure agreement could place 'geographical' limits on the dissemination of intellectual property comparable to those restricting the locale where a salesman may try to drum up customers for a new employer." The court stated.

The agreement was not specific enough but nonetheless enforceable. IDX "has been both too vague and too inclusive, effectively asserting that all information in or about its software is a trade secret." According to the court.

It's understandable that companies are reluctant to include too much information in these agreements because they don't want to "tip off a business rival." The court noted. But "unless the plaintiff engages in a serious effort to pin down the secrets, a court cannot do its job."

However, the Seventh Circuit recognized that because "it is hard to prove that particular information qualifies as a trade secret, many producers of intellectual property negotiate with their customers for additional protection."

Questions: What shall we learn from this case?

实训项目 10
第三方监管账户协议练习①

实训目标

1.掌握第三方监管账户协议的内容。

2.掌握撰写第三方监管账户协议的注意事项。

一、将下列第三方监管账户协议条款翻译成英文

1.本协议的修改需要以书面形式进行。

2.在本协议签署之日，本协议取代以往涉及本协议交易或者标的物的任何书面或者口头协议。

3.本协议的签署意味着其具有法律遵从的、有约束力的、有效的和可执行的义务。

4.ABC负责支付监管账户维护和管理的所有费用和相关税费。

5.本合同不得以口头方式修改，而须经双方签署书面文件后方可修改。

6.当乙方向甲方提供已经存款的证明文件后，甲方将提供给乙方相应的收据。

7.乙方已向母公司交付所有乙方合同及修订的准确和完整的附件。

8.法律顾问参与了本协议的谈判、签署和交付过程。

9.就第2条而言，"土地"并不包括继承财产。

10.如果不存在相反的合同规定，通常不得向赔偿方要求补偿间接损失。

二、将下列第三方监管账户协议条款翻译成中文

1. Subject to Clauses 3.2.1 and 3.2.2, the Escrow Bank shall transfer to such account designated by the ABC the applicable amount of funds from the Escrow Account by wire transfer on the proposed withdrawal date.

2. The ABC hereby instructs the Escrow Bank to apply up to all the Minimum Amount to discharge any amount due and payable by the ABC under any Specific Loan Agreement, provided and to the extent that.

3. This Agreement shall come into force on the Effective Date and remain valid for fifteen (15) years, subject to an automatic extension to the later of the expiry date of the Coal sales

① 张林玲. 商务英语合同翻译与写作 [M]. 北京：机械工业出版社，2009.

contract or when the ABC has discharged all its payment obligations under any Specific Loan Agreement.

4. No terms or provisions of this Agreement shall be varied or modified by any prior subsequent statement, conduct or act of either of the Parties, except that the Parties may amend this Agreement by written instruments referring to and executed in the same manner as this Agreement.

5. The Parties hereby warrant that they are not engaged in and will not engage either directly or through subsidiaries or associated companies, in activities included in the business of the Joint Venture unless upon by the Parties in writing.

6. If the country of either party restricts the remittance of funds to the other country, the Party A may instruct the Party B to deposit sums due into an account Party B's country but in the Party A's name.

7. Except as expressly set forth in the Party B Closing Certificate, each party in the representations and warranties made by the Party B in this Agreement is accurate in all material respects as of the Closing Date as if made on the Closing Date.

8. Except for the stay of the Party B Pending Litigation and the Parent Pending Litigation pursuant to the Stay Order, the Party B Corporations do not commence or settle any Proceeding.

9. In case of default of the Applicant, the Society must first notify the Applicant it is in default and allows the Applicant a thirty-business-day remedy period.

10. Where the Contract provided for payment in whole or in part to be made to the Contractor in foreign currency or currencies, such payment shall not be subject to variations in the rate or rates of exchange between such specified foreign currency or currencies and the currency of the country in which the Works are to be executed.

实训项目 11
股权转让协议练习①

实训目标

1. 掌握股权转让协议的内容。
2. 掌握撰写股权转让协议的注意事项。

一、将下列股权转让协议条款翻译成英文

1. 本股权转让（简称"转让"）总对价（简称"转让价"）详见协议双方约定的本协议附件三第2条。

2. 转让价不含下述第2条第3款规定的应付的转让（可能的）税款。

3. 受让人应于下列第3条第1款第1项所述交割日期，向转让方支付转让价格。

4. 受让人应提交与转让相关的所有必要文件供盖章，应代表转让方依照相关法律，向有关税务部门纳税。

5. 在风险投资中，公司章程是一份重要文本。

6. 公司章程设定了包含但不限于不同种类、不同序列的公司股票所对应的权利、优先权、特权及限制。

7. 衍生证券指任何可转换、执行或兑换为普通股的有价证券或权利，包括期权和认股权证。

8. 股东指持有可登记证券的、为本协议当事方的股东。

9. 发起股东指根据本协议适当地发起登记申请的股东之统称。

10. 首次公开招股指公司根据《中华人民共和国证券法》首次推出股份让公众认购的行动。

二、将下列股权转让协议条款翻译成中文

1. "Key Employment" means any executive-level employee (including division director and vice president-level positions) as well as any employee who, either alone or in concert with others, develops, invents, programs, or designs any Company Intellectual Property (as defined in the Purchase Agreement).

2. "Major Investor" means any Investor that, individually or together with such Investor's

---

① 张林玲. 商务英语合同翻译与写作 [M]. 北京：机械工业出版社，2009.

Affiliates, holds at least shares of Registrable Securities (as adjusted for any stock split, stock dividend, combinations, or other recapitalization or reclassification effected after the date hereof).

3. In the event there is more than one closing, the term "Closing" shall apply to each such closing unless otherwise specified.

4. "Company Intellectual Property" means all patents, patent applications, trademarks, trademark applications, service marks, trade names, copyrights, trade secrets, licenses, domain names, mask works, information and proprietary rights and processes as are necessary to the conduct of the Company's business as now conducted and as presently proposed to be conducted.

5. "Shares" means the shares of Series A Preferred Stock issued at the Initial Closing and any (Milestone Shares or) Additional Shares issued at a subsequent Closing under Section 1.3.

6. For the purposes of these representations and warranties (other than those in Sections 2.2, 2.3, 2.4, 2.5, and 2.6), the term "the Company" shall include any subsidiaries of the Company, unless otherwise noted herein.

7. With respect to the property and assets it leases, the Company is in compliance with such leases and, to its knowledge, holds a valid leasehold interest free of any liens, claims or encumbrances other than those of the lessors of such property or assets.

8. The Financial Statements have been prepared in accordance with generally accepted accounting principles applied on a consistent basis throughout the periods indicated.

9. The share of capital stock of the Corporation shall not be sold, pledged, hypothecated, or transferred.

10. By the contract B shall be entitled to have a general lien on all of the merchandise.

三、实务思考

本案原告 S 和被告 H 都是美国公民。H 提出将其在 FDJ 公司中的 20% 股权转让给原告。原告按 H 提出的价格，先后向 FDJ 公司汇入 40 万美元，以投资人身份被列名为 FDJ 公司的副董事长，但一直未参与 FDJ 公司的经营管理。

2018 年 9 月，原告应邀暂时管理公司时，才发现 H 并未按合同、章程的约定，将其承诺投入的 200 万美元现汇及价值 97 万美元的生产设备注入 FDJ 公司，而是将原告投入的资金当作他个人出资进行验资，并且在经营管理期间还有违规操作以及侵害其他股东权益的情形。为此，原告向 H 要求退出 FDJ 公司，由 H 按原价收购其出让给原告的 20% 股权。H 表示同意，并与原告达成协议，草拟了《股权转让协议》。但在行将签约时，因 H 变更付款条件，签约未成。双方又确定以 H 公司董事会决议案的方式代替股权转让协议。

2019 年 3 月 13 日，H 公司董事会作出两个决议案，同意原告将 FDJ 公司 20% 股权以 40 万美元的价格转让给 H；同意在决议签署后两日内，将公司购买的 S 的房产作价 521 145 元人民币过户给原告，同时将 H 处店面出售款中的 130 万元人民币先支付给原告，余款由则公司向原告开出远期银行汇票，每月支付一次；若有任何一期透支或被退票，原告有权主张全部未到期债权。

由于 H 实际是 FDJ 公司的全额投资人，因此 H 对原告的付款行为，即为 FDJ 公司向原告的付款行为。董事会决议作出后，原告即离开 FDJ 公司，H 也向员工宣布了原告退股的消息。而H并未将S之房产过户给S，FDJ公司也未向原告开出远期银行票据支付余款。原告认为，股权转让协议签订后，虽未到政府相关部门办理变更登记手续，但已经是依法成立的协议，具有法律约束力。现在H和FDJ公司未按协议向原告支付相应的股权转让款，已构成违约；原告为维护自身合法权益，故提起诉讼。

　　问题：从该案例中我们应该吸取什么教训？

实训项目 12
雇佣合同练习①

实训目标

1.掌握雇佣合同的内容。
2.掌握草拟雇佣合同的注意事项。

一、将下列雇佣合同条款翻译成中文

1. In carrying out economic and technological cooperation with the Third World countries, we sign the contract on the principle of equality and mutual benefit stressing practical results, adopting various forms and working for common development.

2. China Corporation shall dispatch for the Works its authorized representative technical personnel and workers, and a necessary number of supporting and administrative staff (hereinafter called the Personnel) in accordance with the occupational categories, number, technical qualifications, departure date and term of service as specified in appendices 1 and 2 attached hereto.

3. If the engaging party finds it imperative to terminate the Contract, then, in addition to bearing the above-mentioned wages and benefits, it shall pay the engaged party three months' extra salary as compensation allowance, and arrange at its own cost for him and his family to go back to their country within one month in case of an emergency involving serious illness, accident or death of Employee. Employer shall notify Employee's next-of-kin immediately.

4. China Corporation shall bear all relevant taxes and levies imposed upon the Personnel by the Chinese Government, whereas the Employer shall bear the same imposed upon the Personnel by the Government of the Project-host country.

5. In the interest of our clients, we would train their technical staff at request. The training may be carried out in this city or at your end, depending upon specific conditions. The training courses include operation and maintenance of individual machines and also industrial administration of a shop up to a complete plant.

6. Employers shall guarantee to let engineers remit dollars up to the ceiling permissible by

---

① 兰天，屈晓鹏. 国际商务合同翻译教程［M］. 大连：东北财经大学出版社，2014.

the Government of necessary procedures on behalf of the engineers in making their income to China in US and shall attend to all the remittances.

7. Party B's personnel shall abide by the laws and decrees prevailing in ... (country), respect the local habits and customs and not partake in local political activities. The Employer shall respect the personnel's habits and personalities and not interfere in their activities in off-duty time.

8. Party B's personnel shall be on probation for 90 days. In case any of them is found incompetent, he will be repatriated to China. Party B shall replace him with a suitable person and pay travelling expenses for the replacement.

9. Party B's personnel shall be entitled to 20-day leave with pay after completing one year's service in ... (country). No such leave can be given to those who have served less than one year.

二、将下列雇佣合同条款翻译成英文

1.如乙方人员在工作中因意外事故受伤，甲方将给予治疗和带薪病假25天。如因违反工地操作规章而受伤，乙方应承担其返回中国和替换人员由中国来到工地的费用。

2.下列任何一条均构成合同的因故终止：

（1）雇员5次无故旷工或10次无故上班迟到；

（2）雇员不完成工作任务；

（3）在这个国家犯下重罪或两项以上轻罪；

（4）雇员放弃工作职责；

（5）身体的或其他方面的极度残酷虐待；

（6）无故拖延支付雇员的工资。

3.如果雇主需要在工作人员工作期限期满之前终止雇用，雇主应在终止雇用之前，提前_____个月书面通知中国公司。

4.雇主应向人员支付每人_____美元的动员费。动员费应在每批人员抵达工地后由雇主随同人员的机票以美元一并汇至中国银行中国公司账户。

5.根据工程的进展情况，通过工地上双方授权代表的协商和达成的协议，雇员可以加班或在夜间工作。每月加班工作总时间原则上不得超过_____个小时。

6.关于劳务合作，我们愿意提供任何行业的工程师、技术工人，为任何工厂或矿物生产线进行工程建设、设备安装和技术指导。

7.劳务合作的方式包括草拟可行性研究、勘探、设计、建筑、设备安装和技术指导。

8.当前承包工程的世界市场很大，中国的劳务合作公司有着广阔的前景。

9.如果雇员死亡，雇主应负担其尸体保存和运送的费用。

三、根据下列情境撰写一份雇佣合同

The School is going to invite Prof. White Johnson to teach in the school as a foreign and you are going to offer an employment to Prof. White Johnson which should include:

1. obligation of the school

2. obligation of Prof. White Johnson

3. working hours and overtime work

4. leave

5. holidays

6. other benefits

7. revision, cancellation and termination

8. severability

9. applicable law

四、实务思考

中国某公司诉巴拿马某航运有限公司船员雇用合同纠纷案

20××年12月17日，中国武汉某公司（以下简称武汉公司）与巴拿马某航运有限公司（以下简称巴拿马公司）在上海签订一份船员雇用合同。合同规定，由武汉公司派出包括船长在内的25名船员前往巴拿马公司的巴拿马籍"帕莫娜"轮工作一年；在受雇用期间，巴拿马公司于每月5日将20 833美元的船员工资汇入武汉公司账户。次年1月14日，武汉公司开始履行合同，船员在受雇期间，接受巴拿马公司的指派和调遣，按照合同各司其职，为巴拿马公司提供劳务。巴拿马公司对船员提供的劳务未表示过任何异议。从开始履行合同起，一直到次年9月16日止，巴拿马公司仅于同年2月1日、6月12日两次寄汇武汉公司21 455美元；还于同年8月21日、9月22日两次供应船员伙食费840.8美元。巴拿马公司尚欠武汉公司的船员工资款190 149.24美元，致使25名船员及其家属的生活受到了影响。武汉公司以此为由，于次年9月16日向上海海事法院申请扣押"帕莫娜"轮，责令巴拿马公司提供20万美元的担保，直至变卖该轮以赔偿其债务。上海海事法院审查认为：武汉公司申请符合扣押船舶的条件，具有合理的依据，并于同年9月28日裁定扣押该轮。

次年10月3日，武汉公司向上海海事法院提起诉讼请求，要求巴拿马公司除偿还拖欠船员的工资外，还应承担武汉公司向该轮提供燃料的费用、扣船申请费、律师费、违约金及有关费用的利息等，上述几项共计为259 636.03美元。

上海海事法院受理此案后，通知被告进行答辩和提供担保。被告未在法定期限内提出答辩，亦不提供担保。为了维护当事人的合法权益，上海海事法院遂于次年10月18日公开拍卖"帕莫娜"轮，保存售得之价款43万美元，同时，公告该轮所有债权人在30日内申请债权登记。

被告经两次合法传唤均未提出任何正当理由而拒不到庭。上海海事法院遂于第3年2月25日对本案进行缺席公开审理。经审理认为，原告（武汉公司）与被告（巴拿马公司）之间签订的劳务合同，符合我国法律的规定，双方应认真履行。原告及其所派船员在"帕莫娜"轮被法院强制变卖前，始终认真地履行合同，由于被告长期拖欠大量劳务费，影响了船员及其家属的正常生活，在被告严重违约的情况下，原告行使其海事请求权，申请扣押被告所有的"帕莫娜"轮，理由正当。被告作为"帕莫娜"轮的所有人，长期拖欠劳务费，违反了合同规定，应对其未尽义务所产生的后果负全部责任。在法院扣押"帕莫娜"轮期间，原告向该轮供油一事，应视其为债权人共同利益保存船舶所做出的行为。上海海事法院根据《中华人民共和国民事诉讼法》，参照国际惯例做法，于第3年9月21日作出以下判决：

（1）被告偿付原告应得劳务报酬 190 149.24 美元；

（2）被告偿付原告燃料供应费用 3 500 美元；

（3）原告请求的其他费用不予支持；

（4）本案受理费为 1 176.87 美元，扣船申请费为 625 美元，其他诉讼费为 139.90 美元。以上费用共计 1 941.77 美元，由被告承担；自本判决生效后，从"帕莫娜"轮所卖价款中扣除。

变卖"帕莫娜"轮及清偿债务所支付的费用 25 185.88 美元，应从该轮所变卖价款中先行扣除。

上述第 1 项的执行，自本判决生效后，由原告与"帕莫娜"轮其他债权人从船舶变卖价款中共同清偿。上述第 2 项的执行，自本判决生效后，从变卖价款中扣除。

判决书送达后，原告与被告均未上诉，判决生效。上海海事法院主持各债权人召开会议，采取由各债权人充分协商的办法，对"帕莫娜"轮案的债务进行了清偿。

问题：

（1）为什么法院这样判决？

（2）从该案例中我们应该吸取什么教训？

实训项目 13

国际借贷合同练习^①

实训目标

1.掌握国际贷款合同的基本内容。

2.掌握草拟国际贷款合同应该注意的事项。

一、将下列国际借贷合同条款翻译成中文

Article 5 Events of Default

Section 1 Events of Default. If one or more of the following events of default (each an "Event of Default") shall occur and be continuing, the agent and the Banks shall be entitled to the remedies set forth in Section 2.

1. The Borrower shall fail to pay any amount payable hereunder as and when such amount shall become payable.

2. The Borrower shall fail to perform or observe any covenant or agreement contained herein to be performed or observed by it other than those referred to in Section 1.1, if such failure is not remedied within thirty days after it occurs.

3. Any representation or warranty of the Borrower in this Agreement or any other documents delivered in connection with this Agreement shall prove to have been incorrect, incomplete any material respects at the time it was made or repeated or deemed to have been made or repeated.

4. The Borrower or any Subsidiary shall fail to perform or observe any covenant or agreement to be performed or observed by it contained in any other agreement involving the borrowing of money or the advance of credit to which the borrower or such Subsidiary is a party as a borrower or guarantor.

5. Any governmental authorization necessary for the performance of any obligation of the borrower under this agreement or the Notes shall fail to remain valid and subsisting in full force and effect.

6. Any governmental authority or court shall take any action which, in the reasonable opinion of Majority Banks, adversely affects the condition of the borrower and the Subsidiaries or the

① 吴敏，吴明忠. 国际经贸英语合同写作 [M]. 广州：暨南大学出版社，2002.

ability of the Borrower to perform its obligations under this agreement or the Notes, if such action is not rescinded within thirty days after it occurs, or if such rescission shall fail to remain in effect.

7. The Borrower shall sell or otherwise dispose of all or a substantial part of its assets or cease to conduct all or a substantial part of its business as now conducted.

二、将下列国际借贷合同条款翻译成英文

1.贷款总额：贷款总额应为20亿美元，如双方同意可以增到40亿美元。

2.贷款期限：贷款期限应为10年零1天，与提作抵押的定期存单（certificates of time deposit）的期限相同。

3.年利：借方应在贷款期内，按存单面额向贷方每年支付2.5%的利息。

4.副本：借方应于存单到期日，向贷方支付20亿美元的本金。

5.协议代号：所有有关交易的文件，均应注明本协议的协议代号：CD99888。

6.抵押品明细表：存单抵押品明细表应按照借、贷双方所同意并接受的内容提供给出具存单的银行。出具存单的银行应按借、贷双方的议定，用密押向其他国家分行发送电传，以便该分行验证、确认和核实该存单；然后由该分行用密押向贷方银行发送电传。

7.贷款提供时间表：贷方银行应于接受借方银行出具的存单以及存单的保管收据后15天内提供贷款。全部贷款由环球同业银行金融电讯协会（SWIFT）从贷方银行划拨到借方指定的银行账户。每次划拨的贷款金额由贷方与借方双方协定。贷款划拨后，借方银行应在7个银行营业日内，将存单正本提交给贷方。

三、选词填空

acquired, advanced, approves, applicant, credit, correspondent, deposits, exchange, drawdown, guidance, laid, leap, number, option, provides, penalty, period, raised, repay, vary

Foreign Currency Loans in China

Like the extending of RMB _____ facilities, the granting of loans in foreign currency to Chinese enterprises is the most important line of business of the Bank of China. The main object of this business is to use, under the _____ of the policies and plans _____ down by the Chinese government, the foreign currencies _____ by the bank to finance the import of _____ equipment and technology and raw materials for the promotion and development of domestic production, the expansion of Chinese export, the acquisition of foreign _____ and the increase of public revenue.

The Bank of China _____ two kinds of foreign currency loan. One is in free convertible foreign currencies and the other in the form of buyer's credit. The funds for the free convertible foreign currency loans come from various sources. They may come from the foreign currency _____ held by the overseas branches of the bank, or the current accounts the bank maintains with its overseas _____ banks, or the money _____ by the bank in the international markets, such as the euro-currency Market.

The term of the loan may be short, medium or long. The interest rates _____ with the term, purpose and economic result of the loans, and may range from a floating rate approximately the same as the London Interbank Offered rate down to a preferential fixed rate of 2.52 per cent per annum. Unlike the buyer's credit, the loan may be used to import from any country goods or services approved by the Chinese authorities.

If the bank _____ the application, a line of credit will be granted to the _____ with a formal agreement. The agreement will stipulate, among other things, for the annual rate of interest, and for the loan to commence from the date of the first _____. If the interest is at a fixed rate, it will be calculated on the actual _____ of days for which the loan is used on the basis of a year of 360 days, as is the noun for U.S. Dollars loan facilities. But for sterling loans, the interest is calculated on the basis of _____ a year of 365 days or 366 days in the case of a _____ year. To encourage the borrower to _____ earlier than the stipulated date, the bank may accept prepayment of any portion of the loan without imposing any _____ or requiring any prior notice. If a floating interest rate loan is granted, the borrower has the _____ to have the interest rate adjusted monthly, quarterly, half-yearly, or yearly; and interest will be calculated according to the floating rate of each interest _____ .

四、单项选择

1. The bank of China is a state-owned enterprise and is the _____ foreign exchange bank in the People's Republic of China.

A. sole exclusive　　B. exclusive　　C. modernized　　D. specialized

2. The number of overseas offices of the bank of China has increased to 26, _____ 18 are in Europe and 1 in Asia, 6 in Europe and 1 in the United States.

A. which　　B. on which　　C. of which　　D. from which

3. The granting of foreign loans is a feasible way to _____ the pace of realizing China's modernization.

A. fast up　　B. speed up　　C. fast　　D. speed

4. By a government supported export credit, we mean a financial mechanism devised by governments to help exporters compete in _____ markets and to protect them against the risk of the buyer's failure to pay.

A. home　　B. domestic　　C. supplier's　　D. foreign

5. In a supplier's credit, the exporter extends credit directly to his overseas _____ by means of a deferred sales contract.

A. agent　　B. bank　　C. supplier　　D. buyer

6. In a buyer's credit, the _____ bank in the exporter's country enters into a loan agreement either with the overseas buyer directly or with a borrowing bank in the buyer's country.

A. buyer's　　B. importer's　　C. ending　　D. borrow

7. The export credits should not be made available for more than _____ percent of the contract value.

A. 75　　B. 80　　C. 85　　D. 90

8. The supplier's credits or buyer's credits are in all cases tied up with the export of capital

goods or services from the _____ country.

　　A. ender's　　　　　　B. borrower's　　　　　C. buyer's　　　　　D. importer's

　　9. In a buyer's credit, the overseas buyer is normally required to pay directly to the supplier from his own funds _____ percent or more of the contract price, including adequate down-payment, on signature of the commercial contract or on an agreed date.

　　A. 5　　　　　　　　B. 10　　　　　　　　C. 15　　　　　　　D. 20

　　10. Export credits are usually financed in the currency of the _____ country, but there have been occasions where U.S. Dollars are used instead.

　　A. import　　　　　　B. export　　　　　　C. third　　　　　D. importers

五、实务思考

　　2016年10月16日，中国香港Sales公司与上海沪川集团公司（以下简称沪川公司）签订的租赁合同规定，由Sales公司从意大利购买一套轧钢设备，然后出租给沪川公司使用，租期是4年，租金为150万美元。货到上海港半个月以内，沪川公司先行给付30万美元，其余120万美元租金从设备到达上海港之日起分4次交清，每年交付一次。租赁期间设备的所有权归Sales公司，沪川公司则享有全部使用权；在租期届满而且沪川公司付清全部租金后，设备的所有权即归沪川公司。同时双方约定，此套设备交货后如发现产品有瑕疵，Sales公司将索赔权转让给沪川公司并协助索赔，但不承担任何责任，沪川公司仍须按期支付租金。

　　2016年10月28日，沪川公司与上海的一家钢铁公司进行谈判。沪川公司称其利用业务关系以及其他特殊关系现已从意大利某机械设备公司弄到一套先进的轧钢设备，价格合理，如出现质量问题概由沪川公司负责。由于该钢铁公司急需一套进口先进设备，又因沪川公司声誉良好，于2016年11月26日双方签订了购货合同。合同约定沪川公司向钢铁公司提供意大利的机械设备公司所生产的先进轧钢设备一套，价格为150万美元，在安装调试完以后的一个月内一次付清。合同同时约定若有质量问题概由沪川公司负责。

　　2017年2月3日，全套设备从意大利运到上海港，沪川公司将设备运到钢铁公司，交原上海市质量技术监督局检验，质量合格。2017年6月1日，设备调试合格，钢铁公司一次性付清货款150万美元至沪川公司。2018年2月3日，沪川公司按时交付Sales公司第1期租金；2019年2月3日，沪川公司没有交付已经到期的第2期租金。Sales公司即派代表到上海要求沪川公司支付到期租金。结果该代表发现归Sales公司所有的租赁设备，已被沪川公司转卖给钢铁公司。后Sales公司以沪川公司未经其同意擅自转卖租赁设备，侵犯其所有权且未付第2期到期租金为由，向上海市中级人民法院起诉。

　　法院经审理认为：2017年10月16日沪川公司与Sales公司签订的租赁合同符合我国法律的有关规定，符合有关融资租赁方面的国际惯例，因而合同合法、有效。根据《中华人民共和国合同法》，当事人双方就合同的条款经过协商一致并签字，合同就成立，该租赁合同是双方在自愿协商一致的基础上签订的，具有法律效力，双方当事人应当认真地全面履行合同所规定的义务。

　　根据租赁合同，沪川公司只享有使用权。合同中虽规定在租期届满而且沪川公司付清全部租金后，设备所有权即归沪川公司，但是这不等于说沪川公司只要能按期支付租金，或者提供有效的担保即可对租赁的设备享有处分权。因此沪川公司将设备转卖给钢铁公司，侵犯了 Sales 公司对租赁设备在租期内的所有权，同时严重违反了租赁合同的规定。钢铁公司不知道承租人沪川公司是在"融资性购买设备"的情形下接受承租人擅自处分的租赁物，这就是说钢铁公司对该套轧钢设备是善意占有。同时，钢铁公司支付了对价，即购买设备款 150 万美元，因此出租人 Sales 公司无权要求钢铁公司返还租赁设备。在弄清事实、明确责任的基础上，法院作出如下判决：

（1）沪川公司在判决生效后 7 日内交付第 2 期租金和延迟利息，在判决生效后 1 个月内付清余下全部租金。

（2）善意第三人钢铁公司对设备的所有双予以确认。

问题：从该案例中我们应该吸取什么教训？

实训项目 14
国际商标许可合同练习

实训目标

1. 掌握国际商标许可合同的特点。
2. 掌握国际商标许可合同的基本内容。
3. 掌握草拟国际商标许可合同的注意事项。

一、将下列句子翻译成中文

1. AAA grants to the joint company the rights to use trademarks and trade names.

2. AAA hereby grants to ZZZ a license under the aforesaid letters patent.

3. The seller may retain ownership of the container, if they are reusable and expensive.

4. The licensee shall take all necessary measures to protect the licensor's trademark.

5. The manufacturer is the owner of the trademark, which has been duly registered in the Patent Office.

6. ZZZ undertakes that it will not sublicense the rights of any other party.

7. Improvement refers to new findings and/or modifications made in the validity period of the Contract by either party in know-how in the form of new designs, formulas, recipes, ingredients, indices, parameters, calculations, or any other indicators.

8. Know-how refers to any valuable technical knowledge, data, indices, drawings, designs and other technical information, concerning the design, manufacture, assembly, inspection of contract products, developed and owned or legally acquired and possessed by Licensor and disclosed to Licensee by Licensor, which is unknown to either public or licensee before the date of effectiveness of the contract, and for which due protection measures have been taken by licensor for keeping know-how in secrecy. The specific description of know-how is set forth in appendix.

9. AAA shall have the right to grant releases for past infringement of ZZZ under the patent of AAA.

二、将下列句子翻译成英文

1.卖方不应由于任何专利申请、专利权或发明证明受到侵犯，而对买方承担责任。

2.有鉴于公司急欲获得发明转让的保证以及验证申请书中发明人专利权的保证。

3.建筑师表示并保证，工程没有缺陷，并且没有侵犯（某国）法律的所有权问题。

4.甲方授予乙方一张豁免特许权使用费的非独家的许可证。

5.许可方应有权从将来的特许权使用费中得到补偿。

6.如果宣判许可证持有方为破产者，那么甲方可立即终止本协议。

三、实务思考

原告中国A有限公司将其所拥有的AAA商标于2009年2月在原国家工商行政管理总局商标局登记注册，取得该商标专用权。商标有限期限至2014年3月，商标使用范围为烟草、烟具、打火机等。2010年6月，中国B打火机厂为新加坡某洋行加工TTT系列重油打火机，该系列打火机外壳图案中，部分地使用了涉讼的黑白两种底色的由原告注册的AAA商标。B打火机厂于同年试生产，2013年开始批量生产。该系列产品的外壳图案由B打火机厂委托被告上海C工艺厂加工印制。自2011年至2013年8月，C工艺厂共为B打火机厂加工印制了带有AAA商标的该系列打火机外壳60余万只，全部外壳均已由B打火机厂组装生产后销售。因B打火机厂无自营出口权，故该系列的部分产品由被告中国技术进出口公司代理出口。在此过程中，进出口公司亦曾直接给B打火机厂下过生产订单。由进出口公司代理出口及自行组织订购出口销售的印有AAA商标的打火机有1 132 000只，余下568 327只由B打火机厂自行销售。进出口公司自B打火机厂收购的印有AAA商标的TTT系列重油打火机的平均价格为每只3.10元人民币，B打火机厂自行销售的该系列打火机单价最高价为520元人民币，最低价为320元人民币。

B打火机厂于2011年月1日经其上级主管部门批准与他厂合并为某市打火机总厂，债权、债务等由打火机总厂负责承担。三被告（打火机总厂、C工艺厂、中国技术进出口公司）在法院审理中，均未举证证明原告曾许可新加坡某洋行使用其AAA商标，原告对此也予以否认。此外，法院委托上海资产评估事务所对系列产品的生产成本进行审核，总结为该产品内销生产成本为每只3.00元人民币。

原告诉称：打火机总厂未经原告许可，擅自使用了原告所注册的AAA商标生产打火机产品1 132 000只。该商标由C工艺厂印制，部分产品由进出口公司销售。经与打火机总厂交涉不成，故认为三被告共同侵犯其注册商标专用权，为此诉请法院判令三被告销毁全部库存商品，登报道歉，赔偿600 000元人民币并承担诉讼费。

被告打火机总厂辩称：其所生产的1 132 000只AAA商标打火机的生产成本高于销售价，是亏损生产，且产品生产后全部交由进出口公司出口销售，现已无库存。

被告C工艺厂辩称：TTT系列重油打火机的AAA商标标识是打火机总厂的，由B打火机厂委托其印制。该厂共印制AAA商标打火机外壳612 327只，这些产品已全部交B打火机厂组装生产，其加工印制成本高于所收加工费，是亏损印刷。

被告中国技术进出口公司辩称：B打火机厂是直接与新加坡商人洽谈打火机业务的，该公司共代理出口有AAA商标的TTT系列重油打火机1 132 000只，单价平均为3.20元人民币，出口价高低不等，最高价为 0.43 美元，最低价为 0.35 美元，所得利润约为 8 000 元人民币。

问题：

（1）法院将会如何判决？

（2）我们从该案例中应该吸取什么教训？

实训项目 15
合资与合作经营企业合同练习①

实训目标

    1.掌握合资与合作经营企业合同的基本内容。

    2.掌握草拟合资与合作经营企业合同的注意事项。

一、将下列句子翻译为英文

    1.外国合营者如以技术或设备进行投资，则必须是确实适合我国需要的先进技术或设备；如有意提供落后的技术或设备进行欺骗，对造成的损失，应予赔偿。

    2.合作双方同意该合作经营公司拥有自己的名称，但不是一个独立的企业法人，而是合作双方共同经营的一个经济实体。这样，合作双方应以各自所拥有的财产为限对合作经营公司的风险亏损和债务承担责任。

    3.合作任何一方向第三方转让其全部或部分出资，或转让其全部或部分合作条件，须经另一方同意，并报原审批机关审批。获得批准后，合作企业应向有关政府机关办理变更登记。

    4.合作经营公司营业执照签发后10日内，乙方应与合作经营公司签订旨在确定合作产品销售条件的销售确认书。销售确认书应作为本合同不可分割的组成部分。

二、将下列句子翻译成中文

    1. The manager and deputy manager of the Company and the director and deputy director of the factory shall be appointed by the joint managerial institution to handle the day-to-day work. The manager shall come from the Foreign Co. and the deputy manager from the Chinese Corp.

    2. The goal of the Company is to sell all cooperatively produced products of which the quality requirements stipulated in this Contract within China or abroad. For the exports, Party B shall procure a reputable bank agreed by both parties to issue a sight, irrevocable, revolving, transferable letter of credit in favour of the Company valid for a period of six months to be opened at the beginning of the sixth month after the Effective Date of this Contract.

---

    ①   [1] 刘川，王菲. 英文合同阅读与翻译［M］. 北京：国防工业出版社，2010.［2］王相国. 鏖战英文合同：英文合同的翻译与起草［M］. 最新增订版. 北京：中国法制出版社，2014.［3］吕昊，刘显正，罗萍. 商务合同写作及翻译［M］. 武汉：武汉大学出版社，2005.

3. The Company shall deduct 8% from the total value of production every year for the Foreign Co. to recover its investment and for the renewal and overhaul of equipment. The balance after the expenses are defrayed shall be distributed to the two parties as profit according to the ratio stipulated in Article 2.3 hereof.

4. The staff and workers of the Company shall, in accordance with law, establish their trade union organization to carry out trade union activities and protect their lawful rights and interests. The Company shall provide the necessary conditions or the company's trade union to carry out its activities.

5. The total amount of capital of the Company shall be USD 50 million including machinery and special equipment, and it shall be contributed by Party B. The first installment USD 30 million shall be paid to the Company's account within 30 days after the issuance of the Company's business license. The rest USD 20 million shall be paid to the Company's account within six months after the issuance of the Company's business license.

三、选词填空

1. comparatively, direct, usually, more, active, foreign, Chinese, small, mutual, incomplete, quick, simple, flexible, huge, long

Since 1979, more and _____ sino‑foreign jointly operated enterprises have been established and they have played an _____ role in the country's maximization drive. The establishment of such enterprises in China is one of the ways of using _____ foreign investment. It is a contract type joint venture. The rights, responsibilities and obligations of each side are prescribed in the form of contract signed through discussions and negotiations, _____ the Chinese partner provides land, factory buildings including equipment and facilities which may be used, labor, right to develop resources, and a _____ amount of capital, and the _____ partner provides fund technology and equipment. The two sides decide on proper ways of management and the way and proportions of distributing profit, according to the cooperation conditions provided by each side and the principle of equality and _____ benefit. As the foreign partner may recover its investment and make profits during the term of cooperation, the total assets of the enterprise will go to the _____ partner after the cooperation term expires. Features of such enterprises are _____ in form and _____ in formalities. It is easy for partners to reach an agreement through negotiations. At present, China's legislation governing this type of enterprises is still _____ . This kind of cooperation form is _____ suitable for projects which require less complicate technology and not very _____ cooperation period, give _____ economic returns and a _____ profit.

2. make, enjoy, assign, undertake, limited, recruit, detailed, invited, appointed, registered, set, speaking, paying, opening, purchasing, deducting, making, getting

Since China began to pursue the policy of _____ to the outside world, it has enacted the law of the People's Republic of China on Joint Ventures Using Chinese and Foreign Investment and the _____ regulations for the implementation of the law and a series of other laws and regulations sino - foreign joint ventures are limited partnership companies. Liabilities of each partner of a joint venture are _____ to the amount of capital it has invested. The partners may _____ their investment with money, buildings, factory workshops, machines and other equipment, materials, industrial property, patent technology and the right to use the construction site. Generally _____ , investment by foreign partners should not be less than 25 of the total registered capital of the venture. Net profit of a joint venture is distributed in line with the proportion of each partner's _____ capital after _____ the venture's income tax according to the country's lay, on taxes and after _____ the reserve fund bonuses for employees, welfare fund and development fund according to the ventures regulations and rules.

Board of directors of the joint venture is the supreme organ of power. Distribution of the number of people to the board of directors is decided through discussion and according to the proportion of their investment. Chairman is _____ by the Chinese partner and vice-chairman, by the foreign partner. President and vice-presidents are _____ by the board of directors and they may be either Chinese or foreigners.

The joint ventures have greater decision _____ power in production and management than state - owned enterprises, and their production and management plans are decided by the board of directors. Relevant authorities' _____ to guide, help and supervise them, but their relationship is not one of the direct leaderships. The authoritative departments at various levels do not _____ any mandatory production quotas. The joint ventures have the right to import machines and equipment, raw materials and parts and accessories they need and have the right to export their products. They _____ equal opportunities with state - owned enterprises in _____ domestic materials and goods and _____ water, electric power, gas supplies and heating and other services at the same price. They sell their products on the domestic market at the prices by the government according to product quality. The joint ventures themselves may _____ employees through examinations and their wages may be 20% to 50% higher than those of the employees of the state-owned enterprises of the same trade in the same region.

四、单项选择

1. The issues related to taxes will be _____ in accordance with the taxation laws in China.

A. dealt   B. dealt in   C. dealt to   D. dealt with

2. An oil refinery wholly owned by the Company will be _____ to refine the crude oil produced by the Company.

A. set off   B. set up   C. set by   D. set forth

3. The Chinese Corp. shall apply to the relevant departments for reductions or exemptions with regard to business and income _____ and customs _____ on imports and exports.

A. tariffs; duties   B. duties; taxes   C. taxes; duties   D. duties; tariffs

4. The joint venture should apply for the extension of term of operation _____ .

A. before expiration six months   B. before six months expiration

C. six months before expiration   D. six months expiration before

5. The company is a _____ liability company and a legal person under the laws of the People's Republic of China.

    A. limit   B. limited   C. limiting   D. incorporation

6. "Joint venture" means a _____ usually temporary but sometimes permanent, formed by two or more persons or companies.

    A. factory   B. partnership   C. firm   D. organization

7. The bank will, as _____ by the national policies, laws and regulations, give joint venture active support.

    A. called at   B. called for   C. called forth   D. called off

8. This contract shall _____ after it has been approved by the examination and approval authority of China.

    A. come to terms   B. come to effect   C. come into force   D. come through

五、实务思考

案例1

中外合营企业未获批准，合营合同应视为无效案

2017年6月20日，韩国××发展有限公司与中国辽宁省××县水产购销公司在广州东山宾馆签订了一份中外合资协议书，创办合资经营企业，企业名称为辽宁省××实业有限公司，同时对企业性质、所在地、经营范围、企业资金、机构设置、经营管理、利润分成等作了规定。2017年8月9日，韩国××发展有限公司将投资款50万元人民币汇入了中国辽宁省××县水产购销公司的账户。2017年9月30日，双方订立了合资经营××实业有限公司的合同。2017年11月14日，××县经济贸易委员会办理了《关于申请核发中外合资经营企业××实业有限公司批准证书的请示》，后因资金不落实，未获批准。在申办合营企业期间，韩国××发展有限公司借用款及其他开支合计348 336.8元人民币，这样，在中国辽宁省××县水产购销公司的账户上，韩国××发展有限公司的实际投资款为151 663.2元人民币。该公司几次催要投资余款未果，由此形成纠纷。

争议：韩国××发展有限公司于2018年8月30日向中国辽宁省××市中级人民法院起诉。该公司诉称：合营企业未获批准，被告中国辽宁省××县水产购销公司应及时返还其占用的剩余投资款并负担滞返期的利息。被告中国辽宁省××县水产购销公司辩称，虽然合营企业未获批准，但原告、被告之间已经形成事实上的合伙经营关系，要求原告赔偿合营造成的损失总额的1/2，即425 000元人民币。

判决：法院在查明事实的基础上认为，双方申请设立的合营企业未获批准，所订立的合营合同应视为无效，被告应及时返还原告的投资款，长期滞返是错误的。至于被告提出反诉，认为双方实际上形成合伙经营关系，并且要求原告赔偿损失，查无事实根据，被告亦未能举出证据，本院不予支持。根据《中华人民共和国合同法》《中华人民共和国中外合资经营企业法实施条例》的规定，判决如下：被告返还原告投资款151 663.2元人民币，并承担滞返该款的银行利息（自2017年9月1日起计算到给付之日，利息率为5.45%）。诉讼费6 007.1元人民币由被告承担。

问题：从该案例中我们应该吸取什么教训？

案例2

假借投资骗取购买设备款案

2017年3月4日，中国A公司（甲方）与法国B公司（乙方）在中国签订了合资经营某建材有限公司的合同。该合同规定，合资企业注册资本为320万美元，甲方为250万美元，乙方为70万美元。出资方式是：甲方以现金、先进设备、厂房、场地使用权作为出资，乙方以先进设备作为出资。乙方负责于2017年10月31日以前从法国引进5条某型号化工设备生产线，并规定了该生产线应达到的技术水平，其中，每条生产线单价为40万美元，共计200万美元。乙方只负责出资设备的70万美元，作为其全部出资，甲方向乙方支付余下设备款的130万美元。合同同时规定：乙方分5批将设备运至合资企业，并于每一次发货后按货价的13/20开具发票。

甲方见单后，支付发票值的85%；全部设备试车合格后，支付货款的10%；质量保证期过后再支付货款的5%。合同签订后，乙方按规定期限首批设备运到，并且开具了甲方应分摊的全部货款130万美元的发票，甲方亦未表示反对。甲方在乙方没有将全部设备交付之前按乙方开具的发票支付了110.5万美元。后来，乙方按期交付了第2、3、4、5批设备。

2017年11月4日，某市出入境检验检疫局根据申请到合资企业进行检验。商检人员经过检查发现以下问题：（1）分5批到货的设备，大部分是零部件，根本不能构成生产线；（2）设备大部分并非法国生产的；（3）所购设备的市场价格远远低于合同价格。鉴于上述严重问题，为维护国家利益，该出入境检验检疫局于2017年11月20日依法查封了这家合资企业的全部设备。

甲方看到全部设备被查封，而且经检验证明并非先进生产线，即电传通知乙方，要求退换设备并且赔偿经济损失。乙方最初回电传给甲方表示愿意协商，而后一直杳无音讯。甲方多次与乙方联系未果，只得在中国境内向某市中级人民法院提起诉讼。

问题：从该案例中我们应该吸取什么教训？

技术贸易合同练习①

实训目标

掌握撰写技术贸易合同条款的方法。

一、将下列技术贸易合同翻译成中文

In licensing, contracts for transfer of patent or know-how alone constitute only a small portion of the total of the licensing contracts, most of which are mixed ones even linking with import of the machines and equipments. This is due to the fact that these elements are closely related. In the absence of any one of them, production cannot be proceeded with. Therefore it is often hard to say whether it is a contract for transferring a patent or know-how or a contract for importing complete plant equipments. In transferring a patent or know-how, a contract or an agreement should be signed between the licensor and the licensee. The differences between the contents of a contract for transferring a patent and those of a contract for transferring know-how are not great. The following conditions are usually included in a contract for transferring a patent or know-how.

1. Definition

2. The scope of technology transferred

(1) The technology transferred

(2) The areas of manufacture and sale of the goods produced by the transferred technology

3. Licence fee and the method of payment

4. Training of licensees personnel

5. Despatch of technical personnel

6. Secrecy

7. Continuing assistance of technology and grant-back

8. Patent infringement

9. Assignment

10. Tax

① ［1］吴敏，吴明忠. 国际经贸英语合同写作［M］. 广州：暨南大学出版社，2002. ［2］吕昊，刘显正，罗萍. 商务合同写作及翻译［M］. 武汉：武汉大学出版社，2005.

11. Duration of the contract

12. Force majeure

13. Arbitration

14. Applicable law

According to different patents, technology or know-how transferred, some modifications and/or addition or deletion of certain conditions may have to be made.

二、选词填空

by, on, for, from, borne, accurate, supplied, showing, fails, manufactured, occur, make, mean, disclose, principal, annum, rate, remittance

ROYALTY AND PAYMENT

1. During the term of this Agreement B shall pay to a royalty on the total sales of PRODUCT _____ by B under the technical guidance of A as net receipt by A after tax reduction in the People's Republic of China. The _____ of royalty shall be 2.5 percent net on such total sales amount excluding packing and transportation fee, and deducting CIF China port price of MATERIAL _____ by A.

2. "Sales" shall _____ delivery of product from B's factory or warehouse.

3. The royalty _____ the sales between January and June shall be paid at the end of the following August and that between July and December shall be paid at the end of the following February.

4. Any and all taxes of whatever nature imposed or levied in the People's Republic of China _____ the payments made by B to under this agreement shall be _____ and paid by B.

5. All payments by B to A shall be made in U.S. Dollars in the form of T.T. _____ to the Bank of London, whose full address is _____ for account of A and all charges which may _____ in connection with such remittance shall be borne and paid by B.

6. In case B _____ to make any payment as specified in this Agreement within the stipulated time, an interest of 10 percent per _____ on such unpaid amount shall be paid by B to A together with the _____.

7. Each payment of the royalty shall be accompanied _____ a report showing the total sales amount during the term and the related CIF China port prices of materials supplied from A to B to be deducted _____ the sales amount.

8. During the term of this Agreement, B shall keep true and _____ books of account _____ all information necessary for preparations of the above reports and upon A's request. B shall _____ these books to A or its agents and shall _____ explanations on any questions about the records mentioned therein.

三、单项选择

1. If the business had been carried out to our satisfaction, we _____ to renew the contract.

A. had agreed   B. already agreed

C. shall agree   D. should have agreed

2. Terms and conditions shall be _____ mutual discussion and agreement between Party A and Party B.

    A. subjected   B. subject   C. subject for   D. subject to

3. Both Parties shall solve any problems _____ from the Contract in a cooperative manner.

    A. rising   B. risen   C. arising   D. arisen

4. Party A and party B shall be _____ by the final decision made by arbitration.

    A. binding   B. bound   C. borne   D. born

5. The "equipment" as used _____ shall mean the following.

    A. hereof   B. hereto   C. herewith   D. herein

6. In such case, no party shall have any claim for damages or other compensation from any party and this agreement shall be considered _____ from the beginning.

    A. non and void   B. null and void   C. valid and void   D. effective and void

7. The method of the payment shall be _____ the irrevocable L/C payable _____ sight _____ U.S. Dollars.

    A. with; at; by   B. by; on; with   C. on; by; with   D. by; at; in

8. DEF Co. shall consider marketing finished products to Europe and Africa when the quality _____ to be satisfactory.

    A. turn   B. turns out   C. turns on   D. turns in

9. We must _____ for all consequence arising therefrom.

    A. hold you responsible   B. ask you to respect

    C. keep you responsibility   D. request you reliable

10. The _____ grants to the _____ an exclusive _____ to make _____ products throughout the territory.

    A. licence; licensed; licensee; licensor   B. licensee; licensor; licensed; licence

    C. licensor; licensee; licence; licensed   D. licensor; licence; licensed; licensee

四、实务思考

案例1

2018年中国××省××公司与荷兰××有限公司草签了一项引进挖泥船设备和制造挖泥船技术诀窍（专有技术）的合同。其中有这样一项条款："对于那些挖泥船用户公司的总机构设在中华人民共和国之外的，假如该公司与荷兰××有限公司无利害关系冲突或将不会产生冲突，那么这些挖泥船的建造和交船可以进行。对上述情况须经双方协商最后判断，该公司与荷兰××有限公司是否存在利害关系冲突或将会产生冲突，最后由荷兰××有限公司单方决定。"有关律师在审查该草签合同过程中提出异议，认为这样的条款几乎剥夺了我方挖泥船出口的权利，即使同意出口，也会借口索取昂贵的补偿，这是极不公平的。后来在正式签订合同时，我方据理力争，最后使荷兰××有限公司不得不同意取消了该项条款。

问题：从该案例中我们应该吸取什么教训？

案例2

申诉人中国某轻工开发公司与被诉人加拿大某公司签订了关于买卖3台新闻纸机的合同，总价款为300万美元。合同签订后，加拿大某公司一直不交货，中国某轻工开发公司遂从其他来源购买了相同规格的新闻纸机作为替代物，但买入价比合同规定的价格高出50%，即后来购买的新闻纸机总价为450万美元。中方要求加拿大某公司赔偿该50%的差价损失。仲裁庭接受了中方依据仲裁条款而提交的仲裁申请，经调查认为加拿大某公司已构成根本违约，中方有权宣布撤销合同并请求损害赔偿。但是，中方购买替代物的价格大大高于同类产品的国际市场价格，超出了合理的限度。仲裁庭裁决加拿大某公司赔偿中国某轻工开发公司新闻纸机应交货日的国际市场价格与合同价格之间的差价损失。

问题：从该案例中我们应该吸取什么教训？

实训项目 17

技术转让与设备材料进口合同练习①

实训目标

掌握撰写技术转让与设备材料进口合同条款的方法。

一、将下列技术转让与设备材料进口合同条款翻译为英文

1. 技术合同的价款、报酬或使用费的支付方式有：（1）一次总算，一次总付；（2）一次总算，分期支付；（3）提成支付；（4）提成支付附加预付入门费。

2. 非法垄断技术、妨碍技术进步或者侵害他人技术成果的技术合同无效。

3. 让与人未按约定转让技术的，应当返还部分或者全部转让费，并应承担违约责任。

4. 供方不得强迫买方接受不合理的限制性要求，如要求买方购买不需要的技术、技术服务、原材料、设备、产品等。

二、将下列技术转让与设备材料进口合同条款翻译为中文

1. Since the successful recovery of the 17th satellite on October 26, 1985, we have been ready to place our satellite-launching service on the international technology market. Our Long March-2 Rocket, 32-meter-long, two-stage, can carry a two-ton satellite into orbits near Earth. Our most advanced rocket, the three-stage long March-343-meter-long, has a payload capability of 1.4 tons for loads to be put into long-distance geostationary orbits. Furthermore, the Chinese People's Insurance Company is ready to provide insurance cover at internationally competitive rates for foreign clients making use of our launching service.

2. In addition, we have a lot of traditional technologies, such as those involved in making the pottery and porcelain, arts and crafts and traditional medicines. As these technologies are rare in the international market, they may turn out to be good sellers in your country.

3. We are glad to learn that you are willing to export your advanced technology and equipment to our country. There is no doubt that China's rich experience in developing her

① [1] 吴敏，吴明忠. 国际经贸英语合同写作 [M]. 广州：暨南大学出版社，2002. [2] 吕昊，刘显正，罗萍. 商务合同写作及翻译 [M]. 武汉：武汉大学出版社，2005.

national economy and technology will be very useful to our country. We share your country's view to supply each other's needs on the basis of equality and mutual benefit that is an important way to promote South-South cooperation.

4. We used to purchase technology and equipment from developed countries at exorbitant prices. Seeing that as China belongs to the Third World, she naturally understands our problems and difficulties and her technology and equipment are likely to be more suitable to our needs. Our company is prepared to switch your terms and conditions are favorable and prices are reasonable.

5. The invention and creation shall mean invention, utility model and design.

6. No patent right shall be granted for any invention-creation that violates the laws of the state, goes against social morals or is detrimental to the public interests.

7. Any entity or individual exploiting the patent of another must conclude a written licensing contract with the patentee and pay the patentee a fee for the exploitation of the patent.

8. If any Chinese entity or individual intends to file a patent application in a foreign country for the invention-creation made in China, it or he shall file first a patent application with the patent administration department agency designated by the said department under the state Council and appoint to act as its or his agent.

9. The dispute on the infringement of the patent right shall be settled through consultation by the parties concerned. If the consultation fails, the patentee may institute legal proceedings in the People's Court.

10. Where any person passes the patent of another person off as his own, he shall bear his civil liability according to the laws and his illegal earnings shall be confiscated.

三、实务思考

案例1

转让方未尽技术指导义务,合同利益未获实现案

20××年7月中国南方新技术开发公司与日本中田株式会社签订了生产彩色玻璃马赛克设备的技术转让合同,双方约定:(1)转让方日本中田株式会社提供一套生产彩色玻璃马赛克的成型设备及技术,负责装机、建炉、试炉、投产的全部技术指导;(2)受让方中国南方新技术开发公司付给转让方设备及技术转让费50万元,负责建炉的材料及厂房的土建工程项目。合同订立后,转让方依约向受让方提供了彩色玻璃马赛克设备一套,收取了技术转让费、材料费等。受让方为实施受让技术,向当地市场监督管理局申报登记成立某彩色玻璃马赛克厂,聘请了技术转让方的3名专家为顾问。同年12月厂子开始试产,至第二年6月,因产品质量不合格停产。该厂成立后受让方先后向该厂投资了211万元,受让方为挽回损失遂向法院提起诉讼,请求转让方赔偿。

法院委托某市建筑材料工业研究所对转让方转让的成型设备和生产技术的实用性、可靠性及工艺配方进行鉴定,鉴定结论为:转让方提供的技术、设备实用可靠,工艺配方能生产各种色调的玻璃马赛克。据此,法院认为双方订立的非专利技术转让合同符合法律规定,依法成立,应具有法律约束力。但是,转让方虽然提供了实用、可靠的技术,却未尽技术指导义务,致使受让方试产不出合格的彩色玻璃马赛克,转让方负有违约的过错责

任。在法院主持调解下，双方达成如下协议：受让方将生产设备返还给转让方，转让方自愿赔偿受让方 80 万元。

问题：从该案例中我们应该吸取什么教训？

案例 2

无技术转让能力，为何偏要转让技术案

2018 年 3 月，中国某公司与美国某公司签订了技术转让协议。该协议规定美方公司向中方公司转让其生产 GBR 型减速器的专有技术，并在 2018 年 6 月 30 日之前将全部技术资料，以及协助中方公司开发产品、设计定型的方案提交出来。中方公司支付美方公司 7.5 万美元的技术转让费。

但是，在签订协议之后，美方公司迟迟不履行协议，至 2018 年 10 月，中方公司起诉到某市中级人民法院。

中方公司诉称：双方签订的技术转让协议约定，美方公司应在 2018 年 6 月底以前向中方公司提供双方约定的技术资料和方案，但时至今日，仍不见美方公司有履约行为，因此要求法院判令美方公司退还中方公司已支付的技术转让费。

而美方公司辩称：该 GBR 型减速器的专有技术转让协议之所以落空，主要是由于中方公司存有单方终止合同的企图，给转让工作造成障碍，并说其已于 2018 年 6 月底以前备齐了全部技术资料，并已完成了设计定型方案及产品开发方案。所以，中方公司应对违约事件负责。

法院经调查，认定了以下事实：

（1）2018 年 3 月，中方公司与美方公司签订了一份《GBR 型减速器制造技术转让协议书》。

（2）根据协议，中方公司于 2018 年 5 月给美方公司支付了 7.5 万美元的技术转让费。

（3）美方公司从未开发和生产过减速器系列的产品，根本没有履行协议约定的技术转让的能力，无法提供有关资料和方案。

（4）中方公司按合同约定支付了技术转让费，并无单方终止合同的意思表示。

（5）由于美方公司不具备履约能力，因而所签订的协议应为无效协议。美方公司的答辩理由不充分，在此案中应负主要责任。

（6）中方公司由于急于引进技术，在未查明美方公司的经营范围和履行能力的情况下，就盲目签订了该技术引进协议，也应负一定责任。

法院据此对双方进行调解，达成协议如下：

（1）撤销双方于 2018 年 3 月签订的《GBR 型减速器制造技术转让协议书》。

（2）美方公司返还中方公司 75 万美元的技术转让费。

（3）双方共同负担诉讼费用。

问题：从该案例中我们应该吸取什么教训？

实训目标

掌握撰写销售合同条款的方法。

一、根据梁晓与 Benjamin 交易磋商的函电往来签署销售合同

（一）函电往来

1.询盘

梁晓先生：

　　我方有意向你方购买 4 560 件货号 AGY509 箭牌电热干手器。若你方能向我方提供货样并报每件 CIF 蒙特利尔最低价，我方将不胜感激！我方此前曾从其他供货商处购买此商品，现我方向你方订购，是因为我方认为你方可以更优惠的价格向我方提供优质的商品。

　　期待你的回函。

加拿大长盛进出口贸易有限公司

Benjamin

Dear Mr. Liang Xiao,

　　We are interested in buying 4,560 PCS Arrow electric hand dryer code AGY509 from you. We would be appreciated if you could forward samples and quote your lowest price per PC CIF Montreal, Canada to us. We used to purchase these products from other sources. We may now prefer to buy from your company because we understand that you are able to supply larger quantities at more attractive price. In addition, we have confidence in the quality of your products.

　　We look forward to hearing from you by returning E-mail.

　　Yours sincerely,

　　CANADA SWATOW IMPORT & EXPORT TRADING CO. LTD.

　　Benjamin

① [1] 陈剑玲. 成员国适用国际货物销售合同公约案例选评 [M]. 北京：对外经济贸易大学出版社，2012.
[2] 刘川，王菲. 英文合同阅读与翻译 [M]. 北京：国防工业出版社，2010.

2. 发盘

Benjamin 先生：

你方 5 月 12 日要求我方报货号 AGY509 箭牌电热干手器海运至蒙特利尔的来函已收悉。现依你方要求，以最优惠价向你方发盘如下：

1. 商品名称：箭牌干手器，货号 AGY509。

2. 数量：4 560 件。

3. 单价：116 美元/件 CIF 蒙特利尔。

4. 包装：出口纸箱装 30 件/箱，0.164 立方米/箱，总箱数：152 箱。

5. 装运：不迟于 2018 年 8 月 15 日。

6. 装运港：广州；目的港：蒙特利尔。

7. 支付条件：买方应在本合同签字之日起，15 天内将本合同总金额 30% 的预付款，以电汇方式汇交卖方，并在收到本合同所列单据后 7 天之内电汇其余货款。

8. 保险：由卖方负责按发票金额的 110% 投保一切险和战争险，以中国人民保险公司 1981 年 1 月 1 日的有关海洋货物运输保险条款为准。

样品已经通过 DHL 快递给你方，快递号为：N12345678。

请注意：发盘有效期至 2018 年 5 月 20 日。

广州美林电器贸易有限公司

梁晓

Dear Mr. Benjamin,

We have received your E-mail of May 12, asking us to offer arrow electric hand dryer code AGY509 for shipment to Montreal, Canada and highly appreciate that you are interested in our products.

To comply with your kindly request, we are pleased to offer you our latest price as follows:

1. Commodity: Arrow electric hand dryer code AGY509.

2. Quantity: 4,560 PCS.

3. Unit Price: USD 116.00/PC CIF Montreal.

4. Packing: 30PCS/CTN, 0.164CBMS/CTN, Total: 152CTNS.

5. Latest Date of Shipment: Aug. 15, 2018.

6. Loading Port: Guangzhou; Destination Port: Montreal.

7. Terms of Payment: 30% of the total contract value as advance payment shall be remitted to the seller through T/T within 15 days after signing this contract by the buyer. Payment to be effected by the buyer shall not be later than 7 days after receipt of the documents listed in the contract by T/T.

8. Insurance: To be covered by the seller for 110% of total invoice value against all risks and war risk, as per and subject to the relevant ocean marine cargo clauses of the People's Insurance Company of China dated 1/1/1981.

The samples have been sent by DHL, relation number is: N12345678.

Noted: Our quotation remains effective until May 20, 2018.

Yours faithfully,

GUANGZHOU MEILIN ELECTRIC TRADING CO. LTD.

Liang Xiao

3.还盘

梁晓先生：

你方2018年5月16日来函已收悉。在此，我方很抱歉地通知，你方所报价格太高，有关资料显示，同类商品的其他供应商以低于你方15%的价格在我方市场上销售。为达成交易，我方还盘如下：152箱箭牌电热干手器，货号AGY509，106美元/件CIF蒙特利尔，其他条件根据你方2018年5月16日的发盘内容确定，以你方答复于2018年5月23日或之前到达我方有效。

期待你的回复。

加拿大长盛进出口贸易有限公司

Benjamin

Dear Mr. Liang Xiao,

We have well received your E-mail dated May 16, 2018. All the contents were duly noted. In reply, we regret to inform you that we find your price much too high. The information indicates that some suppliers have been sold here at a level about 15% lower than yours. To step up the trade, we counter-offer as follows, subject to your reply received by us on or before May 23, 2018. 152 cartons of Arrow electric hand dryer code AGY509 at USD 106. 00/PC CIF Montreal, other terms as per your E-mail of May 16, 2018.

We are looking forward to your early reply.

Yours sincerely,

CANADA SWATOW IMPORT & EXPORT TRADING CO. LTD.

Benjamin

4.接受

Benjamin先生：

感谢你方2018年5月19日的来函。为使我们双方的交易有一个良好的开端，我方接受你方将价格降至106美元/件的建议，其他条件详见我们双方之间的往来电文。祝贺我们之间建立了贸易关系，并期待我们双方进一步的互利共赢。

广州美林电器贸易有限公司

梁晓

Dear Mr. Benjamin,

We thank you for your E-mail of May 19, 2018. To start the hall rolling, we accept your suggestion and reduce the price down to USD 106.00/PC, other terms as E-mail exchanged between us. We send you our warmest congratulations on your increasing business with us and look forward to further increases to our mutual benefits.

Yours faithfully,

GUANGZHOU MEILIN ELECTRIC TRADING CO. LTD.

Liang Xiao

（二）合同签署

经过双方协商，梁晓与 Benjamin 就交易的各项条件达成了一致意见，并根据双方的函电往来所确定的内容签署了以下销售合同：

销售合同 SALES CONTRACT			
卖方 SELLER		编号 NO.	
		日期 DATE	
买方 BUYER		地点 SIGNED IN	
买卖双方同意以下条款并达成交易： This contract is made by and agreed between the BUYER and SELLER，in accordance with the terms and conditions stipulated below.			
1. 品名及规格 Commodity & Specification	2. 数量 Quantity	3. 单价及价格条款 Unit Price & Trade Terms	4. 金额 Amount
Total:			
允许 With		溢短装，由卖方决定 More or Less of Shipment Allowed at the Sellers' Option	
5. 总值 Total Value			
6. 包装 Packing			
7. 唛头 Shipping Marks			
8. 装运期及运输方式 Time of Shipment & Means of Transportation			
9. 装运港及目的地 Port of Loading & Destination			
10. 保险 Insurance			
11. 付款方式 Terms of Payment			
12. 备注 Remarks			
The Buyer		The Seller	

二、将括号内的中文翻译为英文

1. _____ (如果任何一方由于不可抗力而不能履行本合同规定的义务)，such party shall not be considered to be in default under this contract but shall continue to fulfill its other obligations under this contract which are not affected, by the force majeure.

2. _____ (卖方应在货物装船完毕后，立即电告或函告买方合同号码、商品名称、商品数量、发票价格、毛重、船名，以及起航日期等事项). In case the Buyer fails to arrange insurance in time due to the seller not having cabled in time, all losses and expenses incurred shall be borne by the seller.

3. Any dispute arising from the execution of, or in connection with, this contract shall be settled through negotiation. _____ (如果协商不能解决，应提交中国国际经济贸易仲裁委员会，根据该仲裁委员会的仲裁规则进行仲裁). The arbitration shall take place in Beijing. The award of arbitrators shall be final and binding on both the buyer and the seller.

4. _____ (除非由于本合同第十六条规定的不可抗力，卖方如果未按本合同的规定交付货物), the Buyer shall have the right to cancel the contract.

5. Within 90 days after the arrival of the goods at destination should the quality specification or quantity be found not in conformity with the stipulations of this contract except those claims for which the insurance company or the owners of the vessel are liable? _____ _____ (买方有权依据中国海关总署出入境检验检疫局出具的检验证书请求卖方更换商品或者要求卖方予以赔偿，因此发生的所有费用，如检验费、因更换货物产生的费用、保险费、仓储费以及装卸费等，应由卖方承担).

三、选词填空

hereby, hereof, herein, whereof, whereby, thereof

1. The credit shall be available against Sellers, draft(s) drawn at sight on the opening bank for 100% invoice value accompanied by the shipping documents specified in Clause 8 _____.

2. This contract is made by and between the Buyer and the Seller; _____ the Buyer agrees to buy and the Seller agrees to sell the under-mentioned goods subject to the terms and conditions stipulated below.

3. In the event that anything _____ contained is inconsistent with any applicable international convention or national law which cannot be departed from by private contract, the provisions hereof shall to the extent of such inconsistency but no further be null and void.

4. The Seller shall be liable for any damage to the goods on account of improper packing and

for any rust damage attributable to inadequate or improper protective measures taken by the seller and in such case or cases any and all losses and / or expenses incurred in consequence _____ shall be borne by the seller.

5. In case the period of delay exceeds 5 weeks after the stipulated delivery date, the buyer shall have the right to terminate this contract but the seller shall not _____ be exempted from the payment of penalty.

四、将下列销售合同条款翻译为中文

1. The Buyers shall, about 20 days prior to date of delivery, open an irrevocable Letter of Credit with the Bank of China, Guangzhou, in favour of the Sellers. The Credit shall be payable against the presentation of draft drawn on the opening bank and the shipping documents specified in Article 10 of this Contract. The Letter of Credit shall be valid until the 15th day after the shipment is effected.

2. The Buyer is requested to sign and return one copy of this Sales Confirmation immediately after receipt of the same. Objection, if any, should be raised by the Buyer within five days after the receipt of this Sales Confirmation in the absence of which it is understood that the Buyer has accepted the terms and conditions of the Sales Confirmation.

3. This contract is made out in English and Chinese with the English edition being authentic in three original copies, one copy to be held each by the buyer, the end-user and the Seller in witness thereof.

4. In addition, the seller shall, within 7 days after shipment, send by airmail one set of the aforesaid documents to the buyer and the China National Foreign Trade Transportation Corporation at the port of destination respectively.

5. The Seller guarantees that the commodity hereof is made of the best materials with first class workmanship new brand and complies in all respects with the quality and specification stipulated in this contract. The guarantee period shall be twelve (12) months counting from the date on which the commodity arrives at the port of destination.

五、用括号内的词把下列句子翻译为英文

1. 我们期待你方将我方第25号订单的货物在本月底以前装出。（indent）

2. 兹附上我方售货确认书样本，希望你仔细阅读各项备注。（Sales Confirmation, specimen, remarks）

3. 延迟是由于你方未及时开立信用证。（due to, failure）

4. 由于价格不稳定的缘故，大多数买方已退出市场。（in consequence of）

5. 我们希望这个事件对市场没有什么影响。（incident）

六、用恰当的介词填空

1. Amendments to Letter of Credit: Buyers shall open a Letter of Credit in accordance _____ the terms of this Contract. If any discrepancy is found, amendments to the Letter of

Credit should be made immediately by the Buyers upon receipt _____ the Sellers' advice, failing which the Buyers shall lie responsible any losses thus incurred as well as _____ late shipment thus caused.

2. Shipping Advice: Immediately loading is completed, the Sellers or their branches shall notify the Buyers by cable the number of credit, quantity and name of vessel.

3. Force Majeure: Should the Sellers fail to deliver the contracted goods or effect shipment in time by reason _____ force majeure beyond their control, the time of shipment might be duly extended, or alternatively, a part or whole the contract might be cancelled without any liability attached the Sellers, but the Sellers have to furnish the Buyers _____ a certificate attesting such event(s).

4. Arbitration: All disputes in connection _____ this Contract or the execution thereof shall be amicably settled through negotiation, in ease no amicable settlement can he reached between the two parties, the case _____ dispute shall be submitted for arbitration, which shall be held in the country where the defendant resides, or in a third country agreed by both parties. The decision of the arbitration shall be accepted as final and binding upon both parties. The Arbitration Fees shall be borne _____ the losing party.

5. Claims: Should the quality, quantity and/or weight be found not in conformity _____ those stipulated in this Contract, aside from those usual natural changes of quality and weight _____ transit and losses within the responsibility _____ the shipping company and/or insurance company, the Buyers shall have the right within 30 days after the arrival of the goods at the port of destination, to lodge claims concerning the quality, quantity or weight the goods. (Claims for perishable goods are to be put forward immediately after arrival of the goods at destination.)

七、单项选择

1. This Sales Contract is made by and between the Sellers and the Buyers _____ the Sellers agree to sell and the buyers agree to buy the under-mentioned goods according to the terms and conditions stipulated below.

A. whereby   B. that   C. which   D. what

2. Payment is to be made by irrevocable Sight L/C _____ 2,000 M/Ts of steel.

A. under   B. against   C. covering   D. as per

3. Insurance is to be effected _____ seller _____ 110% _____ the invoice value _____ All Risks.

A. with; for; of; against   B. to; of; for; with

C. by; for; of; against   D. in; about; for; with

4. The findings of theirs shall be considered final and binding _____ both parties.

A. by   B. upon   C. about   D. for

5. The contract stipulates that shipment is to be made within one month _____ receipt of the L/C.

A. after   B. during   C. before   D. for

6. Party A agrees to reserve for Party B a commission of 1% on the _____ of FOB value of the business thus concluded.

A. form   B. base   C. basis   D. way

7. All the additional premium shall be _____ the buyer's account.

A. on   B. for   C. at   D. of

8. The buyer lodged a claim _____ the shipping company _____ the loss sustained in transit.

A. to；to   B. before；on   C. of；with   D. against；for

9. We have always honored our commitments to pay the _____ drafts.

A. expire   B. due   C. scheduled   D. valid

10. Payment terms are by irrevocable L/C for 90% of the total invoice value of the goods to be shipped, payable _____ at sight.

A. with draft   B. by draft   C. for draft   D. to draft

实训项目 19
商品购买合同练习[①]

实训目标

掌握撰写商品购买合同条款的方法。

一、翻译下列商品购买合同条款

1. Shipping Documents Required as Follows:

(1)CLEAN ON BOARD FREIGHT TO COLLECT OCEAN BILLS OF LADING marked with Contract and L/C numbers.

(2)PARCEL POST RECEIPT/BUYERS FORWARDING AGENTS' CARGO RECEIPT.

(3)INVOICE bearing Shipping Marks, Contract and L/C numbers.

(4)PACKING LIST or WEIGHT MF. MO showing gross and net weight for each package.

(5)PLANT QUARANTINE CERTIFICATE issued by the Authorized Surveyor. (Aside from certifying the merchandise being itself free from any pest, it must also be certified that the merchandise itself and the packing are free from KHOPR/VBEETLE.)

(6)AUTHORIZED SURVEYORS' CERTIFICATE OF QUANTITY/WEIGHT.

(7)INSURANCE POLICY or CERTIFICATE in accordance with Art. (12) covering 110% of the Invoice Value bearing the clause "In the event of loss or damage, application for survey upon arrival of cargo in Chinese Area must be made to China National Bureau of Entry-Exit Inspection and Quarantine."

2. SHIPPING ADVICE:

(1)On the date of shipment, the Seller or his Shipping Agents shall advise the Buyer immediately by tele printer of the shipping marks, name of commodity, quantity actually loaded, invoice value, name of steamer, date of sailing and port of loading.

(2)In case of transshipment at other port, the Seller should instruct the shipping company at the port of transshipment to advise the Buyer by tele printer, at the time of transshipment, of the shipping marks, name and quantity of commodity, name of vessel and date of sailing.

---

① [1] 陈剑玲. 成员国适用国际货物销售合同公约案例选评 [M]. 北京：对外经济贸易大学出版社，2012.
[2] 刘川，王菲. 英文合同阅读与翻译 [M]. 北京：国防工业出版社，2010.

3. Should the Seller fail to distribute the Shipping Documents and the Shipping advice according to the provisions of Art. (14) and/or (15), the Seller shall be responsible for any loss or damage thus sustained by the Buyer.

4. SELLER'S RESPONSIBILITY, FOB DELIVERY: In the event of Seller's failure to effect shipment of the contracted goods within the stipulated time, unless it is due to bona fide Force Majeure, which is to be dealt with according to Art.(20), the Buyer shall have the right to cancel the Contract. In such case, the Seller is responsible for any loss thus sustained by the Buyer.

5. Quality and Quantity/Weight: The contracted goods are bought on the basis of landed quantity/weight and the certificate issued by China National Bureau of Entry-Exit Inspection and Quarantine shall be taken as final.

6. FORCE MAJEURE: In case of delayed shipment or non-delivery due to Force Majeure generally recognized, the Seller must advise the Buyer immediately by telex of the occurrence, and within 14 days thereafter the Seller must airmail to the Buyer a certificate of the incident issued by the competent government authorities or Chamber of Commerce at the place where the incident occurred as evidence thereof. The Seller shall not be absolved from his responsibility unless such an incident is acknowledged by the Buyer. In case conditions of FORCE MAJEURE continue to last over and above 30 days, the Buyer shall have the right to cancel the Contract. The Seller's failure to obtain export licence shall not be considered as FORCE MAJEURE.

7. ARBITRATION: All disputes in connection with this Contract or the execution thereof shall be settled by way of amicable negotiation. In case no settlement can be reached, the case at issue shall then be submitted for Arbitration to the International Economic and Trade Arbitration Commission, Beijing, China, in accordance with the Rules of Procedure of Arbitration of the said Commission, the award by the said Commission shall be deemed as final and binding upon both parties.

8. Please sign and return one original copy. In case this is not done, it shall be considered that the seller has fully agreed to all the above terms and conditions.

二、用括号内的词将下列句子翻译为英文

1.该轮由于天气恶劣而迟误了。(delay)

2.他们承认你方的索赔或多或少是合理的。(recognize)

3.这是一个没有预料到的事件。(occurrence)

4.有关买方已向主管当局申请进口许可证。(competent, authority)

5.没有充分的证据说明这项损坏是由装卸不慎所造成的。(evidence)

6.我们一定准时执行你们的订单。(execution)

7.我们希望用一种友好的办法解决这个争端。(amicable)

8.我们很抱歉不得不把此案提交仲裁。(case)

9.争论点是延迟交货的原因是否应看作不可抗力。(at issue)

10.我们正在办理例行手续，预计数日后将电告装船通知。(procedure)

11.仲裁的决定对买方有利。(award)

12.我们希望我们不久能友好地解决争端。(reach)

三、用恰当的介词填空

1. Payment: The Buyers, upon receipt from the Sellers _____ the delivery advice specified in Article 14 hereof, shall, in 15-20 days prior _____ the date of delivery, open an irrevocable Letter of Credit with the Bank of China, _____ favour of the Sellers, for an amount equivalent _____ the total value of the shipment. The Credit shall be payable presentation of draft drawn _____ the opening bank and the shipping documents specified in Article 13 hereof. The Letter of Credit shall be valid until the 15th day after the shipment is effected.

2. Guarantee of Quality: The Sellers guarantee that the commodity hereof is made _____ the best materials with class workmanship, brand new and unused, and complies in all respects _____ the quality and specifications stipulated in this Contract.

3. Penalty: If the Sellers fail to effect the delivery at the contracted time _____ delivery, the Buyers shall have the option to cancel this Contract and demand _____ all losses resulted therefrom, or alternatively, the Sellers may postpone delivery _____ the Buyers' consent, _____ condition that the Sellers pay to the Buyers a penalty of 1.5% of the goods value _____ a delay within 30 days and further 0.5% _____ every 15 days thereafter. The penalty shall be deducted _____ the paying bank during the negotiation _____ payment.

四、单项选择

1. Some customers requested us to _____ our price because they considered it too high.

A. make down   B. get down   C. take down   D. bring down

2. Insurance is to be _____ by the buyer if a transaction is concluded on FOB or CFR basis.

A. taken   B. covered   C. done   D. made

3. Please _____ the shipping marks are in strict conformity with those in the L/C.

A. notice   B. be certain   C. see your way to   D. see to it that

4. The _____ of 10% the proceeds is to be paid only after the goods have been inspected and approved at the port of destination.

A. insurance   B. cash   C. money   D. income

5. The sellers shall effect insurance for 110% of the invoice value against All Risks and War Risk _____ the relevant Ocean Marine Cargo Clauses of the People's Insurance Company of China.

A. with   B. of   C. as per   D. as of

6. The decision of the arbitration shall be accepted as final and _____ upon both parties.

A. bound   B. binded   C. bounded   D. binding

7. The sellers are allowed to _____ 5% more or less and the price shall be calculated according to price.

A. make   B. load   C. add up to   D. unload

8. The stipulators of the L/C should _____ those of the contract.

A. agree to　　　　　B. agree in　　　　　C. agree on　　　　　D. agree with

9. The L/C is to be opened _____ Party A's favor and must reach Party A not later than May 4,2018.

A. at　　　　　　　　B. in　　　　　　　　C. to　　　　　　　　D. for

10. We shall _____ if you will do your best to promote this new product of ours.

A. enjoy　　　　　　B. please it　　　　　C. appreciate　　　　D. appreciate it

五、将下列句子翻译为中文

1. If the Seller is unable to obtain the new material necessary for the manufacture of the goods to be sold hereunder, he shall have the right to reduce the amount of the goods to be delivered to the Buyer. If the Buyer refuses to accept delivery of the goods because of such reduction, this agreement shall then be terminated and neither party shall be liable for the other provisions hereunder.

2. To be packed solidly, suitable for long distance ocean / air freight transportation multi - handling and well protected against dampness, shock, rust etc. The Sellers shall be liable for any rust, damage and loss attributed to inadequate packing by the sellers.

3. Certificates of Quality, Quantity, Weight and Origin are required. The Buyers have the right to have the goods reinspected by the Guangzhou Entry - Exit Inspection and Quarantine Bureau of the People's Republic of China at the port of discharge. The relevant Inspection Certificates may serve as the basis of any claim to be lodged by the buyers against the sellers.

4. Any claim by the buyers on the goods shipped shall be filed within 30 days after arrival of the goods at port of destination and supported by a survey report issued by a surveyor approved by the Sellers. Claims in respect of matters within the responsibility of the insurance company or of the shipping company will not be considered or entertained by the Sellers.

5. Should the Sellers fail to make delivery on time as stipulated in the Contract with exception of Force Majeure causes specified in Clause 15 of this Contract, the buyers shall agree to postpone the delivery on the condition that the Sellers agree to pay a penalty which shall be deducted by the paying bank from the payment under negotiation. The rate of penalty is charged at 0.5% for every 7 days, odd days less than 7 days should be counted as 7 days. But the penalty, however, shall not exceed 5% of the total value of the goods involved in the delayed delivery. In case the Sellers fail to make delivery 10 weeks later than the time of shipment stipulated in the Contract, the Buyers shall have the right to cancel the Contract and the Sellers, in spite of the cancellation, shall nevertheless pay the aforesaid penalty to the buyers without delay.

六、实务思考

案例1

2018年6月27日，我国某公司应荷兰某商号的请求，发出某初级产品20公吨，每公吨CIF鹿特丹1 950元人民币，即期装运的实盘（要约）。对方接到我方报盘后，没有表示承诺，而再三请求我方增加数量、降低价格，并延长有效期。我方曾将数量增至300公吨，价格每公吨 CIF 鹿特丹减至 1 900 元人民币，有效期经两次延长，最后延至 7 月 25 日。荷商于 7 月 22 日来电接受该盘，但附加了包装条件为"需提供良好的、适合海洋运输的袋装"。我方在接到对方承诺电报时，发现因巴西受冻灾而影响该商品的产量，国际市场价格猛涨，从而我方拒绝成交，并复电称："由于世界市场的变化，货物在接到承诺电报前已售出。"但对方不同意这一说法，认为承诺在要约有效期内作出，因而是有效的，坚持要求我方按要约的条件履行合同，并提出，要么执行合同，要么赔偿对方差价损失 23 万余元人民币；否则提交仲裁。这项纠纷经过多次的电报往返，争论十分激烈，但最终仍以我方承认合同成立而告结束，只是坚持包装为单麻袋装。如按照我方发盘的价格与当时市场价格比较，其差价损失达 23 万元人民币。

问题：

（1）要约发出可否随意撤回？

（2）接到对方承诺可否置若罔闻？

（3）从该案例中我们应该吸取什么教训？

案例 2

<h3 style="text-align:center">不知对方底细成交，货款两空案</h3>

2017 年 10 月，中国某进出口公司 D 与巴西客商 C 订立国际货物买卖合同，成交商品一批，合同条款订为 CFR 桑托斯，D/P 托收付款。后巴西银行来函通知，客商 C 拒不付款。货物在次年 3 月运抵巴西，对方银行来函告知，货已存入桑托斯海关仓库。某进出口公司于 2018 年 4、5、6 月 3 次去函客商 C，催其尽速付款提货，但皆无回音。D 公司又于 10 月再次去函，客商 C 才来电，对付款事仍推托敷衍。为此，D 公司致电我国驻巴西商务处，询问其可否将此货就地处理。

2018 年 12 月，我国驻巴西商务处来函称："该客商资信不好，资金不足，经营能力差，现在对于此业务，仍是推托。"巴西海关规定，货存关栈超过 120 天，海关就没收处理。以后，D 公司于 2018 年 12 月、2019 年 1 月，再次致函该客商催促其付款，但皆无回音，D 公司损失货款合计 84 000 美元。

问题：从该案例中我们应该吸取什么教训？

实训项目 20
经销合同练习[①]

实训目标

掌握经销合同中的特定词汇表述、固定的表达和用法以及基本条款。

一、根据中括号内的提示词填空

This Distributorship Agreement is (1)_____［订立］ by and between ××× CORPORATION，a U.S.A. corporation incorporated under the laws of the State of Delaware, U.S.A., having its principal place of business at 1,000 ×××× Street, ×××, XX 10,000, U.S.A., (2)_____［下文称］ "Company" and YYY, a corporation incorporated under the laws of China, having its principal place of business at 1,000 ×××× Street, ×××, XX, Beijing, China, 100,071 (hereinafter referred to as "Distributor").

Appointment of Distributor. Subject to the terms and conditions (3)_____［协议中规定的］ and the payment of a non-refundable $ 5,000.00 by Distributor, Company hereby appoints Distributor as a (4)_____［非独家的］ distributor in the People's Republic of China (the "Territory") to distribute and sell merchandise purchased from the Company in the Territory only, excluding merchandise under private labels containing the name "×××" or "××××." Distributor is not an (5)_____［代理人］ of Company and shall not at any time represent itself as such. Nor shall Distributor incur, assume or create any debt, obligation, contract or release of any kind in the name of or on behalf of Company.

Term and Termination...

Orders and Prices. All orders for merchandise placed by Distributor shall be subject to acceptance or non-acceptance by Company at its corporate headquarters, now located in ×××, ××, U.S.A. Company shall cause all items ordered by Distributor to be delivered to Distributor's (6)_____［指定的接收终点］ in the United States. Title to all such merchandise and supplies and risk of loss shall pass to Distributor at the time of delivery to such receiving terminal. Distributor shall pay Company all costs and charges related to the delivery of merchandise and supplies to Distributor's receiv-

———————————
① [1] 徐良霞，李海燕. 实用英语教你写合同［M］. 北京：北京航空航天工业大学出版社，2004. [2] 吴敏，吴明忠. 国际经贸英语合同写作［M］. 广州：暨南大学出版社，2002. [3] 王立非. 国际商务合同实践教程［M］. 上海：上海外语教育出版社，2012. [4] 刘川，王菲. 英文合同阅读与翻译［M］. 北京：国防工业出版社，2010.

ing terminal.

　　Payment. Distributor agrees to pay all amounts shown as currently due on Company's billing statements for purchases of merchandise with such promptness as shall enable Company to receive payment (7)_____［不迟于］the 10th day following the date of the statement (it being understood that all invoices for merchandise purchased on extended payment terms become currently due when other items billed are not paid when due), and pay Company's then current service charge, presently equal to 77%, per bi-weekly billing statement on any past due balance. All prices shall be exclusive of tariffs, customs duties, sales and goods and services taxes, insurance, and (8)_____［运费］, all of which shall be the responsibility of Distributor. All amounts becoming payable by Distributor pursuant to Company's billing statements shall be stated and payable in United States currency. If requested by Company, Distributor shall provide Company with a standby irrevocable letter of credit, issued or confirmed by a bank approved by Company, or with such other instruments or collateral as Company may deem appropriate in order to secure the prompt payment of the indebtedness to it incurred by Distributor from time to time.

　　Minimum Purchase Requirement. The minimum volume of merchandise to be purchased by Distributor hereunder shall be $200,000.00.

　　IN WITNESS WHEREOF, this Distributorship Agreement has been executed by the parties on this day of 20××.

二、将下列句子翻译为中文

　　1. The Manufacturer shall deliver within 30 days to the Distributor all goods for which the Distributor places orders, except when delivery is delayed because of the Distributor's fault or because it becomes impossible as provided in this Agreement.

　　2. The Manufacturer shall deliver the ordered goods by shipment to the locations designated by the Distributor within the Territory, provided the Distributor has complied with its obligations with respect to importing.

　　3. The Manufacturer is responsible for procuring all export licenses and inspections and for completing all export requirements within time to deliver the goods.

　　4. If the Manufacturer discontinues the production of any goods for any reason. The Manufactures will immediately notify the Distributor and will continue for a reasonable time after discontinuance to furnish replacement parts and to offer service for the discontinued Goods already sold to the Distributor.

　　5. The Manufacturer will not sell any goods to any person or entity, other than the Distributor, that sells, resells, leases or rents products identical or confusingly or similar to the Manufacturer's Goods within the Territory.

三、将下列句子翻译为英文

1.双方承认他们意图建立一种互惠互利的关系。

2.双方应努力通过友好磋商方式解决争端。

3.制造商指定经销商作为该地区的独家经销商从事商品的出售、租赁。

4.制造商拥有所有与货物有关的商标、名称、设计、专利和商业秘密等财产权。

5.如果商品在该地域内交付，制造商不得把商品销售给除经销商外的任何人或实体用于直接使用。

四、讨论

1. What are the basic types of distribution agreement?

2. What are the typical clauses of a distribution agreement? Give their headings.

3. What is meant by "Ricital" at the beginning of the distribution agreement?

4. How is a distribution agreement rescinded and/or terminated?

5. What are the main obligations of the parties in a distributorship?

五、实务思考

Case A: Fish V. Blue Pool

A company lost millions of dollars of business because it did not have a formal distributorship agreement in place. The company (let's call it "Fish") was the sole distributor for the Blue Pool range of pool equipment in NSW. However, there was no formal written distribution agreement in place between Fish and Blue Pool.

The distribution arrangement was evidenced by a three-paragraph letter from Blue Pool to Fish confirming that Fish was Blue Pool's sole distribution agent for its range of pool equipment in NSW. In this letter, Blue Pool also reserved the right to appoint an additional distributor after giving Fish 3 months' notice in writing.

For many years Blue Pool and Fish conducted business based on this letter and Fish built up quite a reputation as the sole distributor for the Blue Pool range of pool equipment in NSW. Fish estimated that this sole distributorship was worth $ 4 million to its business.

One day, Blue Pool told Fish that it intended to appoint an additional distributor and gave Fish 3 months' notice in writing. After receiving this notice, Fish did some investigating and discovered that Blue Pool had no intention of appointing an additional distributor, but rather Blue Pool intended to take over the distribution itself.

If Blue Pool took over the distribution of the Blue Pool range of pool equipment, Fish would no longer have its "sole distributor" status but of even more concern, Fish would be competing directly with Blue Pool as the manufacturer and distributor.

Despite Fish's protestations, Blue Pool terminated the distribution arrangement and began to distribute its range of pool equipment. Fish was still entitled to distribute the Blue Pool range of pool equipment, but Fish had lost its "sole distributor" status. When the market found out they could purchase the Blue Pool range of pool equipment directly from the manufacturer Blue Pool and at a cheaper cost than via its agent Fish, Fish lost almost all of its business.

This highlights the need to ensure that you have good distributorship agreements in place which add capital value to your business. Luckly, for Fish it had a large share of the pool equipment market and was able to focus on other areas of its business. But just imagine if Fish had developed its business around promoting itself as the sole distributor for the Blue Pool range of pool equipment in NSW. If that were the case, Fish would not be in business today.

Case B: Jackson Distribution Ltd. V. Tum Yeto

The High Court decision of Jackson Distribution Ltd. V. Tum Yeto Inc. has given some useful guidance on factors to consider when looking at exiting a distribution agreement says Shaw Stapely, Associate at Thomas Eggar LLP. In particular, it has had a significant impact in clarifying what constitutes a reasonable period of notice when terminating otherwise than for breach. This is likely to be an issue where there is no formal written agreement or the contract itself is silent on the issue (which means a "reasonable period" of notice will usually be implied by law).

In this case, the parties agreed that Jackson Distribution would be the sole distributor for certain goods of Tum Yeto via a series of emails, and each sent their own form of draft agreement to the other, neither of which was signed.

Two and a half years later, Tum Yeto purported to terminate the agreement without notice, which Jackson contested. The court considered what was the agreed terms of the arrangement and on what basis could Tum Yeto terminate it? In the absence of a written agreement, the court implied a term that the distribution arrangement should be terminable on reasonable notice.

What is reasonable notice?

The court considered various factors including:

-the length of the relationship between the parties;

-the lack of formal arrangement between the parties;

-the extent of Jackson's early investment;

-the percentage of Jackson's turnover made up of Tum Yeto' supplies;

-that Jackson had agreed not to sell competing products.

The court concluded that a reasonable notice period in this case would be nine months and Jackson was entitled to damages for the nine-month-period from when Tum Yeto had purported to terminate the agreement.

What should the manufacturers do to protect themselves?

Commenting on the case, Shaw Stapely, Associate at Thomas Eggar, LLP stated:

"Termination of distribution agreements can be tricky for manufacturers and this case gives a useful checklist of facts to consider when deciding what is reasonable notice. However, each case will depend on its facts and three and six months periods have been held to be 'reasonable' in the circumstances. For the distributor, a period of notice needs to be sufficient to allow the manufacturer the ability to find alternative business.

Ultimately, there is of course no substitute for having a written contract with defined termination provisions and express notice periods."

Questions:

(1)What is the key issue in Case A? What lessons may be learned from it?

(2)Suppose that you are to draft a distribution agreement in favor of Fish before the dispute arises as it is in Case A, how do you draft?

(3)What is the key issue in Case B? What lessons does the case tell?

(4)In the absence of a written agreement, implied terms will be filled in by courts. Is it wise to rely on implied terms? Why?

实训项目 21
国际货物运输合同练习[①]

实训目标

1.掌握国际货物运输合同的基本内容。
2.掌握草拟国际货物运输合同的注意事项。

一、翻译下列国际货物运输合同条款

1. This insurance attaches from the time the goods hereby insured leave the warehouse or place of storage named in the policy for the commencement of the transit and continues in force in the ordinary course of transit until the insured goods are delivered to the consignee's final warehouse or place of storage at the destination named in the policy or to any other place used by the Insured for allocation or distribution of the goods or for storage other than in the ordinary course of transit.

2. This insurance does not cover loss or damage arising from normal loss, inherent vice or nature of the insured goods, loss of market and/or delay in transit and any expenses arising therefrom.

3. It is the duty of the insured to attend to all matters as specified hereunder, failing which the Company reserves the right to reject his claim for any loss if and when such failure prejudice the rights of the Company.

4. The time of validity of a claim under this insurance shall not exceed a period of two years counting from the time of completion of discharge of the insured goods from the seagoing vessel at the final port of discharge.

5. This Policy of Insurance witnesses that the Insurance Company (hereinafter called "the Company"), at the Request (hereinafter called "the Insured") and in consideration of the agreed premium being paid to the company by the Insured, undertakes to insure the under-mentioned goods in transportation subject to the conditions of this policy as per the Clauses printed overleaf and other special Clauses attached hereon.

---

① [1] 黄文伟，刘美华. 商务英语函电与合同 [M]. 上海：上海大学出版社，2008. [2] 陈剑玲. 成员国适用国际货物销售合同公约案例选评 [M]. 北京：对外经济贸易大学出版社，2012.

二、将括号内的中文翻译为英文

1. This insurance covers _____(直接由战争、类似战争行为和敌对行为、武装冲突或海盗行为所致的被保货物的损失).

2. These clauses are the clauses of an additional insurance to the Ocean Marine Cargo Insurance of the company _____(如本条款与海洋运输保险条款中的任何条文有抵触，均以本条款为准).

3. This insurance is classified into two conditions‐Overland Transportation Risks and Overland transportation All Risks _____(被保险货物遭受损失时，本保险公司按照保险单所载承保险别的条款规定负赔偿责任).

4. The Insured shall take delivery of the insured goods in good time upon their arrival at the port of destination named in the policy _____(当发现被保险货物遭受任何损失，应立即向保险单上所载明的检验、理赔代理人申请检验).

5. Where there is loss or damage to the vessel from a peril insured against or where the vessel is in immediate danger from such a peril, and as a result reasonable expenditure is incurred by the Insured in order to avert or minimize a loss which would be recoverable under this insurance _____(保险人应予以赔付。本条不适用于共同海损、救助或救助费用，也不适用于本保险中另有规定的开支).

三、选词填空

hereof, thereat, therefrom, hereunder, thereof, therein

1. The following documents should accompany any claim _____ made against this Company.

2. The Insured may decide the place of repair of the damaged vessel, however, if the Insured in taking such decisions does not act as a diligent uninsured owner, then the Insurer shall have a right of veto concerning the place of repair or a repairing firm decided by the owner or deduct any increased costs resulting _____ from the indemnity.

3. The Company shall be liable for expenses of removal, lighting or marking of the wreck of the insured ship or obstruction after deduction of the proceeds _____.

4. In no case shall this insurance cover loss, damage, or expense caused by capture, seizure, arrest, restraint or detainment (piracy excepted), and the consequences _____ or any attempt _____.

5. If owing to circumstances beyond the control of the Insured either the contract of carriage is terminated at a port or place other than the destination named _____ or the transit is otherwise terminated before delivery of the goods as provided for in Clause 6 above, then this insurance shall also terminate.

四、实务思考

案例1

威迅公司与商发贸易公司受骗案

2017年5月，我国威迅公司与瑞士洛斯美尔公司签订了进口500吨钢材的贸易合同，合同总价为230万美元，交货期为2017年10月，货物装运港是西班牙港口，目的港为中国某市。但时至2017年11月，货物仍未装运。洛斯美尔公司发来电传声称货物已在装运港备妥待运，装运期为2017年11月21日，要求威迅公司速开信用证。洛斯美尔公司委托一家意大利的泰勒尔船运公司运输货物。泰勒尔公司实际上是一家皮包公司，其船东为一个国际诈骗犯，但我方威迅公司并不知情，航运等一切事宜均由洛斯美尔公司办理。为了取得威迅公司的信任，洛斯美尔公司还进一步让利，每吨钢材降价6美元，合同总价不变，钢材的总数量增加。洛斯美尔公司还承诺，在收到信用证后两周内一次交货。

2017年12月2日至8日，洛斯美尔公司两次来电告知货已备好，要求威迅公司将信用证开往挪威银行卢森堡分行。威迅公司即按合同规定于2017年12月13日通知中国银行上海分行开出了以洛斯美尔公司为受益人的信用证，通知行为挪威银行，信用证金额为230万美元。威迅公司于2018年2月付款，但是货物杳无音信。在威迅公司的一再追问下，洛斯美尔公司发来电信告知运货船只为"纳罗基尔"号，预计于2018年4月到达目的港。根据常识判断，从欧洲到中国一般只需要45天就可完成船舶的海上运输。如果按照双方约定于信用证开出后两周内将货物装运，那么货物应该在2017年12月27日前装运，最迟也应该在2018年2月底之前到达目的港。但是到了2018年3月底，仍不见该"纳罗基尔"号货轮的踪影。在威迅公司一再催问之下，洛斯美尔公司回复说："由于中国港口拥挤，船舶将改变航线，航程有了新的安排，预计货物将于2018年8月抵达目的港。"船舶加速运营是船东赖以赚取运费的主要渠道，所以船东会尽速停泊，迅速完成卸货任务，而不会为了一宗货物在海上漂泊好几个月。很明显这是一场卖方与船东合谋的骗局。

问题：从该案例中我们应该吸取什么教训？

案例2

2019年3月，我国商发贸易公司与美国图瑞斯特贸易公司签订了进口白糖的合同，以CFR价为基础。合同中双方约定：

(1) 由美国图瑞斯特贸易公司向中国商发贸易公司供应450万吨的白糖。

(2) 中方商发贸易公司以信用证分式支付货款260万美元。

(3) 由于是CFR价成交，租船由美国图瑞斯特公司负责。

由于由卖方负责租船，我方无法掌握船舶动态及了解其他情况。而美国图瑞斯特公司根本未去租船。该公司实际上是一家皮包公司，根本没有买方需要的货物，只是想骗取买方商发贸易公司的货款。图瑞斯特公司找到了一家纳卡尔环球航运公司。该航运公司也是个诈骗老手，曾欺诈过许多埃及、印度、巴基斯坦、科威特等国家的买主。图瑞斯特公司给付了该航运公司8 000美元的租金，换取了一套假提单，凭此顺利地通过银行结汇，拿到了260万美元巨款后逃之夭夭了，再也没找到。

问题：从该案例中我们应该吸取什么教训？

实训项目 22
知识产权合同练习

实训目标

1. 掌握知识产权合同的基本内容。
2. 掌握草拟知识产权合同的注意事项。

实务思考

iPad's Road to China: Patent Disputes and Tele Giants Loom①

May 13, 2010, By CSC Staff, Shanghai

The Apple iPad tablet PC entered the market less than a month ago and its sales have already breached the one million unit marked. By the end of the month, it will be sold in 9 countries outside the U.S.A., not, however, in China's mainland.

China's Apple fans are awaiting the iPad launch here, but at the same time a campaign against Apple iPad is developing.

Earlier this year, Shenzhen Great Loong Brother Industrial Company in South China laid a claim that Apple iPad infringed its patents. General Manager Wu Xiaolong said he was also contacting senior management of Proview International, a world top-five display devices producer, hoping to buy China's IPAD trademark. "We are willing to pay a higher price than Apple," he stated, "If Proview does not want to sell, we can work together with them to produce and sell IPAD Tablet PCs in China."

The two sides have not yet reached a price agreement, but once negotiations are settled, Apple iPad will have to pay great money for access to the Chinese market. Wu Xiaolong said his company had the IPAD Tablet PC design patent in China and Proview had the IPAD China trademark, and that paved way for cooperation between the two.

A search for "IPAD" in the Trademark Office of the State Administration for Industry and Commence website showed eight relevant results. Trademarks, with the registered numbers 1,590,557 and 1,682,310, were applied for by Proview Technology Shenzhen Co., Ltd. in January and September of 2000, respectively, with trademark images for "iPad" and "IPAD" and

---

① 王立非. 国际商务合同实践教程 [M]. 上海：上海外语教育出版社，2012.

merchandise categories for computers, computer peripheral equipments, monitors, and cameras, and they will expire on June 20th and December 13th of 2011.

Proview owned the IPAD trademark in Taiwan, China and sold it to Apple last year. Apple apparently thought that purchase also included the IPAD trademark ownership on China's mainland. Proview said it did not. Apple was already suing Proview Hong Kong on this issue in China's Hong Kong. It was reported that Proview International had put $ 3.6 million price tag on the IPAD China's mainland trademark.

However, the contention over the IPAD China trademark ownership was not limited to only Apple and Great Loong Brother. Proview International owed more than one billion yuan to the banks, so any possible sale was being monitored by creditors which would certainly put pressure on the company to get the highest price.

Great Loong Brother's Wu said in addition to his company's newly-released P88, they were cooperating with Japan's Wacom to launch a new generation of tablet PC. The company last year applied to the State Intellectual Property Office for two flat-panel TV appearance patents with application numbers of 200,930,166,516.3 and 200,930,166,757.8. When the Apple iPad hit the market, foreign media discovered that its tablet PC and that of Great Loong Brother were almost identical. Wu said an American law firm had taken the initiative to sue Apple for patent infringement and is collecting evidence and information but had not yet entered into legal procedures.

Wu said that if Apple iPad entered China's mainland, a lawsuit here was a certainty. "The Shenzhen Baoan District government is encouraging us to defend our rights and a legal aid center has been organized." He saw the lawsuit as an inevitable success if the company had the IPAD China trademark.

"In China, the protected fields of Proview's IPAD trademark include domestic production and sales of similar products." said Liu Hui, partner of the Guangdong Jun Yan Law Firm. He said that while iPad was not yet for sale in China, the manufacture of iPad in China was already an infringement, and the trademark owner had the right to raid the factory and ask the Customs to detain and confiscate exported products. However, Liu Hui cautioned that proving identity of appearance infringement was not so easy nor so obvious as proving trademark infringement. The Apple iPad was being produced in Shenzhen, and will certainly be marked with "iPad" in its OEM factory Foxconn.

Since the appearance of iPad in the U.S.A., shanzhai (pirate product) factories have been producing iPad knock-offs at home and abroad, encroaching on any market Great Loong Brother wants to enter. This also daunts any optimism over the appearance patent lawsuit.

Case Discussion:

(1)What is the key issue in the above case?

(2)If Shenzhen Great Loong Brother Industrial Company sued against Apple Inc. over IP infringement, which party is likely to win? Why?

(3)If you were a party in the case, what would you do to deal with the dispute?

(4)What is the value of intellectual property rights? What do you suggest on the protection of intellectual property rights in international contracts?

实训项目 23
劳务出口合同练习^①

实训目标

    1.掌握劳务出口合同的基本内容。

    2.掌握草拟劳务出口合同的注意事项。

一、将下列劳务出口合同条款翻译为中文

Labour service here refers to all non-industrial and non-agricultural economic activities, such as finance, communications, tourism, insurance, transport and technical services. It includes both physical labour and intellectual labour provided by people like professors, specialists, doctors, artists and engineers. Based on the use of manpower, labour service trade is known as invisible trade, distinguished from commodity trade.

Providing labour service abroad has at least three advantages. Firstly, it is a good way to promote friendship and understanding between China and other countries. Secondly, our country can benefit in terms of foreign exchange. Thirdly, useful experience can be gained in methods of construction from foreign countries.

Overseas labour service provided by our country can be carried out in the following forms, in which China will

    (i)provide overseas firms and organizations with Chinese technicians, workers, professors, etc. for various services;

    (ii)undertake construction projects through bidding and send designers and construction and managerial personnel abroad for execution and maintenance of the works.

Contracts for labour services vary with different categories of work to be done. Generally a contract for providing manpower for civil engineering construction should include the following conditions:

    (1)preamble of the contract;

    (2)obligations of the employer and employee;

---

    ① [1] 王立非. 国际商务合同实践教程［M］. 上海：上海外语教育出版社，2012.［2］KIAN C T S，CHIM T S. Contract law，a layman's guide［M］. London: Time Books International，2000.［3］哈格德 T R. 法律写作［M］. 影印版. 北京：法律出版社，2003.

(3)mobilization fee;

(4)visa and other documents;

(5)payment of wages or overtime wages;

(6)travelling expenses;

(7)boarding lodging;

(8)medical service;

(9)social insurance;

(10)taxes & dues;

(11)labour protection;

(12)annual holidays leave;

(13)secrecy of information;

(14)duration of the contract;

(15)termination of the contract;

(16)force majeure;

(17)arbitration;

(18)governing law;

(19)witness clause.

The contents of a contract for labour service are entirely different from those of a contract for selling or buying commodities. For this type of contract, emphasis should be laid on wages, welfare facilities labour protection, holidays, annual leave, medical service, etc. In drawing up a contract for providing labour service, we should take every possibility into consideration, as any negligence will lead to a heavy loss.

二、将下列劳务出口合同条款翻译为英文

1.AA公司在本合同生效后两周内将任命授权代表，负责处理合同范围内发生的问题。

2.乙方人员应遵守伊拉克的现行法律、法令，尊重当地风俗习惯，并且不参加当地的政治活动。雇主应尊重乙方人员的习惯与人格，不干涉他们业余时间的活动。

3.乙方人员将有90天的试用期；如发现不称职，将被遣送回中国，乙方应另派适当人员代替，其费用由乙方承担。

4.乙方负责办理进出中国以及伊拉克的必要手续，并负担由此发生的各种费用。

5.每天正常工作时间为8小时，工作超过8小时则作为加班，加班费按标准工资125%支付。

6.乙方人员在伊拉克工作期满1年，能享受带薪假期20天；不满1年者，不能享受这种假期。

7.工资及加班费75%以美元支付，25%以伊拉克第纳尔支付，该款凭乙方授权代表签字的发票并经甲方工地经理同意后支付。

8.乙方人员每年最多有15天全薪病假、10天半薪病假，以甲方医生确认疾病为有效。

9.如乙方人员在工作中因意外事故受伤，甲方将给予治疗和带薪病假25天。如因违反工地操作规章而受伤，乙方应承担其返回中国和替换人员的费用。

10.雇主应免费向乙方人员提供水、电、煤气、厨房、餐具、冰箱、床、桌子、卫生间、空调机等。伙食由乙方人员自理。

三、用下列词语的适当形式填空

labor, system, differs, form, cooperation, needs, signed, developing, contains, explain, seek, valid, avoiding, used

Labor service cooperation is a _____ of economic and technical exchanges for common development through transferring, supplying each other's _____ and mutual cooperation. In countries of different social _____, such cooperation _____ in content, meaning, form and purpose. Labor service cooperation among the _____ countries of the Third World is part of South-South _____ under the principle of equality and mutual benefit for common development. An effective labor service contract must be jointly _____ by legal and capable sides. The contract must clearly _____ its reason and _____ law protection. A labor service contract generally _____ three parts: the lead, contract clauses and the end. Words _____ in the contract must be accurate, _____ any divergence in meaning. The ending part should stress that the contract texts in Chinese and a foreign language are equally _____. The language of a third country can also be used.

四、单项选择

1. An employer shall remain at his post and persist _____ pursuit of high competency.

A. at   B. on   C. in   D. for

2. In case of sick leave, Party B shall be notified in time and doctor's _____ shall be provided if the leave exceeds 2 days.

A. word   B. wording   C. notice   D. certificate

3. A work day shall not exceed 8 hours and a work week should be _____.

A. longer no than 5 days   B. no longer than 5 days

C. 5 days longer than   D. 5 longer than days

4. Party B undertakes to pay for midnight meal _____ for overtime work extending beyond 10 months.

A. allowances   B. discounts   C. concessions   D. rebates

5. As to those employees who cannot take their annual home leave because of their indispensability work, an extra 10-day _____ shall be paid in lieu thereof.

A. sum   B. amount   C. money   D. wage

6. When an employee is injured while _____ Party B undertakes to pay expenses for medical treatment and nutrition.

A. for duty   B. on duty   C. in duty   D. by duty

7. This contract enters into force upon _____ for a period of one whole year.

A. recognition   B. consent   C. signature   D. acceptance

8. The employer shall complete all the necessary entry procedures and inform BBB

accordingly, so as to _____ for the personnel.

    A. enabling BBB to procure visas   B. facilitate BBB to get visas

    C. benefit BBB to get visas   D. facilitate BBB's procurement of visas

    9. This Agreement is _____ in quadruplicate, each party holding two copies.

    A. made out   B. made on   C. made into   D. made off

    10. This contract is _____ concluded through consultation between the Service Co., Guangzhou and WXY Co., Hong Kong in respect of engagement of Chinese employees.

    A. hereby   B. whereby   C. thereof   D. thereon

五、实务思考
案例1
谎称经营亏损解雇劳务人员案

中国蛇口某区劳动服务公司与泰国新丰酒店签订了劳务合同，由劳动服务公司派出30名劳务人员到新丰酒店工作，期限为3年。2017年12月12日，新丰酒店提出辞退30名劳务人员的要求，解除合同。劳动服务公司以违反合同为由向法院起诉，要求继续履行合同，并赔偿损失。

法院经调查核实，认定事实如下：2014年6月新丰酒店到劳动服务公司联系业务，提出要招聘30名酒店服务人员。劳动服务公司经过多次调查后，于2014年8月同新丰酒店签订劳务输出合同，规定由酒店提供劳务人员的饮食、住宿，合同有效期为3年，即从2014年8月10日至2017年8月9日。同时，新丰酒店提出为了保证劳务人员不中途解除合同擅自回国，需先交纳30 000元作抵押。劳动服务公司经过再三斟酌，最后同意。2015年11月20日，新丰酒店认为生意不好是劳务人员素质不高所致，扬言要解雇劳务人员。2015年11月22日，新丰酒店召开董事会，以当地的一个会计事务所的验资报告和酒店利润统计表为根据，作出了经营亏损并应适当压缩现职员工的决议。后经核查，该验资报告和当利润统计表都是虚假的。验资报告是酒店串通会计事务所所作的，并付给会计事务所的华某、钱某、刘某3 000元作为报酬。利润统计表则是总经理戴某指令史某做的。经核查，该酒店不但没有亏损，还略有盈余。2015年12月12日，新丰酒店除保留本国员工外，将中方劳务人员全部解雇。劳动服务公司与新丰酒店多次交涉，均未达成协议，故劳动服务公司向法院提起诉讼，认为新丰酒店单方面解除合同，违反合同的有关条款，是违约行为，要求返还作保证用的押金30 000元，赔偿劳务人员在被解雇期间的住宿费、饮食费、交通费等共45 000元，并补发劳务人员停工期间共3个月的工资63 000元。

被告辩称经营亏损是由劳务人员素质差所致，酒店经常出现丢失钱物的现象。劳务人员也多次和顾客与酒店管理人员发生口角，严重影响了酒店的形象和声誉。被告律师提出根据中华人民共和国人力资源和社会保障部的文件，外资企业对试用、培训不合格人员，因生产技术条件变化而产生的富余人员，可以进行辞退，因此，新丰酒店辞退合同制劳务人员的做法并没有违反有关的政策和规定。另外，根据双方所签劳动合同第14条"因营业情况变化而产生了富余人员，又不能改换工种的，可以解除合同"，上述做法也是合理合法的。经查，新丰酒店所得到的30 000元的保证合同履行的押金已被投资于其他营业活动，被告所称经营亏损不成立，而所称的经营亏损原因是劳务人员素质太差也与事实不符。劳动服务公司所提供的劳务人员在 2014 年 10 月 10 日合同期限一开始就认真履行合同,接受酒店人员的管理、派遣、调动,按时保质地完成了有关工作,在合同履行期间新丰酒店从未对劳务人员的工作提出过任何异议。至于酒店丢失钱物的事,是曾经一名顾客因看到酒店房间的一套紫砂壶非常精致,就偷偷拿走了一个,被中方劳务人员发现后,该顾客交还茶壶并被罚款,和劳务人员没有任何关系。而劳务人员和顾客及酒店管理人员发生口角之事没有证据,不能认定。

法院经审理认为,酒店所说的经营亏损是歪曲事实,企图以此达到解除合同的目的,是错误的,有欺诈的因素在内。被告所说的劳务人员素质差,丢失钱物的责任在劳务人员的说法也不能成立。新丰酒店中途解除合同,是违反合同的有关条款的,是违约行为,应负违约责任。因被告违约造成的劳动服务公司的劳务人员的损失,新丰酒店应负赔偿责任。根据中国人力资源和社会保障部的文件,外资企业对试用、培训不合格人员及因生产技术条件变化而产生的富余人员,可以进行辞退,但是新丰酒店的劳务人员既不是经试用、培训不合格的人员,也不是因生产技术条件变化而产生的富余人员,因此,不能适用该规定。另外,有关法律规定,当企业因营业情况发生变化,主要指企业因经营不善面临破产时可以解除劳动合同,但必须依照法定程序进行,因此新丰酒店的理由也不能成立。

经法院调解,双方多次协商,达成调解协议如下:

(1)维持新丰酒店的辞退劳动服务公司提供的劳务人员的决定。新丰酒店发给每位员工辞退补偿金,再加发 3 个月的平均实得工资,每人每月按 1 560 元计算。

(2)诉讼费双方各自负担一半。

问题:从该案例中我们应该吸取什么教训?

案例 2

假借对方违约,拒付劳务费案

2014 年 6 月 6 日,中国沿海某公司(甲方)与某国远洋航运公司(乙方)在 M 市签订一份船员劳务合同。合同规定,甲方向乙方派出 30 名船员到乙方所有的"查理 1 号"轮工作,提供劳务时间为 1 年,从 2014 年 10 月 10 日到 2015 年 10 月 9 日。乙方向甲方支付船员劳务费工资,每月合计 30 000 美元,通过银行于每月 15 日将工资汇入甲方账户。当时甲方提出应写明是按月支付工资,乙方以这是人所共知的惯例,不必特意写明为由而拒绝。2014 年 10 月 10 日,甲方开始履行合同。船员在受雇期间,接受乙方的指派和调遣,完全按照合同的规定为乙方提供劳务,乙方对甲方船员提供的劳务非常满意,从未向甲方就劳务问题提过任何意见。从合同开始至 2015 年 4 月,乙方未按履行合同,只发给船员基本生活费;到 2015 年 10 月 9 日合同终止,乙方都没有履行合同,共欠甲方的船员工资款为 180 000 美元,致使 30 名船员及其家属的生活受到了极大的影响。

2015 年 10 月 20 日,"查理 1 号"轮送中国船员回到中国 M 市。10 月 21 日,甲方立即向 M 市海事法院提出申诉,要求诉讼保全,扣押"查理 1 号"轮,责令乙方提供 18 万美元的担保,直至变卖该轮清偿其债务。M 市海事法院审查认为:甲方申请符合扣押船只的条件,并有合理、合法的依据,于 11 月 3 日裁定扣押"查理 1 号"轮,责其提供担保。

2015 年 11 月 7 日,甲方向 M 市海事法院提起诉讼,除要求乙方偿还拖欠船员的工资外,还应承担扣船申请费、违约金、诉讼费、律师费、船员生活补偿费及有关费用的利息共20万美元。

M市海事法院在接到甲方的起诉后，审查合同，发现合同中没有仲裁条款，产生纠纷后双方没有达成书面仲裁协议，根据《中华人民共和国民事诉讼法》，当事人可以向人民法院提起诉讼。依据《中华人民共和国民事诉讼法》：因合同纠纷或者其他财产权益纠纷，对在中华人民共和国领域内没有住所的被告提起的诉讼，如果合同在中华人民共和国领域内签订或者履行，或者诉讼标的物在中华人民共和国领域内，或者被告在中华人民共和国领域内有可供扣押的财产，或者被告在中华人民共和国领域内设有代表机构，可以由合同签订地、合同履行地、诉讼标的物所在地、可供扣押财产所在地、侵权行为地或者代表机构住所地人民法院管辖。M市海事法院于2015年11月12日受理了此案。M市海事法院通知被告（乙方）进行答辩和提供担保。被告在法定期限内提出了答辩，内容如下：被告认为在合同期间原告未执行合同，在提供劳务过程中给被告造成了损害，因而拒绝向原告（甲方）支付船员工资。被告列举了损害事实：被告（乙方）所有的"查理1号"轮于2015年5月5日在为丙国运送货物的过程中由于甲方船员驾驶船舶不当而触礁，严重受损，停靠丁国修理，以致未能如期到达丙国，造成直接经济损失100多万美元。

经查：被告所答辩的内容与事实不符，2015年5月5日被告的"查理1号"轮确实发生了触礁事件，但当时并非中国船员操作不当所致，而是由于轮船突发意外事故。在发生事故后，根据有关专家所做出的鉴定结论，当时被告已申明与原告船员无关，现在又将"查理1号"轮触礁责任推给原告，实属无理。

由于被告拒绝提供任何担保，为了维护原告（甲方）的合法权益，M市海事法院于2015年11月25日在M市公开拍卖"查理1号"轮，拍卖价款为70万美元；与此同时，公告"查理1号"轮所有债权人在30日内申请撤销权登记。

在公告债权人期间，被告方律师提出M市海事法院无权审理被告与原告的劳动纠纷案件，应由被告所在国有关法院管辖。M市海事法院认为依照《中华人民共和国民事诉讼法》，M市海事法院完全拥有此案的管辖权。

被告经M市海事法院两次合法传唤，均未提出任何理由而拒不到庭。2016年3月1日，M市海事法院对本案进行了缺席公开审理。经审理认为：原告（甲方）与被告（乙方）之前签订的劳务合同，符合我国法律的规定，双方应该认真履行。不按月支付工资属于欺诈，被告答辩的理由不成立。原告及其所派船员在"查理1号"轮上始终认真地履行合同，而被告长期拖欠大量劳务费，影响了船员及其家属的正常生活。在被告严重违约的情况下，原告行使了海事请求权，申请扣押被告所有的"查理1号"轮，要求赔偿所受到的损失，理由合理、合法。被告作为"查理1号"轮的所有人、劳务合同的雇佣一方，应该认真履行合同，但其故意歪曲事实，以达到不履行合同的目的。被告故意长期拖欠船员工资的行为违反了合同的规定，应对其行为所产生的严重后果负责。

M市海事法院根据《中华人民共和国民事诉讼法》，参照国际惯例，于2016年6月5日作出如下判决：

（1）被告偿付原告应得的劳务报酬共180 000美元。

（2）被告偿付原告违约劳务报酬利息共12 000美元。

（3）本案受理费、扣船申请费、其他诉讼费4 300美元由被告承担。

（4）原告请求的其他费用不予支持。

自判决生效后，以上费用从"查理1号"轮所拍卖得款中扣除。判决书送达后，原告与被告均未上诉，判决生效。M市海事法院根据最高人民法院《关于海事法院拍卖被扣押船舶清偿债务的规定》，对"查理1号"轮案的债务进行了清偿。

问题：从该案例中我们应该吸取什么教训？

实训项目 24
租赁合同练习①

实训目标

1. 掌握租赁合同的基本内容。
2. 掌握草拟租赁合同的注意事项。

一、将下列租赁合同条款翻译为中文

Advantages of Leasing Trade

In order to meet the needs of China's current economic development and to promote technical transportation of existing enterprises by importing advanced technologies and equipments, we are developing the new economic form of leasing trade. This form has the following advantages:

1. It can speed up importation of advanced technologies and equipments to promote technical China's medium-sized and small enterprises. At the safety time, it provides opportunities to lease out China-made equipments to other countries to open up a new outlet for our export trade.

2. It can make up for the inadequacy of the traditional credit practices. The leasing corporation plays the dual role of a China/domestic and a foreign trade company. The corporation helps its clients procure credits needed for importing equipments and perform import or export formalities, including signing contracts on their behalf with foreign firms for equipments to be leased in or out.

In addition, it can help its clients raise funds at a fixed interest rate to 100% of the value of the equipments. While banks ordinarily grant medium and long-term loans at a floating interest rate, a fixed interest rate has the advantage of enabling enterprises to make closer calculation in deciding the investment.

3. Leasing makes it possible to open up a practical way for absorbing foreign capital. To import equipments by leasing is tantamount to importing foreign capital for a sum equal to the cost of the equipments.

There are basically two types of leasing:

---

① [1] 吴敏，吴明忠. 国际经贸英语合同写作 [M]. 广州：暨南大学出版社，2002. [2] 索普，贝利. 国际商务合同 [M]. 段佳陆，等，译. 北京：华夏出版社，2004. [3] 王秉乾. 国际商事合同 [M]. 英文版. 北京：对外经济贸易大学出版社，2013.

a. Direct leasing: The leasing corporation procures funds from the international money market, including making use of the equipments seller's export credit, to purchase the equipments and to lease them to the lessee at home.

b. Sub-leasing: The leasing corporation sub-leases the equipments leased from foreign leasing companies to Chinese lessees.

Both types fall within the category of making use of foreign capital to obtain the needed foreign equipments without much tapping on the national resources of foreign exchange.

According to China's policy of encouraging absorption of foreign funds, enterprises which lease equipments from abroad may apply for reduction of/or exemption from customs duty, and Industry and Commerce Unified Tax. Gross profits are to be appropriated first for repayment of debts before being dealt with as profit sharing. In addition, competent authorities have granted a certain amount of flexible right for examining and approving items eligible for absorption of foreign investment in this manner.

4. Leasing helps promote technical transformation of China's existing enterprises and updating their equipments.

5. Flexible and convenient methods are adopted in the Leasing Trade. The leasing corporation provides its clients with convenient funds on flexible terms. With their productive capacity and available funds as the basis, the enterprises can set the terms of leasing and the ways of repayment. Leasing can meet specific needs by working in combination with seller's export credits, compensatory trade, processing with supplied materials and joint investment.

The leasing trade has many advantages and there is great potential for its development in China.

二、将下列租赁合同条款翻译为英文

1.在租赁期内，租赁设备的所有权属于甲方，乙方对设备租赁使用，没有所有权。乙方不得在租赁期内将租赁设备进行转让等任何侵犯所租赁权的行为。

2.在租赁期内，由于我国政府或租赁机器出口国政府增减关税，必须变更租金时，甲方和乙方应通过协商定出新的租金。

3.乙方延迟支付租金时，甲方将计算每日加收租金额的利息。

4.如果乙方在验收时发现租赁物件的型号、规格和技术性能等与合同不符，如出现不良或瑕疵等情况，属供货商的责任，乙方应在30天内与出入境检验检疫局取得检验证明。乙方应立即将上述情况通知甲方。甲方将协助乙方对外进行交涉，办理索赔等事宜。

5.在租赁期内设备由乙方使用，乙方应负责日常保养，使设备保持良好状态，并承担由此产生的全部费用。

6.在租赁期满时续租或买下租赁的机器设备，承租人都可以通过支付优惠的租金或价款继续使用或获得租赁对象。

7.在租赁对象发生毁损或毁坏时，乙方应立即通知甲方，甲方可选择下列方式之一由乙方负责处理，并由乙方承担其一切费用：

（1）将租赁对象复原或修理至完全能正常使用的状态；

（2）更换性能相同的部件，使租赁对象能正常使用；

（3）当租赁对象灭失或无法修复到原有的程度时，乙方应按附表第九项规定的预定损失金额赔偿甲方。

三、选词填空

lessee, lessor, equipment, contract, companies, trade, use, basis

A lease trade is conducted between a ＿＿＿＿ and a ＿＿＿＿ granting the lessee the ＿＿＿＿ of the equipment for a specified term in return for a rent to the ＿＿＿＿with an adequate guarantee usually provided. Nowadays, much of the lease is mainly carried out by specialized lease owned by leading commercial banks, insurance companies, industrial or commercial organizations. A lease company is, generally, not a manufacturer.

It, after concluding a lease ＿＿＿＿ with a lessee, will usually make an order of the leased ＿＿＿＿ from a manufacturer. The lease company, as a ＿＿＿＿, then rents the purchased equipment to the ＿＿＿＿on a rent basis.

四、单项选择

1. The Lessor agrees to ＿＿＿＿ and the Lessee agrees to take in the equipment stated in the Appendix.

A. let out　　　　B. lend to　　　　C. lease out　　　　D. lease to

2. ＿＿＿＿ this Agreement is made out in the Chinese and English languages, ＿＿＿＿ each in two originals and one original of each is to be held by Party A and Party B.

A. both; and　　　B. either; or　　　C. not only; but also　　　D. neither; nor

3. The lessee shall not ＿＿＿＿the equipment to a third party without the Lessor's written permission.

A. sub-let　　　　B. sub-lease　　　　C. transfer　　　　D. offer

4. The lease company, as a Lessor, then ＿＿＿＿ the purchased equipment to the Lessee on a rent basis.

A. gives　　　　B. offers　　　　C. rents　　　　D. presents

5. At the expiration of the lease, the equipment should ＿＿＿＿ to us in good condition.

A. be sold　　　　B. be lent　　　　C. be given　　　　D. be returned

6. In the primary term of a financial lease, the ＿＿＿＿ cover the full cost of the equipment, plus the interest and the Lessor's profit.

A. income　　　　B. rentals　　　　C. cash　　　　D. expenses

7. The term of the lease shall be ten years commencing from the date of the B/L ＿＿＿＿ in Article 4.

A. refining　　　　B. referring to　　　　C. refer　　　　D. referred to

8. If the lessee fails to make payment on time, the lessee shall pay to the lessor as overdue fine one percent interest more than the rate ＿＿＿＿ by the lessor's bank for long-term loans.

A. put off　　　　B. put on　　　　C. put up　　　　D. put out

9. AA Leasing Co., New York ＿＿＿＿ (called the Lessee), ＿＿＿＿(called the Lessor) and

BB Plant，Guangzhou hereby enter into this Contract according to following terms.

A. hereinafter; hereinafter   B. thereinafter; thereby

C. thereby; thereto   D. herein; herewith

10. The defaulting party shall be caused by such a breach, liable to _____ the terminating party for the financial losses.

A. pay   B. paying   C. be paid   D. being paid

五、实务思考
案例 1
由质量欺诈引起的融资租赁纠纷案

2016 年 4 月，A 国际租赁公司（以下简称 A 公司）（甲方）同 B 棉纺厂（以下简称 B 厂）（乙方）签订租赁合同，租赁物件为浆纱机、整经机、剑杆织机等纺织设备，由甲方向 C 公司于 2016 年 2 月购入，租赁计息成本为 705 646.01 美元，租赁期限为 3 年，分 3 次支付租金。合同还规定：如卖方延迟租赁物件的交付或在验收期内发现租赁对象不符合合同规定或有不良、瑕疵等情况，甲方不负责任；乙方若因此受损害，甲方将对卖方的索赔权转让给乙方，并协助乙方向卖方索赔。即使发生此情况，乙方仍须按本合同规定向甲方支付租金及履行合同规定的其他义务；租赁对象运抵目的地后，由甲方向 D 保险公司投保财产险等，保险费由乙方负担。乙方在未能按本合同规定支付到期租金和其他应付款项时，应付延迟支付期间的延迟利息；租赁期满时乙方向甲方交付租金及其他款项，支付完毕，并支付 50 万元人民币，租赁对象所有权自动移交乙方。某建行于 2017 年 4 月向 A 公司出具了"不可撤销外汇配套人民币担保书"。该担保书称："我单位将按照租赁合同之条款担保承租人切实履行该合同各项条款之规定，如承租人因无外汇配套人民币而无法支付租金，我单位在接到贵公司书面通知后 5 日内，无条件向贵公司提供所需的外汇配套人民币。"

2016 年 9 月，租赁物件被运到火车站，同年 10 月 19 日，A 公司、C 公司、B 厂及 D 保险公司四方代表对租赁物件进行检验，于当日写了检验说明。第二天，四方代表签订了备忘录。四方代表经检验发现，租赁物件有 5 箱外包装严重破损，内货外露，39 号锡林烘筒脱位，34 号锡林烘筒被刮伤，29 号机头倾斜，浆轴、左手轮轴、变速箱弯曲变形，并有不少缺件，货损原因系在运输过程中粗鲁装卸而碰撞、挤压。在安装过程中又发现一些质量问题，四方代表均签订了备忘录。2017 年 4 月 3 日，D 保险公司、A 公司、C 公司就租赁物件的货损赔偿达成协议：由于货损主要是运输途中野蛮装卸及碰撞等造成的，总计损失 81 000 美元，D 保险公司愿对保险条款责任内的一切损失负责，又鉴于卖方包装标记不清，使野蛮装卸成为可能，故应负一定责任。D 保险公司负担损失额的 70%，即 56 700 美元，C 公司负担 30%，即 24 300 美元。2017 年 8 月 10 日，A 公司向 B 厂发出了第一期租金通知书，金额为 308 426.11 美元，B 厂同年 9 月 24 日付给 A 公司 235 215.33 美元。2017 年 9 月 15 日，A 公司、C 公司和 B 厂各方达成将索赔期限延长为将来试车验收合格后一年为止的协议。2017 年 10 月 30 日，B 厂、C 公司、A 公司就索赔问题签订备忘录，C 公司应赔偿 B 厂 40 000 美元，没有被接受。2017 年 11 月 2 日，A 公司与 B 厂共同正式向 C 公司提交了索赔意见书，要求赔偿 360 440 美元。2019 年 7 月 25 日，A 公司向 B 厂发出第二期租金到期通知书，金额为 281 082 美元，B 厂没有支付。2019 年 2 月 25 日，B 厂、A 公司共同向中国国际经济贸易仲裁委员会申请仲裁，已开庭审理，尚无结果。

2019 年 10 月 15 日，B 厂和 A 公司就向 C 公司索赔问题达成协议：（1）根据租赁合同规定，甲方将索赔权转让给乙方。（2）仲裁结果如何，不影响租赁合同项下乙方应履行支付租金的义务，乙方保证仲裁所得赔偿金优先偿付甲方。（3）甲乙双方应积极配合向 C 公司索赔。A 公司在 B 厂不支付到期租金的情况下，曾多次书面通知某建行要求分别就配套人民币和外汇额度承担连带责任。某建行答复其在承租方因无外汇配套人民币而无法偿付时，将负责履行合同。

原告诉称：2016 年 4 月 25 日，原告同第一被告 B 厂签订了 A89003CK 号租赁合同。合同约定原与 C 公司签订的购货合同项下的对象由第一被告租用，承租期限为 3 年，货到保定车站日为起租日，租金按平均本金下期付款方式支付，每 12 个月支付一次，3 次付清。租赁物件于 2016 年 9 月 4 日抵达保定站。到 2017 年 9 月 4 日，第一期租金到期，第一被告应支付 308 426.11 美元，但只付给 235 215 美元，尚欠 73 211.11 美元，未付租金新增延迟利息 972 244 美元。截至目前，第二期租金已逾期，租金为 28 108 233 美元，延迟利息为 16 260.61 美元。原告为第一被告垫付的保险费及延迟利息共计 836 939 美元，虽多次交涉，第一被告仍未支付。原告认为租赁合同是有效的。根据租赁合同，第一被告所持不支付租金的理由不能成立，应按合同规定按期如数支付租金及延迟利息，上述各项总计诉讼请求标的为 39 万美元。根据租赁合同和第二被告某建行向原告出具的不可撤销外汇配套人民币担保书，第二被告应就第一被告所欠租金的配套人民币承担连带责任。

第一被告辩称：

（1）租赁合同在履行中因购货合同违约而实质中止。原告虽然在签订购货合同和租赁合同后履行了协议，将 90 万美元货款支付给 C 公司，但由于 C 公司违约，设备无法安装调试，这一事实的发生使租赁合同预定的租赁日期发生变更。按有关规定，租金应从设备安装完备后能够操作运转时开始分期支付，因此设备没有安装完毕，不能操作运转，则租赁合同事实上中止，因中止合同造成的损关应由 C 公司承担。

（2）租赁合同部分条款违背平等互利、等价有偿的原则，应当修改。尽管租赁合同规定对索赔权进行转让，同时规定无论设备是否符合合同或是否有瑕疵，都应当照付租金，被告认为这是不应当的。租赁关系必须以买卖合同全面、及时履行为前提，而租赁合同中不管租赁物有无瑕疵，能否使用租赁物，到货日即为起租日，这不符合平等互利原则，权利、义务不对等。

（3）原告在索赔方面态度消极，致使索赔进展缓慢，因此，被告认为，租赁合同在事实上中止，合同某些条款应予以修改，在对外商索赔仲裁已开庭的情况下，被告不支付租金是完全应当的。

第二被告辩称：原告收取外汇不符合《中华人民共和国合同法》的规定，应以人民币结算。由于 B 厂正向 C 公司索赔，租金应待仲裁结束后支付，如届时不能支付，第二被告将负责提供有外汇额度的配套人民币，第二被告担保的价值不含额度使用费。

某市中级人民法院经审理认为：

（1）根据《最高人民法院关于审理融资租赁合同纠纷案件适用法律问题的解释》第一条，对名为融资租赁合同，但实际不构成融资租赁法律关系的，人民法院应按照其实际构成的法律关系处理。本案中的租赁合同符合此规定，出租方和租赁方是在自愿、互利、协商一致的基础上签订合同的，因此具有法律效力。

（2）根据《最高人民法院关于审理融资租赁合同纠纷案件适用法律问题的解释》第六条，承租人对出卖人行使索赔权，不影响其履行融资租赁合同项下支付租金的义务，但承租人以依赖出租人的技能确定租赁物或者出租人干预选择租赁物为由，主张减轻或者免除相应租金支付义务的除外。同时，第八条规定，出租人转让其在融资租赁合同项下的部分或者全部权利，受让方以此为由请求解除或者变更融资租赁合同的，人民法院不予支持。

因此，此合同的转让索赔权条款无效，不影响合同其他条款的效力。

（3）租赁合同的双方应按照租赁合同明确规定的权利、义务全面地、适当地履行。承租人无权以租赁合同的设备质量出现瑕疵等问题拒付租金。支付租金与质量责任承担是两个独立的法律关系，尽管二者有一定联系，但不构成因果关系，这是由租赁合同的特点决定的。参照《国际融资租赁公约》第八条第一款关于"出租人不应对承租人承担设备的任何责任，除非承租人依赖出租人的技能和判断以及出租人干预选择供应商或设备规格而受的损失"的规定，承租人即使在对外索赔不着的情况下，也应该自己承担此商业风险。因为租赁设备的供应商和设备的规格是由承租人选定或认可的，出租人只是出面代其签订购货合同，处于代理人的地位。

（4）某建行为B厂担保外汇配套人民币，具备代为履行和代偿能力，并不违反法律规定，担保有效。

（5）租赁合同规定用美元支付租金，符合《中华人民共和国合同法》第二百四十八条规定：承租人应当按照约定支付租金。承租人经催告后在合理期限内仍不支付租金的，出租人可以要求支付全部租金，也可以解除合同，收回租赁物。故某建行的答辩理由不能成立。

（6）根据查证事实，A公司已经适当履行了租赁合同规定的义务。货款已以外汇形式付给供应商C公司。对租赁对象出现的瑕疵，A公司已与B厂共同向C公司索赔。在索赔协商不成时，双方共同向中国国际经济贸易仲裁委员会申请仲裁，并已开庭审理。B厂以租赁设备质量问题为由不支付到期租金、应付款项及延迟利息，不符合租赁合同的规定，属违约行为。对A公司由此造成的经济损失，B厂应负主要赔偿责任。对造成索赔权转让条款无效，A公司有一定过错，按照过错责任原则，A公司也应承担相应的责任。

根据租赁合同第七条第三项，关于租赁物件出现瑕疵，乙方仍应按本合同向甲方支付租金且履行本合同规定的其他义务及其他有效条款的约定；参照《国际融资租赁公约》第八条第一款的规定，法院在查明事实、分清责任的基础上依法调解，原被告四方当事人在平等自愿的基础上达成如下协议：

（1）B厂支付给A公司第一期、第二期所欠租金及延迟利息共计36万美元，于2019年11月8日前付清。某建行对36万美元的配套人民币承担连带责任（按给付之日国家汇率计算）。

（2）上述款项届时不能付清，按2018年11月9日的双倍LIBOR（伦敦银行国际同业拆借汇率）计算利息，至付清为止。

（3）诉讼费2 500元人民币，原告负担500元，3个被告负担2 000元。

问题：从该案例中我们应该从中吸取什么教训？

案例 2

<h3 style="text-align:center">釜底抽薪，借租赁偷梁换柱案</h3>

2016 年 4 月 14 日，日本森田电机公司（以下简称电机公司）和莱阳机械厂（以下简称机械厂）签订了一份财产租赁合同，合同规定：电机公司将属其所有的、暂时归其驻中国办事机构使用的两辆丰田牌豪华高级轿车出租给机械厂使用，租期为 54 个月，租金为 31 000 美元，租期内汽车的牌照费、养路费和维修费均由机械厂负责交纳，汽车的所有权仍属电机公司，54 个月期满后收回两辆轿车。合同生效后，电机公司按约交付了汽车，机械厂也于 4 月 30 日交清了租金。2017 年 10 月，机械厂财务紧张，资金周转不开，负债累累。为了偿还到期债务，机械厂决定将两辆轿车转卖出去。2017 年 11 月，机械厂以 120 万元人民币的价格将两辆轿车通过地下途径卖出。2018 年年初，机械厂为了归还两辆轿车，从市场上买了两辆即将报废的同一型号轿车。2018 年 10 月，电机公司前去收取出租的两辆汽车时发现车已非常破旧，因而电机公司到广通律师事务所咨询，并聘请律师代为起诉机械厂

原告电机公司诉称：根据租赁合同，电机公司将两辆汽车租给机械厂使用，并在合同中明文约定租期届满时，收回出租的两辆汽车；但原告采用偷梁换柱的欺骗手法将所有权属于电机公司的两辆汽车非法转让，而用两辆即将报废的汽车顶替。机械厂的行为违反租赁合同的约定，严重侵犯了原告电机公司的财产所有权，对所造成的损失应付完全责任。

法院经审理认为，电机公司与机械厂依法签订的租赁合同合法、有效，当事人双方应认真履行。电机公司按约提供租赁对象，机械厂按期交清了租金。租赁公司明确约定租赁对象的所有权仍属于电机公司，承租人机械厂在租赁期满时应将租赁物件原物返还。然而承租人机械厂擅自处分了租赁物件，在承租期将至之时，又从市场购得另外两辆破旧车准备作为原租赁物件返还出租人，这已构成商业欺诈行为，因而法院认为对出租人所造成的损失，承租人机械厂应付全部责任，根据有关法律规定，作出如下判决：

机械厂于本判决生效之日起一个月内，向电机厂返还扣除已付租金的两辆丰田牌豪华轿车价款 120 万元人民币。

问题：从该案例中我们应该吸取什么教训？

实训项目 25
咨询合同练习^①

实训目标

1.掌握咨询合同的基本内容。
2.掌握草拟咨询合同的注意事项。

一、阅读

How to Write a Consulting Contract[2]

1. Spell out the terms of the contract verbally with the client. This should ideally occur during a face-to-face meeting, but can also be done by telephone or even through an email exchange. Go over each of the relevant aspects of the contract and make sure you and the client are in agreement. If the consultation takes place in person or by telephone, take thorough notes of the conversation.

2. Begin the consulting contract by including the full legal names of the consultant(s) and the client(s). A statement as simple as "This contract constitutes an agreement between Consultant X and Client Y to contract the services of X in executing Project Z" is fine for an opening statement.

3. State each task to be completed separately or in a bullet point or item in a numbered list. Include the expected date of completion and the type of delivery, or final product, to be presented to the client. If the consultant is expected to attend specific meetings on behalf of the client, include the meeting dates and locations.

4. List the procedure for the approval of each step and payment after each stage of the contract (if applicable). Also, list the procedure if revisions or changes are required for approval. If the partial payment will be made even with revisions, state this as well.

5. Spell out the procedure for the client initiated changes that are not the result of required revisions. If the additional payment will be reduced, spell out the amount of the additional payments and the procedure for making the payments.

6. State the total payment amount, the date(s) of the payment and the method of the payment.

① [1] 徐良霞，李海燕. 实用英语教你写合同 [M]. 北京：北京航空航天工业大学出版社，2004. [2] 王立非. 国际商务合同实践教程 [M]. 上海：上海外语教育出版社，2012.
② BLANK C. How to write a consulting contract [EB/OL]. (2017-07-05) [2019-10-17]. http://www.ehow.com/how_4928673-write-consulting-contract.html.

If an invoice from the consultant is required to the initiate payment, it includes a description of the required format of the invoice.

7. Spell out any provisions for termination of the contract before or at the end of its term, including the disposition of any work product renewal of the contract at the end of the term. Also, state whether there will be an option for and how renewal will be negotiated.

8. State the grievance and/or mediation procedures of the contract in case of disagreement about the performance of the consultant and/or payment by the client. Spell out whether the legal recourse will be available to either party in the case of a complete breakdown in communication.

9. Include the terms of confidentiality concerning the project, if applicable. State whether the terms of the confidentiality will extend beyond the term of the contract. Also, state any consequences, legal or otherwise, for violations of confidentiality.

10. State any no compete clause or provisions to the contract if applicable. A noncompeting clause limits the options of the consultant to contract for similar projects or with competing clients for a specified period of time.

11. Make two copies of the contract for both the consultant and the client to sign. Give one copy of the signed contract to the client and keep one signed copy for your files. Having the signatures notarized provides extra assurance, but is not legally necessary.

Consulting Agreement (Sample)

The Consultant is recognized as _____ [area of expertise, e.g., an authority on matters related to direct mail and other direct response advertising activities];

WHEREAS, the Company desires to retain the Consultant to provide services related to and in support of efforts in which the Consultant has expertise.

NOW, THEREFORE, in consideration of the premises, the mutual conditions and promises herein contained, the parties hereto agree as follows:

1. Consulting Services. The Consultant shall furnish the Company with his best advice, information, judgment and knowledge with respect to _____ [services provided by consultant, e.g., marketing via direct mail and other direct response advertising vehicles].

2. Term. The term of this Agreement shall begin on _____ [begining date] and shall, subject to the provisions for the termination set forth herein, continue until it terminates on [end date].

3. Compensation. For all services that the Consultant renders to the Company or any of its subsidiaries or affiliates during the term hereof, the Company will pay Consultant a retainer of $ 5,000 per month, payable on the first day of the month.

4. Confidential Information and Intellectual Property.

The Consultant shall maintain in strict confidence and not use or disclose except pursuant to written instructions from the Company, any Trade Secret (as defined below) of the Company, for so long as the pertinent data or information remains a Trade Secret, provided that the obligation to protect the confidentiality of any such information or data shall not be excused if such information or data ceases to qualify as a Trade Secret as the result of the acts or the omissions of the Consultant.

5. Relationship of Parties. The Company and the Consultant are independent contractors. Both parties acknowledge and agree that Consultant's engagement hereunder is not exclusive and that either party may provide to, or retain from, others similar such services provided that it does so in a manner that does not otherwise breach this Agreement. Neither party is, nor shall claim to be, a legal agent, a representative, a partner or an employee of the other, and neither shall have the right or authority to contract in the name of the other nor shall it assume or create any obligations, debts, accounts or liabilities for the other. IN WITNESS WHEREOF, the above first written parties have executed this Agreement effective as of the date.

Questions:

(1)When writing or drafting a consulting contract, what clauses are typically used to protect both the client and the consultant?

(2)In the sample consulting agreement above, why are there many archaic words, such as whereas, herein and hereof?

二、实务思考

Plaintiffs:William Michael Turner and Technology Engineering Corporation

Defendant:Isoflux, Inc.

Supreme Court:State of New York Monroe County[①]

Facts

Plaintiffs were hired for a three-year period by the Defendant pursuant to a Consulting Agreement executed by the parties in January, 2001. The Defendant terminated the Consulting Agreement in November, 2001, alleging that Plaintiffs had misled and defrauded it, shared confidential information, and thereby breached the Consulting Agreement. Plaintiffs had commenced this action, alleging wrongful termination and that such termination constituted a breach of the Consulting Agreement.

Defendant's Motion for Summary Judgment

The Defendant sought summary dismissal of Plaintiffs' Complaint under two theories. First, the Defendant alleged that it was entitled to summary judgment because the Consulting Agreement lacked definiteness and was consequently unenforceable as a matter of law. The Defendant also alleged that it was entitled to summary judgment because Plaintiff Turner committed illegal acts when he shared the third-party confidential information with the Defendant.

Definiteness of the Consulting Agreement

The Defendant contended that the Consulting Agreement lacked objective criteria against which to measure the reasonableness of Plaintiff Turner's efforts, thus leading the Agreement to be unenforceable...

In this case, the Consulting Agreement did not lack the objective criteria which would render it indefinite and unenforceable. The Consulting Agreement entered into by these sophisticated

---

① 严明. 国际合同实践教程 [M]. 上海：上海外语教育出版社，2012.

parties set forth Plaintiff Turner's experience that the Defendant deemed relevant in entering into the Agreement:

Whereas, TEC/Turner had experience in the field of coating systems applications and Isoflux the commercial, industrial research and development, systems applications, equipments and services, sales, consulting, marketing, engineering desires to use TEC/Turner's experience in manufacturing and marketing of its coating.

Moreover, the Consulting Agreement set forth the following criteria:

(1)Isoflux agreed to use TEC/Turner's services as a consultant on an independent contract basis. This was not a sales performance type agreement and Turner would not be titled as such.

(2)This agreement should be for a period of three (3) years commencing January 1, 2001.

(3)TEC/Turner agreed to use available resources and reasonable efforts to promote Isoflux to existing customers (both of Isoflux and TEC/Turner) with the intent to enhance customer relations and to develop new customers as well.

The Defendant had failed to establish that the Consulting Agreement was unenforceable due to lack of definiteness. While the Defendant might have been disappointed with the quality of the services provided by Plaintiff Turner, it couldn't avoid the promises contracted for in the Consulting Agreement. Despite the Defendant's contentions, the terms of the Consulting Agreement were reasonably certain.

The Defendant's motion for summary judgment on the issue of the definiteness of the Consulting Agreement was denied.

Helga Acts

The Defendant also contended that it was entitled to summary judgment as a result of Plaintiff Turner's breach of the Consulting Agreement by his participation in alleged illegal acts. The Defendant alleged that Plaintiff Turner's decision to share confidential information belonging to other companies with the Defendant constituted an illegal act and justifies terminating the Consulting Agreement.

The Consulting Agreement allowed the Defendant to terminate the agreement if TEC/Turner engaged in any illegal activity ... Black's Law Dictionary defined illegal as against or not authorized by law. The Consulting Agreement also permitted termination under separate provisions if TEC/Turner was convicted of, or engages, in any conduct, constituting a felony ... or was convicted of a crime involving moral turpitude, immoral conduct or dishonesty ... Therefore, in order to give full meaning to all of the contract terms, the illegal activity referred to the Consulting Agreement must encompass not only criminal action, but also any other conduct that was not authorized by law.

Activity Unauthorized by Law

The Defendant's motion for the summary judgment was granted on the issue of the Plaintiffs' disclosure of the confidential information and the participation in the illegal acts.

Violations of the Penal Law

To the extent the Defendant sought the summary judgment and a determination by this Court that Plaintiff Turner violated various provisions of New York's Penal Law that motion DENIED.

This Court would not make a determination on a civil summary judgment motion as to whether the Plaintiff violated Penal Laws.

Questions:

(1)The case involves a consulting agreement. Who are the parties to it? What are the allegations of each party in the case?

(2)The Defendant contends the agreement is unenforceable. Is there an enforceable consulting agreement between the two parties? Why?

(3)What is the key to determine whether "plaintiffs' disclosure of the confidential information constituted an illegal activity"? Which party will win the case? Why?

实训项目 26
国际许可证合同练习①

实训目标

1.掌握国际许可证合同的基本词汇和重点句子。

2.掌握国际许可证合同的分类:专利许可证合同、商标许可证合同以及专有技术许可证合同。

3.熟悉国际许可证合同的形式、结构和重点条款的起草和翻译。

一、将下列国际许可证合同条款翻译为中文

1. This Contract is composed of the Contract proper and the Annexes. The Annexes and the Contract proper have the same validity. In the event that any contradictions should arise between any provisions of the Annexes and the corresponding provisions of the Contract proper, the Contract proper shall be definitive.

2. Should all or part of the contract be unable to be fulfilled owing to the fault of one party, the breaching party shall bear the responsibilities thus caused. Should it be the fault of both parties, they shall bear their respective responsibilities according to actual situations.

3. Any additional agreements and/or amendments to this Contract shall be valid only after the authorized representatives of both parties have signed written document(s), forming integral part(s) of this contract.

4. The Licensor has agreed to grant the License the Licence and the right to use the trade mark of Licensor, and use the combination trade mark of both parties or mark the wording production according to the Licensor's licence on the Contract Products.

5. The Licensor guarantees that the Licensor is the legitimate owner of all the Patent Technology and the Documentation supplied by the Licensor to the Licensee in accordance with the Contract, and that Licensor is lawful in a position to transfer all such Technology and Technical Documentation to the Licensee. In the course of the Implementation of the Contract, if any third party accuses the Licensee of the infringement, the Licensor shall be responsible for approaching the third party about the accusation and bear all the economic and legal

① 黄文伟,刘美华. 商务英语函电与合同 [M]. 上海:上海大学出版社,2008.

responsibilities which might arise.

二、将括号内的中文翻译为英文

1. In the course of the implementation of the contract, _____
_____ (如 受
让方需要出让方提供技术服务或一部分生产所需的原材料,出让方有义务以最低价向受让方
提供). When the time comes, both parties will sign a new contract through friendly consultation.

2. The Contract is made out in both English and Chinese in four originals, two for each party
_____ (在 合
同有效期内,双方通信以英语进行,正式通知须以书面形式航空挂号邮寄,并一式两份).

3. _____
_____(如双方通过协商不能达成协议,则应提交中国的仲裁机构或中国
的有关法院解决). If the arbitration is chosen, the case shall be submitted to the Foreign Economic and Trade Arbitration Commission of the China Council for the Promotion of International Trade
for the arbitration in accordance with its provisional rules of procedure. _____
_____
(如果进行诉讼,则由受让人所在地的人民法院根据中国的有关法律进行审理).

4. _____
_____(本合同自签字之日起6个月如仍不能生效,双
方均有权撤销合同). The patent documents stipulated in Section 6.1 to the Contract shall be returned by the Licensee to the Licensor once the Contract has been canceled.

5. The Licensor guarantees that the Technical Documentation supplied by the Licensor to the
Licensee in accordance with the Contract shall be of the latest Technical Documentation which is
actually used by the Licensor, _____
_____(并保证在合同执行过程中及时向受让方提供其改进和发展的技术资料).

三、选词填空

thereafter, henceforth, hereof, hereunder, hereto, therefrom

1. The Licensor guarantees that it is the legitimate owner of know - how supplied to the
Licensee according to stipulations of the Contract and that it is lawful in the position to transfer the
know - how to the Licensee. If there is any accusation of infringing the right of a third party, the
Licensor shall bear the full legal and economic responsibility arising _____.

2. Both parties shall exert their best efforts to obtain the approval within sixty (60) days and
inform the other Party by e-mail and confirm _____ the same by a letter.

3. This Agreement contains the entire agreement and understanding between the Principal
and the General Agent relating to the Acquisition of the Technology by the Principal, and
supersedes all previous agreements or arrangements between the Principal which shall
cease and terminate with effect from the date _____. This Agreement may not be amended or
modified except by written instrument signed by each of the Parties _____.

4. Notwithstanding the expiration or termination of the Agreement for whatever cause, any term or provision of this Agreement which is capable of being performed or observed after the date of such expiration or termination of the Agreement shall survive the same and shall continue to be binding on the parties _____ and remain in full force and effect.

5. The methods of payment for fee of technical service and personnel training _____ are detailed in Annex 5 to the Contract.

四、填空练习

Licensing Agreement[①]

This Agreement is made on March 15th, 2010 between Bookbinders Inc. (hereinafter termed the Publishers) of one part, and Jones and Company (hereinafter termed the Proprietors) of the other part. WHEREAS the Proprietors are the proprietors of a work entitled: (hereinafter termed the Work), now (1) _____ [双方特此同意如下]:

1. Subject to the terms detailed in this Agreement, the Proprietors hereby grant to the Publishers the (2) _____ [排他性许可] to product and publishing a single printing of 10,000 copied only of the Work in paperback form in the English language under the Publishers' own imprint (hereafter termed the Licensed Edition) for sale throughout United Kingdom only. This restricted circulation is to be clearly indicated on the outside of the cover and on the reverse of the title page of the Licensed Edition by the following words: "(3) _____ [仅限英国许可销售] not for export."

2. This Agreement shall not (4) _____ [生效] until the Proprietors have received the (advance) payment detailed in Clause 9 hereof.

3. The Publishers shall produce the Licensed Edition at their own expense. They shall cause it to be reproduced faithfully and accurately and shall not abridge, expand or otherwise alter the Work, including illustrations where applicable, without the prior written consent of the Proprietors.

4. Should the Publishers fail to issue the Licensed Edition within 12 months from the date of this Agreement, all rights granted under this Agreement shall revert to the (5) _____ [所有者] without prejudice to any money paid or due to Proprietors.

5. The Proprietors (6) _____ [特此保证] to the Publishers that they have the right and power to make this Agreement and that according to English law the Work will in no way whatever give rise to a violation of any existing copyright, breach of any existing agreement and that nothing in the Work is liable to give rise to a civil prosecution or to a civil action for damages or any other remedy and the Proprietors will indemnify the Publishers against any loss, injury or expense arising out of any breach of this (7) _____ [担保].

6. The License hereby granted to the Publishers shall not be (8) _____ [全部或部分转让] or extended to include any other party nor shall the Licensed Edition appear under imprint other

① WIDDOWSON R. Market leader: business law [M]. New York: Pearson Longman, 2010.

than that of the Publishers, except with prior written consent of the Proprietors.

7. The License herein granted shall continue for a period of five years from the date of first publication by the Publishers of the Licensed Edition and thereafter may be subject to renewal by mutual agreement between the parties hereto.

8. If any difference shall arise between the Proprietors and the Publishers touching the meaning of this Agreement or the rights and liabilities of (9) _____ ［协议当事人］, the same shall be referred to the arbitration of two persons (one to be named by each party) or their umpire, in accordance with the provisions of the Arbitration Act 1996 or any subsisting statutory modification or reenactment hereof, provided that any dispute between the parties hereto not resolved by arbitration or agreement shall be (10) _____ ［提交给］ the jurisdiction of the English courts.

五、将下列句子翻译为中文

1. Subject to the terms detailed in this Agreement, the Proprietors hereby grant to the Publishers the exclusive license to product and publishing a single printing of 10,000 copied only of the Work in paperback form in the English language under the Publisher's own imprint (hereafter termed the Licensed Edition) for sale throughout United Kingdom only.

2. Should the Publishers fail to issue the Licensed Edition within 12 months from the date of this Agreement, all rights granted under this Agreement shall revert to the Proprietors without prejudice to any monies paid or due to the Proprietors.

3. Upon the terms and conditions hereinafter set forth, the Licensor hereby grants to the Licensee as a related company, and the Licensee hereby accepts the right, license and privilege of utilizing the Name solely and only upon and in connection with the manufacture, sale and distribution of the following articles.

4. The Licensee agrees that it will not make, or authorize, any use, direct or indirect, of the Name in any other area, and that it will not knowingly sell articles covered by this agreement to persons who intend or are likely to resell them in any other area.

5. This license shall be automatically renewed for a one-year term expiring December 31st of the following year, unless either party hereto shall be given a written notice to the contract at least thirty (30) days prior to the expiration date.

六、将下列句子翻译为英文

1.被许可方同意在协议有效期内及其后，不质疑许可方就该商标享有的所有权和其他权利，不质疑本协议的有效性。

2.根据第十二条所述条款，终止许可合同将不影响许可方对被许可方拥有的其他权利。

3.当本协议到期时，如果被许可方届时能够完全遵守合同，那么双方当事人可以协商对本协议进行延期。

4.所有的广告和促销资料都必须先征得许可方的批准。

5.被许可方应及时将有关侵犯或者威胁知识产权的信息汇报给许可方。

七、讨论

1. What is the subject matter of a licensing agreement?

2. What is the difference between a licensing agreement and a franchising agreement?

3. What are the key terms of a licensing agreement?

4. What are the primary obligations of the licensor and the licensee?

5. Find online a sample licensing agreement, such as KFC Licensing Agreement, and discuss its key provisions.

八、实务思考

Background[1]

If you are in China, chances are that you drink at least one bottle of Wahaha brand water, or perhaps the company's iced tea, fruit drinks, or its Future Cola. If you go to the United States, you may even come across Future Cola in New York or Los Angeles, because the company that first set up shop in an elementary school in Hangzhou, Zhejiang, is going global.

The Hangzhou Wahaha Group Co., Ltd., China's leading domestic beverage producer, didn't achieve success overnight. The company's predecessor, the Hangzhou Shangcheng District School-Run Enterprise Sales Department, funded its start-up operations in 1987 with a government loan. Zong Qinghou, the company's founder, and two retired schoolteachers initially sold milk products and popsicles out of a school store, but to benefit the students' health the group soon began producing and selling nutritional drinks. The company's success selling nutritional products in school shops led to its first big expansion: with Hangzhou government's support, the company acquired a large, 30-year-old state-owned enterprise, the Hangzhou Canned Food Product Co., in 1991. The company then changed its name to the Hangzhou Wahaha Group Co. (The word "Wahaha" is meant to mimic the sound of a baby laughing and is taken from a children's folk song.) Wahaha's second large-scale expansion occurred in 1994 when the company merged with three insolvent companies in Fuling, Sichuan, to set up its first factory in Chongqing.

The Wahaha joint venture (JV) was formed in February, 1996. At the start, there were three participants in the JV: Hangzhou Wahaha Food Group (Wahaha Group), led by its chairman Zong Qinghou; Danone Group, a French corporation (Danone); and Bai Fu Qin, a Hong Kong corporation (Baifu).

In 1996, the two parties signed a trademark transfer agreement, with an intention to transfer the "Wahaha" trademark to the joint ventures. The move, however, was not approved by the State Trademark Office.

For this reason, the two parties signed in 1999 the trademark licensing contract. According to the law, the same subject cannot be synchronously transferred and licensed the use to others by

---

① 严明. 国际合同实践教程 [M]. 上海：上海外语教育出版社，2012.

the same host. Therefore, the signing and fulfillment of the trademark licensing contract showed that the two parties had connived the invalidation of the transfer agreement. The "Wahaha" brand should belong to the Wahaha Group, while the joint ventures only have the right of use.

In October, 2005, the parties inked the No. 1 amendment agreement to the trademark licensing contract, in which it confirmed Party A (Hangzhou Wahaha Group Co., Ltd.) as the owner of the trademark. In addition, the second provision of the amendment agreement clearly stated that the several Wahaha subsidiaries listed in the fifth annex of the licensing contract as well as other Wahaha subsidiaries (referred to as "licensed Wahaha enterprises") established by Party A or its affiliates following the signing of the licensing contract also have the right granted by one party to use the trademark. The "licensed Wahaha enterprises" involved in the amendment agreement refer to the non-joint ventures.

According to the related files, the Wahaha owns the ownership of the "Wahaha" trademark, while its non-joint ventures have the right to use the trademark.

The Danone-Wahaha Feud-Trademark License

From May, 2007, when the Danone initiated legal proceedings against the Wahaha, the both sides have carried out several dozen lawsuits worldwide. As of May, 2009, Danone not only lost a series of cases against Zong Qinghou and the non-joint ventures in China, but directors of the Danone were deemed by many courts to have violated the non-compete obligation of directors, and litigations filed in the U.S.A., Italy, France and British Virgin Islands (BVI) were also dismissed. Now, the Wahaha defeats the Danone in the lawsuits in and out of China.

The ownership and use right of the Wahaha trademark is one of the "Danone-Wahaha feuds."

The Danone often insisted that the Wahaha trademark belonged to the joint ventures, so the use of the trademark by non-joint ventures constituted infringement.

But the Wahaha Group disagreed with that, and emphasized that it was the true holder of the trademark, and the use of the trademark, but the use of the trademark by non-joint ventures was legal.

At the beginning of the Danone - Wahaha "marriage," the Wahaha signed a transfer agreement on the ownership of the Wahaha trademark with the joint ventures, and filed a trademark transfer application with the State Trademark Office, which , however, was not approved. "It actually declared the termination of the transfer contract, and the Wahaha trademark is still owned by the Wahaha Group." said Ye Zhijian, a lawyer who knew the case.

Afterward, the two parties signed a trademark licensing contract in 1999 to substitute the original transfer agreement. Both the licensing contract and the consequent No. 1 amendment agreement clarified that the non-joint ventures of the Wahaha have the right to use the Wahaha trademark.

"It was known to and recognized by the Danone that the non-joint ventures OEM for the joint ventures, so how could it be possible for the non-joint ventures to use a different trademark from the joint venture?" Ye noted.

To confirm the ownership of the Wahaha trademark, the Wahaha referred to the Hangzhou

Arbitration Commission for arbitration in accordance with the trademark transfer agreement. In December, 2007, the commission made a decision that the trademark transfer agreement between the Danone and the Wahaha had terminated, and the Wahaha trademark belonged to the Wahaha Group. Later, the Hangzhou Intermediate People's Court affirmed the ruling.

Questions:

(1)From 1996 to 2005, the Wahaha and the Danone signed several contracts on the license of trademark "Wahaha." What are the content of them respectively?

(2)Is the trademark licensing contract valid? Who owns the trademark "Wahaha?"

(3)What are the requirements for a trademark licensing contract to be valid in China?

实训项目 27
寄售协议练习①

实训目标

1. 掌握寄售协议的基本内容。
2. 掌握草拟寄售协议的注意事项。

一、将括号内的提示词翻译为英文

Consignment Agreement

China National Light Industrial Products Imp. & Exp. Corp., Beijing Branch (hereinafter called Party A) held talks with U.S. Max Factor & Co., (hereinafter called Party B) about the consignment of Max Factor Cosmetics. Through friendly negotiation, both parties (1) _____ [确认约定的要点如下]:

1. Item for Consignment. It mainly covers four product categories i.e. Treatment, Fragrance, Cosmetics, and Toiletries. Party B shall provide the (2) _____ quantity of the above goods in a list to Party A. After (3) _____ [详细说明], unit price and _____ [甲方确认], a concrete contract signed by both parties will then be effective.

2. Terms of Consignment

(1)Period of Time

Both parties agree that sales of Max Factor Cosmetics will commence on or about January 15, 1999 and continue through December 31, 1999. Party A agrees to (4) _____ [专门销售] Max Factor Cosmetics during this one year time in Beijing and agrees that no other cosmetics lines including perfumes, beauty cosmetics, cosmetics for protecting skin, hair lotions and nail enamel will be sold in Beijing Hotel, Beijing Friendship Store or any other locations in Beijing.

In order to facilitate Party A's work of starting the consignment sales on time, Party B should ship the first lot of (5) _____ [寄售货物] to Party A before December 31, 1998. On or about March 15, 1999, Party A and Party B shall meet to mutually determine on acceptable sales level for the remainder of the consignment period.

① [1] 严明. 国际合同实践教程 [M]. 上海：上海外语教育出版社，2012. [2] 王立非. 国际商务合同实践教程 [M]. 上海：上海外语教育出版社，2012.

二、将下列句子翻译为中文

1. The Consignee shall aggressively promote and sell the goods to customers in the Territory.

The Consignee will utilize, at its discretion, various selling strategies, including retail outlets, catalog, mail order, telephone, and electronic sales within the Territory.

2. The Consignee shall be responsible for procuring and maintaining all import licenses, transport permits, business licenses, and other similar permits required for the import, transport, storage, and sale of the Goods in the Consignee's country.

3. The Consignee assumes all risks of the loss for all the Goods consigned. The Consignee will pay for all Goods damaged, destroyed, or stolen from the consignment inventory as if such Goods were sold.

4. The Consignee shall indemnify, hold harmless, and defend the Manufacturer against all claims and damages for injury to, or death of, one or more persons and for damage to, or loss of property arising from or attributed to the conduct, operations, or performance of the Consignee.

5. The Consignee must not represent that he or she owns any rights in the Manufacturer's Intellectual Property. Nor is the Consignee permitted to use the Manufacturer's name as any part of its own name.

三、将下列句子翻译为英文

1.制造方同意按合同条款将货物提供给寄售商，寄售商亦同意在指定地区内销售货物。

2.寄售商应按制造方提供的统一格式提交订货清单，说明寄售商想要从制造方处收取货物的类型和数量。

3.制造方应将所有货物交运到该区域内寄售商指定的地点。

4.除第一次订货外的其他6次订货都必须先付清上月售出货物的全额款项，并减去寄售商约定的适当折扣比例。

5.寄售商在提交存货报告单时应同时提交月度报告，写明上月所售货物的型号和数量。

四、讨论

1. What is a consignment contract?

2. What is the difference between a consignment agreement and a distribution agreement?

3. What does a consignment contract usually cover?

4. Who retains the title to goods in a consignment contract?

5. What are the obligations of the consignee?

6. If the buyer (the consignee) defaults on the payment of the purchase price, what can the seller (the consignor) do?

五、阅读

A Consignment Agreement

Consignment agreements are generally entered into by two parties. One is a retail business owner; the other is a person or business wanting to sell a product to the business owner's customers. The agreement typically allows the business owner an opportunity to bring more stocks into his store without having to spend money on it upfront. The person with something to sell can get his product seen by potential customers without having to lease retail space to display the product. Consignment agreements are inexpensive ways for both parties to increase their business and bottom line.

Significance

Neither the business owner nor the seller pays each other money until or unless the item on consignment sells. When the customer pays for the consigned item, the business owner takes a percentage of the sale price and then pays the seller the rest. The significance of this arrangement is that risks are low for all involved. The seller is risking only the cost of the item he is trying to sell, and the retailer is risking only the use of a little retail space for the term of the agreement. It's a good way to do business in tough economic times when credit is tight. Before putting together a consignment agreement, don't forget to check with your local and state government to see if there are legal guidelines that must be followed ...

Features

Consignment agreements should contain the following basic information: the name of the parties; the date of the agreement; the name of each item consigned and a description of its condition; the asking price of each item consigned; the percentage of the asking price that will go to the retailer and the percentage that will go to the seller if a sale is made; the time each item is allowed to be consigned and the date it should be picked up if it does not sell; a description of what happens to items that are not sold and not picked up by the specified date; how often checks are issued to sellers by the retailer and on what dates; and the signatures of both parties.

The agreements often include a statement that absolves the retailer of any liability related to the product for sale. Some agreements request the seller give the retailer 24 hours or more notice prior to picking up an item. Some also have provisions for renewal of the agreement if the item has not sold by the initial time frame of the agreement. Some may also include provisions for reducing the initial price to a sale price if the item does not sell by a certain date.

Considerations

Other provisions you may want to include in the consignment agreement would clarify what happens if the consigned item is shoplifted, or broken or damaged by the retailer or one of the retailer's employees. Even if the retailer is compiling and issuing monthly reports on consignments, the seller will want to keep careful records, too. Everyone makes mistakes, and it is easier to keep track of many details if both parties are recording everything. Other things to consider are whether the items will be advertised and who pays the cost. If the retailer goes bankrupt and the merchandise is seized, what happens to the seller's items since they are not owned by the retailer? These questions should all be answered in a comprehensive consignment agreement.

Potential

The time and effort spent in putting together a good consignment agreement is well worth it for the result. Consignment arrangements allow business owners and product distributors an opportunity to keep costs low while growing their individual companies. Good agreements that are fair to both parties make good economic sense and can be the beginning of business partnerships that last for decades.

Agreement of Consignment

This Agreement is entered into between ＿＿＿＿＿＿＿＿＿＿＿＿＿＿＿＿＿ Co. (hereinafter referred to as the Consignor), having its registered office at ＿＿＿＿ , China and ＿＿＿＿＿＿＿＿＿＿＿＿＿＿＿ Co. (hereinafter referred to as the Consignee), having its registered office at ＿＿＿＿ , on the following terms and conditions:

1. The Consignor shall from time to time ship ＿＿＿＿ (commodity) to the Consignee on Consignment basis at the prevailing international market prices on CIF terms. The interval between each shipment shall be approximately ninety days.

2. The Consignee must try to sell the consignments at the best possible prices after obtaining the approval of the Consignor as to price, terms, etc.

3. Each shipment by ship at the initial stage will not exceed USD ＿＿＿＿ and outstanding liabilities on the Consignee shall be in the vicinity of not more than USD ＿＿＿＿ only.

4. The Consignor shall at no time be responsible for any bad debts arising out of credit sales to any ＿＿＿＿ buyers. Making payments to the Consignor shall at all times be the sole responsibility of the Consignee.

5. The Consignee shall accept the Bills of Exchange drawn by the Consignor on him at ＿＿＿＿ days' sight with interest payable at ＿＿＿＿% per annum.

6. The Consignee shall collect the shipping documents including B/L from the Consignor's bank against Trust Receipt duly signed by the Consignee.

7. The Consignor shall absorb insurance premium and warehousing charges up to the date of the delivery to customers.

8. Arbitration: Any dispute arising from or in connection with the Contract shall be settled through friendly negotiation. In case no settlement is reached, the dispute shall be submitted to China International Economic and Trade Arbitration Commission, South China Sub-commission, for arbitration in accordance with its rules in effect at the time of applying for arbitration. The arbitral award is final and binding upon both parties.

9. This Contract is executed in two counterparts each in Chinese and English, each of which shall be deemed equally authentic. This Contract is in being signed/sealed by both parties.

A Co.: ＿＿＿＿ (Signature)　　　　　B Co.: ＿＿＿＿ (Signature)

Questions:

(1)In Text A, what should be taken into account when drafting a consignment agreement?

(2)What are the key clauses which are different from a sales contract?

(3)When making a consignment with a foreign trader, what problems usually happen for a Chinese trader? Give an example.

六、实务思考

2010年11月，我国某农业有限公司（以下简称A公司）与日本某公司（以下简称B公司）签署寄售协议，出口切花。协议约定：每两周交一批货，标准海运包装，每批两个标准20′集装箱（冷冻箱）；目的港为日本港口；寄售手续费（handling fee）为（不含消费税）销售额的7%；货物销售款以最终发票计收，以T/T方式支付，由B公司在每月15日和30日汇付A公司；协议期为6个月。在业务操作中，货物的进口清关手续由B公司代为办理，并垫付所产生的税费，所垫付费用日后在货物销售款中扣减。

从2010年12月初开始，A公司每两周发货一批，货物运输事务委托锦海国际货运代理公司办理，锦海公司安排了中国台湾阳明海运公司的船只将货物运往日本。装运港为厦门，目的港为东京。直至2011年2月下旬，该出口项目运行正常：A公司按期发货，货到东京港后，B公司清关、提货。货物顺利销售，B公司按合同约定如期将应付货款汇付A公司。

2011年3月10日，A公司价值31.32万元人民币、数量为4 000枝的鲜菊花分装两个20′标准箱，再次在厦门港完成装船；11日，日本东北部海域发生强烈地震；12日，海轮离港，14日抵达日本东京港。

此时，地震对日本东北部地区造成的巨大灾害以及影响已经开始波及全日本，考虑到该批花卉将面临销售困难，B公司不予清关提货，并建议A公司将此批花卉运回。考虑到在无其他销售渠道的情况下货物运回的货物和费用损失，A公司未接受B公司的建议，随即通知承运人将货物暂存东京港口仓库，希望地震灾害影响很快过去，此批货物还可获得销售收入。然而，直至3月下旬，灾害影响日益严重，此批切花市值一再下跌；同时，由于货物仓储费用开始发生，承运方敦促A公司，要求告知货物处置方法。随时间推移，A公司获知该批货物已经完全丧失商业价值，于是与B公司协商，寻求帮助。B公司称其受地震影响，不能再对此批货物承担任何协助处理义务，而对此情况，A公司束手无措。

由于损失严重，此间，A公司多次要求B公司、承运人为此批货物分担部分损失，均遭拒绝。3月26日，承运人最后通牒：要求A公司授权处置货物并承担费用。而对继续产生的费用损失、承运人的不断催促，A公司选择了逃避并拒绝支付运费。

2011年6月，承运方代表锦海公司将A公司告上法庭，提起诉讼，请求赔偿其为此批货物善后处理垫付的货物仓储费、垃圾清理费、劳务费以及海运费等共计112 350.00元人民币。

此案不仅造成了A公司整批货物的全部损失，又使其而临承运方10余万元人民币的诉讼请求。

问题：从该案例中我们应该吸取什么教训？

实训项目 28
加工贸易合同练习①

实训目标

1.掌握加工贸易合同的特点。
2.掌握加工贸易合同的基本内容。
3.掌握草拟加工贸易合同的注意事项。

一、将下列内容翻译为中文

Processing supplied materials and assembling supplied parts play a very important role in expanding China's foreign trade. They concern both import and export commodities. The Chinese enterprise is supplied with materials and parts by the client abroad and turns them into finished products for export to that foreign client. For this, it receives fees which may include the cost of additional materials it provides. The benefit to the Chinese enterprise is that it can keep itself in touch with changes in the world market and is also provided with an opportunity to learn advanced technology and scientific management, thus helping it to raise the competitiveness of its products abroad.

The characteristics of the industries of processing supplied materials and assembling supplied parts, viewed from the point of import and export, are as follows:

1. The two industries embody both import and export in a single transaction. The purpose of importation is to create exportation.

2. As the ownership of the supplied materials or parts remains with the foreign client and the Chinese enterprise can only use them for processing or assembling, it is important that the foreign client should effect the necessary insurance to cover them against risks from the time they leave their stowing place abroad up to the time they are shipped out as finished products.

3. The foreign client is both the exporter of materials or parts and the importer of finished products, and the Chinese enterprise is both the importer of materials or parts and the exporter of finished products.

① [1] 吴敏，吴明忠. 国际经贸英语合同写作 [M]. 广州：暨南大学出版社，2002. [2] 刘川，王菲. 英文合同阅读与翻译 [M]. 北京：国防工业出版社，2010.

4. If the foreign client provides the Chinese enterprise with the equipment in addition to materials or parts, this kind of processing or assembling parts of the nature of compensation trade. The Chinese enterprise can use the processing or assembling fee to pay the price of the equipment.

二、将下列内容翻译为英文

来料加工和来件装配是指由中国企业采用外商提供的全部或部分原料、辅料、零件和部件，按外商要求的质量、规格和图样进行加工或装配，而且把成品归还给外商。加工装配所需的设备、技术、工具和仪器常由外商供应，其价款由中国企业从所收取的加工装配费中偿还。从这个意义上讲，这也是吸收外国投资的一种形式。

三、在横线上填入恰当的介词

Both sides have agreed to conclude business _____ means of assembling supplied components. Party A shall _____ its own expense, provide Party B with all components, auxiliary materials together with blue prints and other technical data. Party B shall assemble them _____ finished products and then send the same to Party A. Most _____ the components and auxiliary materials sent by Party A and used by Party B shall arrive _____ Guangzhou the end _____ May, 2018.

四、单项选择

1. After expiration of the contracted period of two years, the supplied equipments and tools will become our property _____.

A. with charge   B. free charge   C. uncharged   D. free of charge

2. All parts and components made in Guangzhou must _____ the standards of quality, and be approved by Party A beforehand.

A. add up to   B. measure up to   C. be measured up to   D. be made of

3. Our system of mass production will render low prices _____.

A. to be possible   B. able   C. possible   D. to be impossible

4. Our invoice amounting to $20,000 _____ the first consignment per S.S. "East Wind."

A. pays   B. covers   C. includes   D. comprises

5. Parts and components either to be supplied by Party A or to be purchased in Guangzhou by Party B are _____ the list attached.

A. as for   B. as to   C. as per   D. as yet

6. We must make a liberal allowance _____ such unforeseen circumstances arising during transit.

A. off   B. for   C. on   D. of

7. They have mutually agreed that Party A _____ Party B with the manufacturing of TV sets in Guangzhou with all necessary parts and components supplied by Party A.

A. entrusts   B. gives   C. authorizes   D. appoints

8. If both parties are _____ breach of a contract, each party shall bear its respective

liability.

A. to
B. at
C. on
D. in

9. On taking over the products, your representatives shall give us a receipt _____ that the finished products have been inspected.

A. certified
B. certifying
C. having been certified
D. being certified

10. Your claim for the loss sustained is to be _____ with the insurance company.

A. met
B. compensated
C. filed
D. satisfied

五、实务思考
案例1

中国深圳某公司诉中国香港某公司来件装配合同纠纷案

原告中国深圳某公司与被告中国香港某公司在2017年6月至2018年9月间先后签订了8份来件装配合同。合同分别规定：乙方按加工成品数支付加工费给甲方；对乙方提供的设备，甲方需在每份加工合同中扣除加工费的30%作为价款，直至还清为止。如果乙方提供材料不足，造成甲方停工超过3个工作日的，从第4个工作日起，每天按每个工人20元港币补偿停工费给甲方。

在来件装配生产期间，原告从加工费中偿还被告设备费133 066元港币。原告实际收到加工费3 251 022元港币，被告尚欠加工费、停工补助费和其他费用折合83 896元人民币，仓库租金为9 000元人民币，共计9 289 622元人民币。原告在多次催促而被告终未付款的情况下，采取了停止出货的措施，留置被告的原材料和机械设备，并要求被告先付款后出货，不付款不出货。而被告则坚持先出货后付款，不出货不付款。在此情形下，原告采取了进一步的措施，单方处理留置被告的某型号手机1 019部以抵充欠款，并起诉到深圳市中级人民法院，要求留置被告的财产，以抵偿原告因对方违约造成的损失。

法院认为被告欠款属实，原告在被告违约的情况下，中止履行自己的义务，并留置对方财产，是一种在对方违约时如果继续履行合同会给自己造成更大损失的情况下采取的自力救济措施，是完全合理的，应予允许。但原告未经任何部门批准，单方处理被告留置物资，是违法行为。鉴于原告将该部分物资折价如数返还被告，已认识错误，并补交了关税等相关税费，可不予追究责任。由于被告未应诉，人民法院缺席判决如下：

（1）解除中国深圳某公司与中国香港某公司签订的8份来件装配合同。

（2）被告留置物资作价2 359 002元人民币，扣除原告加工费、停工补助费和仓库租金92 896元人民币和原告已交的设备费35 050元人民币，尚余108 026元人民币，由原告代被告缴纳关税和诉讼费后，余款交本院暂管，限被告在本判决生效后1年内领取，逾期上交国库。

（3）被告所说的是40日后才补偿停工费用的说法没有根据，不予支持。

（4）诉讼费由被告承担。

本判决宣判后，原告和被告均未提出上诉，一审判决发生效力。

问题：从该案例中我们应该吸取什么教训？

案例2

来料加工中请他人代为加工是否欺诈案

——中国G市金银首饰社诉中国香港M实业有限公司来料加工合同纠纷案

2018年2月7日、4月20日及5月13日，中国G市外贸总公司协同市金银首饰社与中国香港M实业有限公司订立的85C001A、85C002Y、85003C来料加工金银饰品合同经市外贸局批准生效。同年6月20日、7月24日、9月5日，市经济技术开发区商业贸易公司协同市金银首饰社与中国香港M实业有限公司又订立了85新G0-003、85新G0-010号来料加工金银饰品合同，经市经济技术开发区管理委员会批准生效。上述合同均订明由M公司向市金银首饰社提供原、辅料和部分加工工具，金银首饰社按M公司所提供的式样进行加工；加工费及交货日期另议。但金银首饰社接到M公司来料后，自己加工很少部分，将大部分饰品发往外埠加工。对此，M公司曾多次提出异议，但金银首饰社均不予理睬。在履行第一份饰品加工合同中，金银首饰社按合同约定交付了加工的饰品，但M公司未及时付清加工费，尚欠港币26 000余元。在履行第二份加工合同过程中，M公司又未按合同中约定的时间交付所需原、辅料，以致金银首饰社未能按期交付该合同中的加工饰品。同年11月，金银首饰社将M公司交来的银料加工饰品交付后，M公司以金银首饰社违约延期交货为由，拒付加工费123 355元港币，并对第二份合同中断来料供应。金银首饰社遂留置M公司来料的剩余银料，并向G市人民法院提起诉讼，要求M公司付清其为M公司加工金银首饰的加工费。

本案经G市人民法院主持调解，在弄清事实、分清责任、双方当事人明确各自过错的基础上，金银首饰社与M公司之间在自愿的基础上达成了如下协议：金银首饰社与M公司所订立的来料加工85新G0-005、85新G0-009、85新G0-010号金银饰品加工合同终止。所有合同中还未履行的部分也不再履行。

（1）M公司在收到本调解书10日之内，将其所欠加工费123 355元港币支付给金银首饰社。

（2）金银首饰社在收到M公司汇付的加工费款项之日起，7天内将M公司的剩余银料，由金银首饰社负责一切过关方面的手续，交还给M公司。

问题：从该案例中我们应该吸取什么教训？

实训项目 29
补偿贸易合同练习①

实训目标

1.掌握补偿贸易合同的特点。

2.掌握补偿贸易合同的基本内容。

3.掌握草拟补偿贸易合同的注意事项。

一、将下列协议翻译为中文

Agreement on Compensation Trade

This Agreement is made by and between AA Corporation, Shantou (hereinafter called Party A) and BB Company, Macao (hereinafter called Party B) whereby the two Parties agree to enter into the compensation trade under the terms and conditions set forth below:

1. After friendly discussions, Party A agrees to make for Party B each month from January 20×× to December 20×× approximately 2,000 to 3,000 dozen Ladies' Blouses according to the supplied samples. Party B guarantees to place orders with Party A for the above quota each month. Party A shall give priority to filling Party B's order for blouses provided that Party B advises Party A of its requirements half a year in advance, failing which Party A will not reserve the productive capacity for Party B.

2. In order to improve the quality of the products, Party B agrees to supply Party A with 100 machines (for details see the attached list) valued at HKD 220,000 on credit basis. Party A shall compensate Party B for the total value of the 100 machines amounting to HKD 220,000 plus freight and interest at ××% per annum before the end of 20×× with the proceeds of the finished products delivered to Party B.

3. Party B shall guarantee that the machines to be supplied are in accordance with Party A's requirements and specifications. If there is any defect in the performance of the machines, Party A shall be entitled to laying a claim against Party B for any losses sustained.

4. Party B shall send technicians at its own expense to supervise installation and effect

---

① [1] 吴敏，吴明忠. 国际经贸英语合同写作 [M]. 广州：暨南大学出版社，2002. [2] KARLA C, SHIPPEY J D. International contracts [M]. 上海：上海外语教育出版社，2000. [3] FARNSWORTH E A, YOUNG W F. Selections for contracts: statutes, restatement second, forms [M]. Westbury, NY: Foundation Press, 1992.

repairs to the machines.

5. The two Parties agree that the first 10,000 dozen blouses shall be made under cut-make-trim terms and the rest of the orders under normal terms.

6. The specific quantities, specifications, prices, terms of payment, time of shipment, etc. shall be stipulated in detail in separate Sales Contracts which will be concluded at the beginning of each quarter during the terms of this Agreement.

7. Any complaints or disputes in connection with this Agreement or the execution thereof shall be settled through friendly negotiation.

8. This Agreement shall become effective as soon as it is signed by the two Parties. The validity of this Agreement is for three years (from January 1, 20×× to December 31, 20××). This Agreement is renewable for a further period of two years upon mutual consent after consultation between the two Parties.

Party A   Party B
（Signed）   （Signed）
Shantou, November 28, 20××

二、将下列内容翻译为英文

按中国的现行规定，凡是中国企业利用外国投资者提供的或用外国出口信贷购进的生产设备和技术进行生产，并以返销其产品的方式分期偿还上述设备和技术的价款或信贷本息的交易方式，都属于补偿贸易。通过补偿贸易购进的技术和设备，必须是先进而适用的，而且必须有利于改造中国的现有企业以及提高生产能力和技术水平。用作补偿的产品，原则上应当是使用引进的设备和技术所生产的直接产品；但必要时，经双方磋商和同意，并经中国政府有关部门批准，可以用其他产品偿还。

三、选词填空

equipment, enterprises, payment, trade, cash, purchase, products, technology, exchange, buyback, discussions, transformation

There are two basic forms of compensation trade. One is product _____ , that is, what is used for payment is the _____ manufactured directly by using the imported equipment and technology. The other is called counter _____ , that is, what is used for _____ is not products manufactured directly by using the imported _____ , but other products decided upon through _____ by both sides. As the equipment and _____ in compensation trade are not imported with _____ , the trade does not cause any direct slate debts. Flexible in form and easy to conduct, this form of _____ is conducive to small and medium _____ in their technical _____ and in their export trade for more foreign _____ .

四、单项选择

1. Party B undertakes to compensate Party A for the contract amount by exporting 3,000

cartons of Canned Asparagus _____.

    A. in two lots   B. in two lot   C. with two lots   D. with two lot

2. The stipulations of this reciprocal L/C shall be in _____ with those in this Agreement.

    A. conformation   B. confirmations   C. conformity   D. conform

3. In case the delivered value of feather exceeds that of machinery equipment _____, Party B shall ship such additional spare parts as indicated by Party A to the difference.

    A. get off   B. set off   C. get up   D. set up

4. Both Parties shall _____ the terms and conditions agreed upon.

    A. carry on   B. carry out   C. lake on   D. take out

5. An irrevocable Letter of Guarantee will be issued in your favour by the Bank of China to _____ timely payment of the installments with the interest due.

    A. demand   B. claim   C. guarantee   D. offer

6. They will compensate you _____ the loss according to the provisions of the insurance policy.

    A. for   B. on   C. with   D. in

7. Party B shall establish in favour of Party A an irrevocable Banker's Acceptance L/C in payment _____ the equipment an amount not less than HKD 22 million.

    A. of; for   B. to; for   C. for; at   D. for; for

8. The B/L is to be made out to _____ and blank endorsed.

    A. instruction   B. offer   C. mark   D. order

9. Party A will put five local fitters _____ the two specialists' disposal.

    A. for   B. at   C. on   D. within

10. Party B shall after effecting shipment, _____ forthwith to Party A through C Bank the under-mentioned documents.

    A. ship   B. forward   C. give   D. transfer

五、实务思考

某电视机厂与法国某电器公司合同纠纷案

2018年，我国某电视机厂与法国某电器公司签订了一份补偿贸易合同，合同规定由电器公司提供一套电视机生产线并辅以30万台主要元器件，由电视机厂分期分批于3年内偿还设备及元器件价款；规定采用对开信用证分别购买设备、元器件和成品的办法结算价款，即由电视机厂每期（批）开出90天远期信用证向对方购买设备、元器件，对方开出向电视机厂购买成品的即期回头信用证。电视机厂开出的远期信用证有如下附加条件：“须在电视机厂收到以它为受益人的由电器公司开立的不可撤销的信用证才可付款。”信用证开出后，电器公司忽然提出，电视机厂的信用证有上述附加条件，在回头信用证没有开出前，不能视作有效，该国银行不同意凭该信用证融资，无法贷款生产元器件，以致经营上产生困难，无法保证在合同期内交货，要求电视机厂重新开出信用证并取消该附加条款，否则不能如期履约。电视机厂不同意修改信用证条款。我国银行也认为如取消以上附加条款会带来很大风险。然而电器公司态度十分坚决，双方相持不下，贸易陷入僵局。此时，电视机厂通过其他客户了解到该电器公司曾采用同样形式与我国另一电视机厂进行过

16 000台电视机的补偿贸易，电器公司完全按合同的规定履行了其他所有义务。该电视机厂认为电器公司的信誉是可靠的，另考虑到对外贸易要有一定的灵活性，如果顾虑到太多，势必耽搁贸易机会。为使业务不致搁浅，电视机厂最后同意，接受电器公司的要求，将支付条款改为："双方必须按期开出信用证，如任何一方不及时开证，则由此造成对方损失应承担责任。"随后开出了没有附加条款的远期信用证。电器公司可凭远期跟单汇票使用后，当汇票到期时没有开回头信用证，由于电视机厂的信用证没有附加约束性条款，只得由我国银行垫出外汇兑付票款。

问题：从该案例中我们应该吸取什么教训？

实训项目 30
代理合同练习①

实训目标

1.掌握代理合同的特点。
2.掌握代理合同的基本内容。
3.掌握草拟代理合同的注意事项。

一、将下列内容翻译为中文

1. The color, design, quantity, quality, shipment, terms of payment for the above-mentioned goods under each order placed by Party B shall be valid only when officially confirmed and approved by Party A.

2. The agent shall have the right by written instrument to delegate any or all of the foregoing powers involving discretionary decision making to any individual or organizations that the agent may select but such delegation may be revoked by the agent at any time.

3. The manufacturer shall assist the employees of the agent to acquire technical knowledge of the Products. The agent will cover their traveling expenses and salary while the Manufacturer provides board and lodging.

4. The agent shall act as full agent on Shanghai market. He shall promote the Manufacturers products, perform informative work and carry out his utmost sales work to obtain enquiries. He shall learn technical knowledge of the products. The agent shall cover from his commission any expenditure or promotion necessary.

5. In case one or more provisions of this contract are invalid, the validity of the remaining provisions of the contract shall not be affected thereby. This agreement is made out in two identical copies, of which each party keeps one copy.

二、将括号内的中文翻译为英文

1. _____

---

① ［1］张林玲. 商务英语合同翻译与写作［M］. 北京：机械工业出版社，2009.［2］徐良霞，李海燕. 实用英语教你写合同［M］. 北京：北京航空航天工业大学出版社，2004.［3］兰天，屈晓鹏. 国际商务合同翻译教程［M］. 大连：东北财经大学出版社，2014.

_____(ABC 公司应支付该地区代理商修理各种船舶总价值 10% 的佣金), commissions for bulk contracts shall be decided upon separately; 5% of the commission shall be paid first, _____(余额待修船结算价格收款后支付).

2. _____

_____(代理商无权就合同之价格条款、时间、规格或其他合同条件对 ABC 公司进行干涉); the acceptance of business shall be at the sole discretion of ABC Company.

3. The Agent hereby declares that the Agent shall not represent any other ship repairing yard that is or that could reasonably be constructed as being in conflict with ABC Company's interest during the period of this agreement. _____ _____ (代理商同意在承签其他代理合同前征求 ABC 公司之意见). The Agent undertakes that he shall not, without the consent of ABC Company, disclose to any third Party information that could be prejudicial to ABC Company's commercial dealings.

4. _____

_____(当需要由 ABC 公司付给业主的经纪人及第三方介绍人等佣金时), the Agent shall advise ABC Company in advance and the commission will be paid at ABC Company's discretion.

5. The Agent shall solicit customers situated in the territory_____ _____(代理人应将接收到的报价或订单转送给制造商). He has no authority to make contracts on behalf of or in any way to bind the manufacturer _____(代理人应告知用户制造商规定的销售条款 (包括装运期和付款方式)). The manufacturer shall be free to reject any offers or orders transmitted to him by the agent.

三、选词填空

herewith, hereunder, hereof, hereto, hereby, hereinafter

1. All disputes arising from the implementation of or related _____ preferably shall be settled through friendly consultation between the Principal and General Agent.

2. The General Agent shall not, without the express prior written consent of the Principal assign or transfer any of its obligations or duties _____ and shall not appoint sub-agent.

3. The party of the first part (_____ called the Company) _____grants to the party of the second part (_____ called the Agent) the exclusive right to sell the "Forever" bicycles in New York, U.S.A. for the period of three years from the date _____.

4. The Principal _____ appoints the General Agent, and the General Agent _____ accepts appointment, as the principal's sole exclusive General Agent to negotiate on behalf of the Principal, with the Seller, the price and all other terms and conditions of the sale.

5. The expiration or termination of the General Agents appointment under this Agreement for whatever reason shall be without prejudice to any pre-existing rights and obligations of either Party _____.

四、实务思考

Case Study on Sales Representative Agreement[①]

Case Story

In this fast-paced world of lucrative international deals, busy executive with a firm understanding of core legal issues enjoy a competitive advantage. Abdul Jami, PLLC's "Busy Executive Guide" series provides decision-makers with the information they need to understand key legal issues and know when to call in back-up.

This report is the first in the "Busy Executive Guide" series. The report focuses on core legal issues that impact the negotiation of sales representative and distributor agreement. It is presented as a case study in question and answer format. After reading this short report you will have a good understanding of (1) the laws that impact sales representative and distributor agreement, (2) key differences between the two types of agreement, and (3) how you should negotiate so that you keep the dollars rolling in and leave the headaches to your competitors.

Background

Arvind, the owner of an India-based company that manufactures electronic equipment, is eager to boost sales in the United States. Arvind is currently negotiating with Joe, a United States citizen, who says he can help Arvind gain a strong presence in the U.S. market. Arvind conducted due diligence and concluded that Joe's claims are legitimate. Now Arvind and Joe, eager to begin generating sales and making profits and commissions, are about to sign an agreement. Arvind's cousin Niraj told Arvind about a website where he could buy a Sales Representative Agreement for $10 and save a bundle on legal fees. Arvind bought the contract, but after reading it, is not sure if it will protect him. He approaches Abdul Jami, PLLC, a law firm that advises on international commercial transactions, and tries to figure out whether it makes sense to spend $500 or so for Mr. Abdul Jami to review his $10 agreement.

Case Discussion

Suppose you were Mr. Abdul Jami, try to discuss the questions raised by Arvind.

Below are the questions that Arvind asked:

1. I bought a sales representative agreement online which seems to cover everything that I can think of. Will having a lawyer review do anything to help better protect my business?

2. What is the basic law that supports my planned business relationship with Joe?

3. My cousin Niraj thinks that I should have bought a distributor agreement instead of a sales representative agreement. What's the difference? Is there any legal affect on my business relationship with Joe?

4. Joe wants me to change the agreement so that his sales company, Bleu Sales Co., is my sales representative. This seems like a minor point. The agreement is not set up in that way and I think I should leave it the way it is. Does it matter whether Joe or his company is the sales

---

① 王立非. 国际商务合同实践教程 [M]. 上海：上海外语教育出版社，2012.

representative?

5. Because Joe is located in the U.S. and I am based in India, I will not be able to manage Joe as I do my other sales employees. What can I do to contractually ensure Joe represents my company in the way that I'd like him to?

6. Besides agency law which you mentioned earlier, are there any other laws that may impact my contractual relationship with Joe?

7. Laws change. I'm worried that a change in U.S. import or India export laws will change and affect the profitability of my agreement with Joe. How can I change my agreement so that I'm protected?

8. My contract manager has trouble in reading contracts that are written in English and therefore I like to have all my contracts translated into Hindi and presented in two languages. If I have to go to court, will this cause a problem?

9. Joe has asked me to change the agreement so that it says that his commission payments will be split between two accounts, one in the U.S., and one in Seychelles. What's the best way for me to write this into the agreement?

10. The contract currently says that all disputes are to be litigated in Alaska and that Alaska law will apply. Joe says that he loves Alaska, but I'm not sure that I'm comfortable with this since I am based in India. What should I do?

11. My cousin Niraj thinks that I should make the contract good for 1 year. Joe wants a 10-year contract. The contract currently says that it is good until termination. I'm confused. What should I do?

12. You have been very helpful and I may have you review my agreement or draft me a new one. What is your procedure for reviewing an agreement? What about drafting an agreement? What are your fees?

Questions: What shall we learn from this case?

主要参考文献

[1] 葛亚军. 合同英语手册 [M]. 天津：天津科技翻译出版公司，2002.

[2] 吕昊，刘显正，罗萍. 商务合同写作及翻译 [M]. 武汉：武汉大学出版社，2005.

[3] 王相国. 鏖战英文合同：英文合同的翻译与起草 [M]. 最新增订版. 北京：中国法制出版社，2014.

[4] 吴敏，吴明忠. 国际经贸英语合同写作 [M]. 广州：暨南大学出版社，2002.

[5] 乔焕然. 英文合同阅读指南：英文合同的结构、条款、句型与词汇分析 [M]. 最新增订版. 北京：中国法制出版社，2015.

[6] 王秉乾. 国际商事合同 [M]. 英文版. 北京：对外经济贸易大学出版社，2013.

[7] 索普，贝利. 国际商务合同 [M]. 段佳陆，等，译. 北京：华夏出版社，2004.

[8] 刘川，王菲. 英文合同阅读与翻译 [M]. 北京：国防工业出版社，2010.

[9] KARLA C，SHIPPEY J D. International contracts [M]. 上海：上海外语教育出版社，2000.

[10] FARNSWORTH E A，YOUNG W F. Selections for contracts: statutes, restatement second, forms [M]. Westbury, NY: Foundation Press, 1992.

[11] 龚柏华，陶博. 法律英语：中英双语法律文书制作 [M]. 上海：复旦大学出版社，2004.

[12] 哈格德. 法律写作 [M]. 影印版. 北京：法律出版社，2003.

[13] 王立非. 国际商务合同实践教程 [M]. 上海：上海外语教育出版社，2012.

[14] 徐良霞，李海燕. 实用英语教你写合同 [M]. 北京：北京航空航天工业大学出版社，2004.

[15] 张林玲. 商务英语合同翻译与写作 [M]. 北京：机械工业出版社，2009.

[16] 兰天，屈晓鹏. 国际商务合同翻译教程 [M]. 大连：东北财经大学出版社，2014.

[17] 陈剑玲. 成员国适用国际货物销售合同公约案例选评 [M]. 北京：对外经济贸易大学出版社，2012.

[18] 黄文伟，刘美华. 商务英语函电与合同 [M]. 上海：上海大学出版社，2008.

[19] KIAN C T S，CHIM T S. Contract law, a layman's guide[M]. Dulles, Virginia: Books International, 2000.

[20] BLACK H C. Black's law dictionary[M]. 5th ed. St. Paul: West Publishing Co., 1979.

［21］CURRY J E. A short course in international negotiating［M］. Traverse City: World Trade Press，1999.

［22］MITCHELL C. A short course in international business culture［M］. Traverse City: World Trade Press，1999.

［23］SITARZ D. The complete book of small business legal forms［M］. 3rd ed. Carbondale, IL: Nova Publishing Co.，2001.